Why the Crimean War?

A Cautionary Tale

Why the Crimean War?

A Cautionary Tale

NORMAN RICH

Brown University

McGRAW-HILL, INC.

New York   St. Louis   San Francisco   Auckland   Bogotá   Caracas
Hamburg   Lisbon   London   Madrid   Mexico   Milan   Montreal   New Delhi
Paris   San Juan   São Paulo   Singapore   Sydney   Tokyo   Toronto

Why the Crimean War? A Cautionary Tale

1 2 3 4 5 6 7 8 9 0   DOH DOH 9 5 4 3 2 1 0

ISBN 0-07-052255-3

This book was set in Caledonia by Yankee Typesetters and
J. M. Post Graphics, Corp.
For the paperback edition, the editors were David Follmer and
Suzanne Thibodeau;
the production supervisor was Denise L. Puryear.
The cover was designed by Gayle Jaeger.
R. R. Donnelley & Sons Company was printer and binder.

Cover photo: Battle of Sevastapol by George Dodd, The Newberry Library,
Chicago.

Library of Congress Cataloging-in-Publication Data

Rich, Norman.
    Why the Crimean war?: a cautionary tale / Norman Rich.
      p.   cm.
    Includes bibliographical references (p.   ) and index.
    ISBN 0-07-052255-3 (paper)
    1. Crimean War, 1853–1856—Diplomatic history.   2. Crimean War,
1853-1856—Causes.   I. Title.
DK215.R53   1991
947'.073—dc20   90-38924

To Peggy Hitchcock

About the Author

Norman Rich is Professor of History at Brown University, co-editor of *Documents on German Foreign Policy* (1949 ff.) and *The Holstein Papers* (1954–1961), and author of *Friedrich von Holstein* (1965), *The Age of Nationalism and Reform, 1850–1890* (1970, 1977), and *Hitler's War Aims* (1973, 1974).

Contents

Editorial Notes

Dates. The Julian (Old Style) calendar, used in Russia and the greater part of the Ottoman Empire in the mid-nineteenth century, ran twelve days behind the Gregorian (New Style) calendar used in the West. Thus 4 October (Russian) was 16 October (Western). To avoid confusion and pedantry, I have altered all Old Style dates used in Russian or Ottoman documents to conform to the New Style system of dating.

Communications. By the mid-nineteenth century all major European capitals were connected by telegraph, but there was no direct telegraph connection between Constantinople and the West until September 1855. Thus there was generally a time lag of eight to twelve days between the dispatch and receipt of communications to and from the Turkish capital.

Orthography. For the most part I have adopted the names and spelling of persons and places in use in the mid-nineteenth century. For Russian names, however, I have adopted recent usage in transliteration (Gorchakov instead of Gortschakoff or other variations), except in the case of names of obvious non-Russian origin, such as Meyendorff or Brunnow. In doubtful situations I have tried to be clear rather than consistent.

Quotations. Spelling, punctuation, and emphasis (italics) have been reproduced as found in the document collections or other works from which they have been taken.

Maps

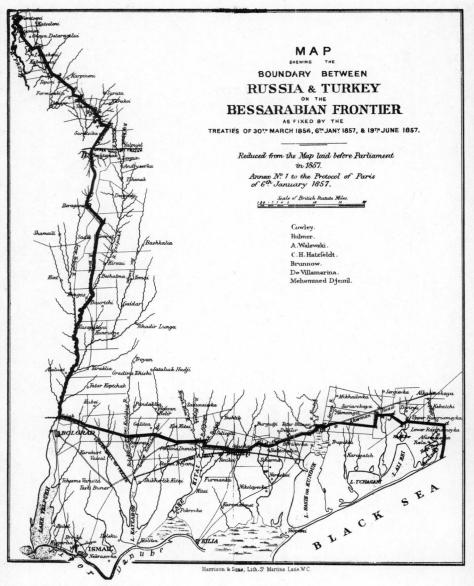

From Edward Hertslet, *Map of Europe by Treaty*. London, 1875.

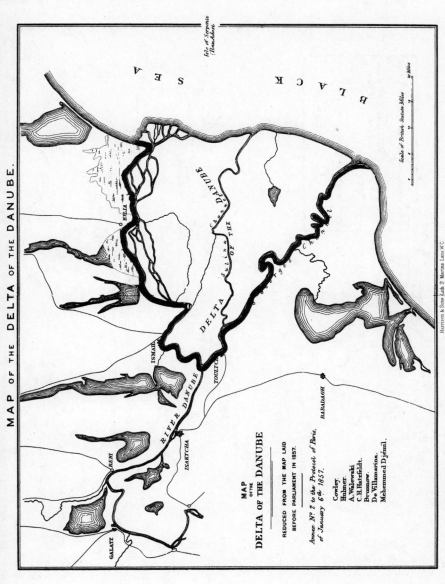

MAP of the DELTA of the DANUBE.

MAP
OF THE
DELTA OF THE DANUBE.

REDUCED FROM THE MAP LAID
BEFORE PARLIAMENT IN 1857.

*Annex. No. 2 to the Protocol of Paris,
of January 6th 1857.*

Cowley.
Hubner.
A.Walewski.
C.B.Hatzfeldt.
Brunnow.
De Villamarina.
Mehemmed Djemil.

Isle of Serpents
(Ilan Adasi)

BLACK SEA

DANUBE

DELTA OF THE DANUBE

Suline Channel of the DANUBE

St George's Channel

TOULTCHA

ISMAIL

ISATCHA

RIVER DANUBE

RELIA

REMI

GALATZ

KARADAGH

Scale of British Statute Miles

Harrison & Sons Lith St Martins Lane W.C.

From Edward Hertslet, *Map of Europe by Treaty.* London, 1875.

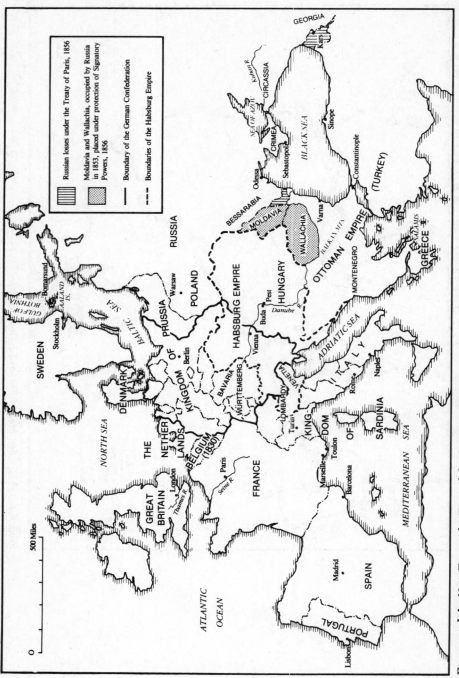

Europe and the Near East at the Time of the Crimean War.

THE BALKAN AREA

```
0      50        150 Miles
```

—·—·— Boundary of 1829 (Treaty of Adrianople)
············· Bessarabia Boundary of 1856

Prulb R.

BESSARABIA

MOLDAVIA

Lake
Salsyk
Kilia
Sulina
St. George's

BOSNIA

SERBIA

WALLACHIA

•Bucharest

Danube R.

HERZEGOVINA

Varna

BALKAN MTS.

BULGARIA

BLACK SEA

MONTENEGRO

ADRIATIC SEA

Constantinople

*SEA OF
MARMARA*

*AEGEAN
SEA*

GREECE

Athens•

IONIAN SEA

*BAY
OF SALAMIS*

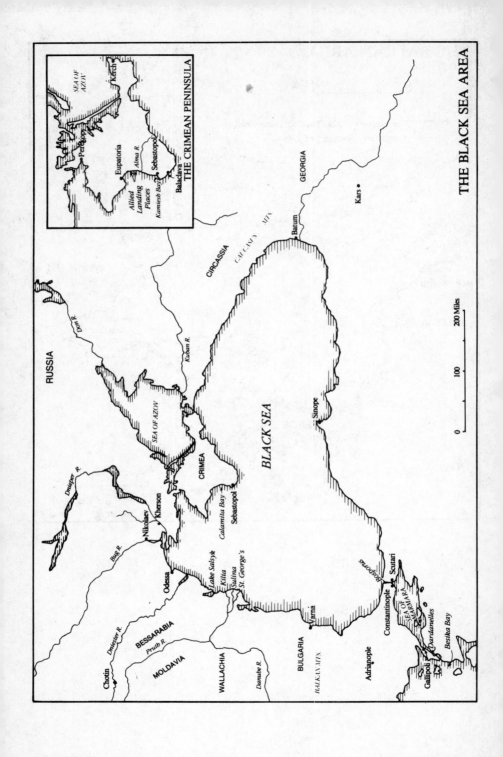

THE BLACK SEA AREA

THE CRIMEAN PENINSULA

SEA OF AZOV

Kerch

Perekop

Eupatoria

Alma R.

Sebastopol

Allied Landing Places

Kamiesh Bay

Balaclava

GEORGIA

Kars

CIRCASSIA

CAUCASUS MTS.

Batum

RUSSIA

Don R.

Kuban R.

SEA OF AZOV

CRIMEA

BLACK SEA

Sinope

200 Miles

0   100

Dnieper R.

Bug R.

Nikolaev

Kherson

Calamita Bay

Sebastopol

Dniester R.

Odessa

Lake Salsyk

Kilia

Sulina

St. George's

Bosporus

Scutari

Constantinople

SEA OF MARMARA

BESSARABIA

Prut R.

Chotin

MOLDAVIA

WALLACHIA

Danube R.

BULGARIA

BALKAN MTS.

Varna

Adrianople

Gallipoli

Dardanelles

Besika Bay

Preface

There is an immense historical literature on the Crimean War, but to the general reader that war is known, if at all, for the charge of the Light Brigade and the humanitarian labors of Florence Nightingale. This book does not deal with either of these subjects or with the course of the war itself except in the most cursory fashion. Instead it concentrates on problems of politics and diplomacy in an attempt to answer the question posed by its title.

It is no longer fashionable to require that scholarly investigations be relevant to the concerns of our own era, but I confess that much of my own fascination with the subject of Crimean War diplomacy stems from the fact that the problems raised in the course of the Crimean crisis and the very language used by the statesmen involved are remarkably—and frighteningly—contemporary.

The Crimean War was a mid-nineteenth-century conflict between the West and Russia, but unlike the campaigns of conquest waged by Napoleon or Hitler, it was fundamentally a war fought on behalf of what we would today call the containment of Russia, an objective many Western leaders believed required rolling back the frontiers of the Russian Empire and liberating the non-Russian nationalities of that empire's frontier regions—the Finns, the Poles, and the peoples of the Balkan and Caucasus areas.

Following the destruction of Germany and Japan as great powers and throughout the years of what became known as the Cold War, the containment of Russia was once again generally regarded as the West's most formidable foreign policy problem. But even as the Cold War seems to be winding down, Russia, if only because of its immense size and geographical position, remains a formidable problem which may actually have grown more volatile as a result of the apparent disintegration of Russia's satellite empire in Eastern Europe and revolutionary turmoil in Russia itself. In our nuclear age, however, the conditions for conducting a policy of containment have changed in one decisive respect: we can no longer afford the luxury of war against Russia. For us, therefore, it should be particularly pertinent to study how statesmen of an earlier age attempted to deal with the problem of containment of Russia through peaceful means and to consider how European leaders in the mid-nineteenth century allowed a routine and seemingly trivial international crisis to erupt into a major European war.

Despite the profusion of historical studies dealing with all aspects of the Crimean War, including its diplomacy, the most authoritative of these studies are relatively specialized and concentrate on a single state, a limited period of time, or a particular issue. Given the immense amount of documentary material on the war available in the archives of Western Europe, such specialization is inevitable, for no conscientious historian can expect to work through, much less digest, the entire body of existing records. Yet concentrating on a single country or issue frequently precludes adequate consideration of the policies of other countries or of other issues. Moreover, the wealth of detail offered in many monographs is so overwhelming that the general reader often finds it difficult to follow the principal themes of the narrative or to perceive the fundamental issues at stake.

The present book developed out of my own efforts to understand the origins of the Crimean War. It represents an attempt to provide a clear and concise analytical account of the main lines of the diplomacy of that war and to tell the story in the round, as it were, by dealing with the policies and motivations of the leaders of all the major powers concerned. Much of the story remains complicated, but complications cannot be eliminated altogether for the sake of clarity because without some appreciation of their intricacy it is impossible to understand the maneuvers of the statesmen compelled to cope with them.

In attempting to be clear and concise, I have omitted all detail I did not consider essential to an understanding of the central political and diplomatic problems. I have not dealt with the policies of those states that were not at the center of the decision-making process (for example, Prussia, Sardinia, or the Scandinavian states), important as they often were, if only through their very existence, in affecting major policy decisions. For those interested in the policies of these ancillary states, a number of excellent monographs exist, which are cited in the bibliography. Throughout my text, wherever it seemed necessary, I have alluded to different or conflicting interpretations, but otherwise I have omitted all discussion of the historiography of the Crimean War. Finally, I have paid only scant attention to the domestic problems of the major powers or to the social, economic, or intellectual forces at work in their societies that may have influenced the decisions of their statesmen, although I have attempted to describe those forces when their impact on policy was obvious. To have dealt adequately with these problems would have required a larger and very different book.

The present study is essentially a work of synthesis and interpretation, and the evidence on which it is based derives in large part from the archival research of other scholars. My dependence on and gratitude to these scholars is, I hope, adequately expressed in my text and footnotes.

I have been asked to whom this book is addressed. Alas, the people to whom it is addressed in the first instance—the present-day formulators of foreign policy—will certainly never read it. It is therefore addressed, with scarcely less presumption, to the future leaders of the world—in other words, to students—in the hope that they and all others interested in international affairs will find this Cautionary Tale as fascinating—and as cautionary—as did the author.

Norman Rich

Why the Crimean War?

A Cautionary Tale

Chapter 1

The Background of the Conflict

After the Napoleonic Wars the leaders of the European great powers, conditioned by almost a quarter-century of revolution and warfare, had become convinced that the primary objective of their diplomacy must be the preservation of international peace and stability, for only through peace could the civilization they cherished, and their privileged position within it, be maintained. To this end they generally agreed to cooperate in the suppression of every kind of revolution, which they regarded as a major threat to international as well as domestic peace, and to settle differences among themselves at the conference table through negotiation and compromise.[1] Because all the great powers were drawn into the system and because their leaders attempted to act in concert when confronted with international crises, the relationship among the great powers in the early nineteenth century became known as the Concert of Europe. Although that concert did not succeed in preventing all revolutions and wars, and although the dissonances within it often seemed to drown out the harmonies, the leaders of the concert nevertheless succeeded in their primary objective of preserving the general peace of Europe. Shortly after the midpoint of the nineteenth century, however, diplomacy broke down over one of the perennial crises in the Near East, and a major international conflict took place that has become known in history as the Crimean War.

In attempting to understand the failure of diplomacy in the mid-nineteenth century and the origins of the Crimean War, we

1

are confronted, as in all historical situations, with a multitude of explanations. But for the Western powers involved in that war, at the heart of the matter, embracing and overriding all other considerations, was fear of Russia.[2]

Fear of Russia is no new phenomenon in history. Since the days of Peter the Great, foreign statesmen have been looking with increasing apprehension at the mammoth power arising in the east, and at the gradual but steady extension of Russia's frontiers in every direction. Finland, the east coast of the Baltic, and a large part of Poland had come under Russian control in the late eighteenth and early nineteenth centuries. For some two hundred years there had been a war between Russia and Turkey almost every twenty years, as Russia extended its influence at the expense of the Ottoman Empire into the Middle East, the Balkans, and toward the Mediterranean. While Russia remained economically and technically backward, it was still possible for the smaller states of Europe and Asia to defend themselves and prevent any serious Russian encroachment on their interests. But if Russia were to overcome this backwardness, the tsarist empire with its preponderance of natural resources and large population might be more than a match for the countries of Europe, especially if by that time its power were solidly established not only on the Baltic but in the Balkans and at the great strategic base of Constantinople, from which Russia might be able to dominate the entire Mediterranean basin.

By 1850 Russia had not yet overcome its economic and technological backwardness, but its relative strength among the states of Europe seemed to have increased enormously. Russia was the only great power in continental Europe whose government had not been overthrown or severely shaken by the revolutions of 1848. In the course of those revolutions Russia had come to the aid of Austria to suppress revolution in the Habsburg dominions, and it had provided support and encouragement for the suppression of revolution everywhere else. In so doing, Russia seemed to have extended its influence over the entire Continent and to have emerged from the revolutionary era as the arbiter of Europe: the friend of Prussia, the protector of Austria, and the reservoir of support for all monarchical and conservative governments.

Power produces curious paradoxes. Russia's strength, or appearance of strength, proved to be a serious political liability, for it tended to make other countries even more fearful of Russia and anxious to prevent any further increase in its strength and influence. Austria, although deeply indebted to Russia for military aid in the suppression of revolution in Hungary in 1849 and for diplomatic support in maintaining its supremacy in German affairs, had no desire to sink to the status of a Russian protectorate, and to preserve Austria's political independence and freedom of action Austrian leaders sought to strengthen their diplomatic ties with other powers. Prussia, under the irresolute leadership of King Frederick William IV, played a negligible role in the diplomacy of the period, but Prussia too had reason to fear a further extension of Russian power and was resentful of Russian support for Austria in German affairs. Napoleon III, the ruler of France, saw in Russia the chief defender of the existing international order and of the restrictions imposed on France following the Napoleonic Wars. To break out of those restrictions and break up the existing international order designed to preserve them, he systematically sought to weaken Russia, disrupt the Concert of Europe, and secure allies of his own against the eastern colossus.[3]

Curiously enough it was Britain, farthest away from Russia and least directly menaced, that was to become the most rabid opponent of Russia among the great powers of Europe. British suspicion and fear of Russia had been vigorously stoked by journalists and other spokesmen for British vested interests in the Near East, but the British had legitimate reasons for concern. They feared the Russian threat to the European balance of power, the possible establishment of Russian control over the Ottoman Empire, and the consequent threat to their overland routes to India, their trade in the Near East, and their sea power in the Mediterranean. These British fears were compounded by the belief that Russia had gained control of the Concert of Europe, and that Austria as well as Prussia had fallen under Russian influence and would support or at least not hinder Russian efforts to extend that influence still further.

It was primarily to halt the process of Russian expansion and eliminate the Russian threat to the security and interests of the states of Europe and the Ottoman Empire that the Crimean War was fought. The tragedy of that war was that it was both unnecessary and useless. It was unnecessary because it accomplished almost nothing that could not have been, and in fact actually had been, accomplished through peaceful negotiation. It was useless because it did not halt Russian expansion or even diminish, much less eliminate, Russia's capacity for aggression. Even more tragic were the political repercussions of that war. The hatreds it engendered dealt a catastrophic blow to the precarious international stability established after the Napoleonic Wars and to the Concert of Europe, that informal system of mutual cooperation among the great powers which, for all its weaknesses, provided an arrangement for the peaceful settlement of international disputes at the conference table. The Crimean War destroyed the mutual confidence among the statesmen of Europe essential to such cooperation; it destroyed their belief that their own as well as their mutual interests were best safeguarded through respect for international treaties designed to preserve international order and therewith also international peace. The destruction of the European concert opened the gates for two decades of war and revolution that permanently altered the European states system and the international balance of power.

The process whereby the chief powers of Europe became involved in the Crimean War was complicated and many issues remain unclear and controversial, but one theory about its origins can definitely be eliminated: the war was not an accident, the result of bungling incompetence or misunderstandings on the part of the statesmen involved, although all of the participants can be charged with serious errors and miscalculations. Yet rarely in history has a war been preceded by so lengthy a period of diplomatic crisis which provided time for passions to cool and statesmen to settle their differences at the conference table through negotiation; and rarely in history have so many sincere and vigorous efforts been made by responsible leaders of the great powers to arrange a compromise settlement throughout the period of prewar crisis and the entire course of the war itself.

The principal reason for the failure of all efforts to preserve or restore peace through negotiation was that there were statesmen in Europe who did not want them to succeed, who were dedicated to the breakup of the existing international order or who were not content merely to halt Russian expansion but wanted to eliminate the Russian threat permanently. Neither of these aims could be achieved through peaceful negotiation, for both required revolutionary changes in the European power structure that could only have been implemented through war. The latter objective especially—the permanent elimination of the Russian threat—would have required the annihilation of the Russian armed forces and the dismemberment of the Russian Empire or equally radical measures that would not only have necessitated war but war on an immense scale.

Among those statesmen who blocked efforts to arrange a peaceful resolution of the Near Eastern crises of the 1850s and who believed in the desirability or necessity of war with Russia, those in the forefront were the Turks. For the two previous centuries they had suffered a succession of military defeats at the hands of Russia as that power steadily expanded its territories and spheres of influence at the expense of the Ottoman Empire. When in the course of the crises of the 1850s the Turks saw reason to believe that they would receive the support of two of Europe's great powers in resisting Russia's demands, the temptation was great—indeed, it proved irresistible—to take advantage of this singular opportunity to provoke a renewal of their wars with Russia in order to recoup some of their losses and roll back the Russian menace.

The European power that first aroused Turkish hopes for more active support against Russia in the 1850s was France, the traditional ally of the Ottoman Empire prior to the nineteenth century. During the era of the French Revolution, the French government had abandoned its policy of friendship with the Turks in the course of war against Britain and had authorized Napoleon to attack Egypt, at that time still part of the Ottoman Empire, in an attempt to sever some of Britain's most important economic and strategic lifelines. For several decades after the fall of Napoleon, French influence in the Ottoman Empire languished, but in the mid-nineteenth century a new Napoleon came to power in France who sought to restore France's traditional ties with Turkey and set out to challenge Russian influence in the Near East. This new Napoleon was Louis Napoleon Bonaparte, a nephew of the first Napoleon, who had been elected president of the Second French Republic in December 1848. On 2 December 1851, the anniversary of his uncle's great victory at Austerlitz and his coronation as emperor, Louis Napoleon made himself dictator of France through a coup d'état, and exactly two years later he himself assumed the imperial title of Napoleon III.

The Napoleonic name had been an important and perhaps decisive political asset in Louis Napoleon's rise to power and his election as president. But the name Napoleon also carried with it a fateful political legacy, for it aroused popular expectations of a new era of glory and empire. Napoleon III left few records that can be considered reliable guides to his political thinking, but the entire course of his foreign policy suggests that he believed his regime was obliged to fulfill the popular expectations associated with his name and to restore France to a position of dominance in Europe.

In seeking to realize this objective, Napoleon III employed three major strategies in his foreign policy: first, he sought to cultivate better relations, even to conclude an actual alliance, with Britain, the country he believed had been the major obstacle to his uncle's success, in the belief that the removal of that obstacle would facilitate the success of his own policies; second, he endeavored to harness to his cause the ideological principle of nationalism, whose potential power his uncle had recognized but failed to exploit, by making himself the champion of nationalities seeking freedom from foreign rule and reorganizing

Europe along the lines of nationality under the political and moral leadership of France; and finally, closely linked with his nationalities program, he sought to disrupt the international order that had been established after the Napoleonic Wars to prevent future French aggression and that still constituted the major obstacle to the reestablishment of French dominance in Europe. Because Russia was the foremost champion of this international order, a primary objective of Napoleon's foreign policy was to weaken Russia's ability to defend it. Such a program did not necessarily require war with Russia, although Napoleon was well aware that the tactics he employed always involved the risk of war. In deliberately provoking a crisis with Russia in the Near East in the spring of 1850, he may have wanted nothing more than a diplomatic victory, an occasion to sow discord among the powers. He was soon to find, however, that he was unable to remain in control of the situation, for in fomenting that crisis he not only aroused the expectations of the Turks but gave them— and others—the opportunity to manipulate the crisis to their own advantage.

Napoleon's challenge to Russia evoked no immediate enthusiasm among British leaders, who were if anything more apprehensive about the imperial aspirations of the new Napoleon than about the ambitions of the tsar. Since the Napoleonic Wars, British statesmen had generally acted on the assumption that British interests in the Near East could be defended most cheaply and effectively through the preservation of the Ottoman Empire. British support had been limited by and large to diplomatic intervention and naval demonstrations; it was not designed to roll back Russian influence or recoup previous Turkish losses to Russia. There was no sign in the early 1850s that British leaders saw any need for more active support, much less war, on behalf of the Ottoman Empire, and during the initial phase of the Franco-Russian crisis in the Near East they attempted to cooperate with other powers anxious to arrange a peaceful settlement.

In the course of that crisis, however, the more pacific British leaders allowed the direction of British foreign policy to pass to more bellicose spirits, men who needed no prompting from Napoleon III to arouse their suspicions of Russia and who were eventually to advocate far more radical measures against Russia than anything conceived by the French ruler. Among the anti-Russian forces in the British government, two men were to play the most critical roles in influencing the course of British policy before and during the Crimean War: Henry John Temple, Viscount Palmerston; and Stratford Canning, since 1852 Lord Stratford de Redcliffe.

Palmerston had served as lord of the admiralty from 1807 to 1809 and as secretary of war from 1809 to 1829. He had frequently held the post of foreign secretary between 1830 and 1851, and in 1852 he was appointed home secretary in the Aberdeen cabinet. Affectionately called "the most English minister," Palmerston seemed to embody all the virtues his fellow countrymen liked to believe were typically English—courage, good nature, generosity, a love of horses and hunting, a mistrust of and a certain contempt for foreigners. But it was above all his patriotism, his bold and unquestioning championship of British interests on every conceivable issue in every part of the world that made him one of the most popular statesman of his day. Palmerston might not always perceive where the true interests of Britain lay, he might fail to understand the limitations of Britain's capacity to defend those interests as he conceived them, but there can be no doubt about the sincerity or consistency of his concern.[4]

Stratford Canning, Lord Stratford de Redcliffe, was a cousin of George Canning, the former British foreign secretary and prime minister who had died in 1827. Stratford served as a member of the British Parliament for twelve years, but it was primarily through his diplomatic career that he earned his reputation as a statesman, especially through his service in Constantinople, where he had represented his country intermittently since 1810 and where over the years he had gained enormous prestige and influence. Stratford's attitude toward the crisis that led to the Crimean War was more parochial than Palmerston's, for he had spent so much time in the Near East that he had come to regard the region as something of a personal preserve. Although like Palmerston, he perceived the tsar's policies in the Near East as a threat to the interests of Britain, he appears to have resented them far more as an intrusion into his own domain, a personal insult that made the entire crisis in the Near East a power struggle between himself and the Russian autocrat. A man of inordinate vanity, Stratford assumed the role of mentor and protector of the Ottoman government and believed that his influence reigned supreme in Constantinople. It never seems to have occurred to Stratford that the Turks might be exploiting his vanity and pretensions in order to use him to play off Britain as well as France against Russia.

Personal animosities in general may have played a critical role in Stratford's conduct of policy. In 1832 he had been appointed ambassador to St. Petersburg, a more prestigious post than Constantinople, but the tsar had refused to accept him because of Stratford's well-known hostility to Russia, a rejection that can only have fed the flames of his Russophobia. Twenty years later he was led to believe that he would be given the post of foreign secretary or be appointed ambassador to Paris, but he received neither position. Instead he was raised to the peerage as Lord Stratford de Redcliffe (the title coming from a parish church, St. Mary Redcliffe in Bristol, a family association), hollow compensation indeed for so ambitious a statesman. As a result of these personal frustrations, Stratford may have developed a hostility to members of his own government comparable to his hostility of Russia; and when he agreed to resume his post in Constantinople early in 1853, he may have been imbued with renewed determination to demonstrate his own diplomatic prowess to the world.

Unlike Napoleon III, Palmerston and Stratford did not desire the breakup of the existing international order. On the contrary, they were primarily concerned with its preservation, and their fear of the Russian threat to that order was their major motive in seeking to frustrate suspected Russian designs in the Near East. As the crisis with Russia developed, they became convinced that

Russia could only be stopped through war; and once involved in war, they decided that the only goal which could justify waging it would be the permanent elimination of the Russian menace. To realize this objective, they were to advocate policies quite as radical as anything conceived by Napoleon.

Another force in Britain working against a peaceful resolution of the Crimean crisis was British public opinion. The American historian John Howes Gleason has shown that British popular hostility to Russia had a long tradition, nourished by fears of Russian threats to British interests in the Near East and by the popular conception of tsarist Russia as a land of tyranny and oppression, a conception powerfully reinforced by reports of Russia's brutal suppression of the Polish revolution of 1830.[5] In the mid-nineteenth century that hostility had been inflamed anew, this time against Austria as well as Russia, when these countries demanded the extradition of Hungarian and Polish refugees who had fled to the Ottoman Empire after the Austro-Russian suppression of the 1848–49 revolution in Hungary. Encouraged by Stratford, the Ottoman government had refused to yield to'these demands, and the British government (with Palmerston as foreign secretary) had sent a naval squadron to the Near East to back up Turkish resistance.

Public opinion is fickle, however, and can swerve violently from one direction to another with disconcerting speed. With the rise of a new Napoleon in France, British public opinion for a time shifted its animosity toward him, only to accept him happily as an ally when the popular mood once again turned against Russia in the course of the Crimean crisis.

In a brilliant analysis of British public opinion during this period, the British journalist Kingsley Martin argues convincingly that much of this popular hostility toward Russia was stirred up by British journalists in the Near East and their editors, and that Palmerston catered to this feeling and used the popularity he gained thereby for his own political purposes.[6] But the question remains as to how British public opinion was stirred up so successfully and into such frenzied antagonism toward Russia. The official press of the Napoleonic dictatorship in France tried to drum up anti-Russian sentiment in a far more systematic manner but was singularly unsuccessful in arousing French opinion, which remained relatively apathetic throughout the Crimean crisis.[7]

Why was anti-Russian feeling so much more extreme in Britain than in France? The most convincing explanation is the one provided by Gleason. Given the background of Russophobia in Britain, the British public was far more receptive to the cries of alarm expressed by their journalists and by Palmerston. The French, on the other hand, were far more skeptical about accepting the opinions voiced by their own press, perhaps for the very reason that it was official. But there were more compelling reasons for the French lack of enthusiasm for the Crimean War. Unlike the English, the French were drafted to fight in it; they resented the personal and financial burdens it entailed; and they intensely disliked the alliance with England, for so many centuries the traditional enemy of France and still bitterly resented for the defeat of the first Napoleon. By the end of the Crimean War, most French appear to have been far more favorably disposed toward Russia than toward Britain, despite the official anti-Russian propaganda.

Throughout the Crimean crisis one European state worked persistently to avoid war, and after war broke out, continued to work persistently to bring it to an end. That state was Austria (the Habsburg Empire), whose efforts at pacification were not so much motivated by humanitarian concerns as by an acute awareness of how much Austria had to lose by almost any changes in the existing international order—and nothing was more likely to effect such changes than a major European war.

Despite having suffered a harrowing series of defeats at the hands of Napoleon, the Habsburg Empire had emerged from the Napoleonic Wars as one of the acknowledged great powers of Europe and with tacit international sanction to serve as something of a guardian of postwar treaty arrangements in both Germany and Italy. The empire acquired this seemingly powerful position not through its intrinsic strength but, rather, through the skill of its diplomats, most notably Prince Metternich, whose name became synonymous with the entire postwar era. During this period, Austrian leaders became painfully aware of the inadequacy of their empire's resources to preserve its European position or even to maintain its existing territorial status. Not only did the empire lack the economic resources of Britain and France or the manpower resources of Russia, it also lacked the institutions to mobilize effectively those resources it did possess. The empire was made up of provinces with widely diverse administrative and economic systems, and inhabited by populations with widely different ethnic, linguistic, and cultural backgrounds.

By far the greatest of the empire's weaknesses was its multinational character. The nineteenth century was an era of rising national self-consciousness, when nationalities that had lived for centuries under foreign rule began to voice demands for independence through the establishment of their own sovereign states. The threat of nationalist aspirations to the Habsburg Empire was dramatically demonstrated during the revolutions of 1848, when Italians, Hungarians, and Czechs rose against the German-dominated Habsburg government. Imperial forces succeeded in suppressing those uprisings, though in the case of Hungary only with the aid of Russia; but to Austrian statesmen the threat of nationalism to the empire's survival was now manifest.

At the head of the Habsburg government was Emperor Francis Joseph, who had come to the throne in 1848 in the course of the revolutionary disturbances. Although the very embodiment of imperial dignity, he had serious deficiencies as a statesman. He was a conscientious bureaucrat, who appeared to assume that meticulous attention to detail was the prime requisite for governing his country. Unimaginative and inconsistent in his conduct of affairs, he was always prepared to try new experiments to extricate his empire from its perennial difficulties and dilemmas but never showed a sound understanding of the nature of those problems.

At the emperor's side as foreign minister during the Crimean crisis was Count Buol, an experienced diplomat (he had earlier been Austria's ambassador to St. Petersburg and London), who was allowed to conduct foreign policy with a great deal of independence and who, so far as one can judge from the official documents, was the chief formulator of Austrian policy in the Near East.[8] According to the testimony of his associates, Buol was unusually reserved about his personal affairs, and he reveals almost nothing about himself in his private papers; as a result, he remains an elusive historical personality. More surprisingly, he remains almost unknown as a political figure, although he emerges from the official records as a diplomat of great professional skill and tenacity, who demonstrated a high degree of resourcefulness in his efforts to preserve and restore peace. Both Buol and the emperor, however, failed to perceive, as Metternich had done, that their empire's very existence depended on retaining the confidence, friendship, and support of the other conservative powers of Europe. Both shared the fears of other European states about the apparent menace of Russia, both were alarmed by the tsar's occasional pronouncements on behalf of the subject Christian nationalities of the Ottoman Empire, and both made the cardinal error of allowing their fears of Russia to obscure their fundamental need for Russian friendship—even at the cost of seeming to become a Russian protectorate.

During the initial stages of the Crimean crisis, Metternich from retirement warned his government in the strongest possible terms of the need for Austria to work for the preservation of peace. "There is only one course we must cling to and that is *the political,* which means in fact the *maintenance of treaties and the prevention of a European war from Oriental causes."* Once the war had begun, he thought Austria's primary task was "the quickest possible restoration of peace" and believed that this could be done most effectively through international conferences, preferably in Vienna, with carefully conceived agenda. Austria, he warned, should not become actively involved in the war under any circumstances or allow itself to be towed off either to the East or to the West: "We are called to the *task of restoring peace* . . . but we must never let ourselves be used as the shock troops of East against West or West against East."[9]

Buol was to make Metternich's advice a guideline for many of his own policies, but as the Crimean crisis developed he became increasingly obsessed about the Russian menace and was ultimately to disregard the most crucial feature of that advice by advocating Austria's participation in the war on the side of Britain and France in the hope of curbing the power of Russia. He was prevented from taking this course by his more conservative emperor, whose other advisers drew his attention to his empire's miserable financial and military position. Under the guidance of Buol, however, Austria did send ultimata to Russia that, although they brought the war to an end, did so at a cost to Austria of converting Russia from a staunch ally into an implacable enemy.

How justified were Turkish and Western fears of Russia? As the Turkish experience over the previous two centuries had shown—and as had the experience of almost every other neighbor of Russia—they were very justified indeed. Moreover there was every reason to remain fearful of Russia, because Russia's very existence—its sheer size and power—constituted a permanent threat to the security of the states of Europe and the Ottoman Empire. But how immediate was that threat in the 1850s? Was the tsar actually planning another incursion into the Ottoman Empire at this time? Was he for his part unwilling to compromise and prepared to risk war to realize his ambitions?

Tsar Nicholas I has been described as an unimaginative bureaucrat, a simple and straightforward military man who believed the state should be organized and administered like a well-drilled army. It is difficult to understand how he could have acquired this reputation, for in many ways he was as complex and unpredictable as his brother and predecessor, the mystic-romantic Tsar Alexander I. He was possessed by sudden hatreds and enthusiasms; he suffered from severe bouts of depression; his ideas could veer with diconcerting suddenness from one extreme to another. Although he regraded himself as a supreme autocrat and insisted on keeping all decision-making powers, even for comparatively minor matters, in his own hands, he could be easily influenced by his advisers, and some of his sudden shifts in policy may be explained by shifts in the nature of the advice he was receiving.

Among his weaknesses as a diplomat was his predilection for dealing directly with other monarchs or their representatives, his confidence that he could solve the most complicated international problems through such personal diplomacy, and his belief that he could trust his fellow monarchs as he believed they trusted him. In these personal negotiations he allowed his ideas to flow freely, and in doing so he indulged in indiscretions that frequently seemed to contradict previous assurances about his intentions and thereby destroyed the trust he thought he enjoyed.

A far more serious and ultimately fatal flaw in the tsar's diplomacy, however, was his exaggerated sense of pride and honor, his need to save face and his insistence on exacting grim retribution for real or fancied humiliations to himself and his country. While inordinately sensitive about his own honor, he seemed incapable of understanding or sympathizing with the pride and honor of others or of perceiving how his own behavior and statements might be interpreted by the leaders of foreign powers. Quick to take offense, he often gave offense apparently without even realizing he was doing so.

In his conduct of diplomacy, the tsar had a stabilizing influence at his side in the person of Count Charles Nesselrode, Russian foreign minister and chancellor of the empire. With skill and tact Nesselrode tried to guide the tsar along a consistent political course; he provided him with sound advice which the tsar all too frequently ignored; he made valiant efforts to cover up or explain away the tsar's indiscretions; and upon occasion he demonstrated a rare degree of moral courage in contradicting or opposing his sovereign.

Nesselrode himself was a statesman in the tradition of Metternich. He viewed political problems in their European perspective; he recognized the desirability of working with and through the Concert of Europe; and he took into account the probable reaction of other powers to any policies Russia might pursue. His frequent analyses of the international situation and anticipation of the policies of other states were often uncanny in their prescience. Unlike Metternich, however, Nesselrode was never allowed a free hand in the conduct of affairs. The major decisions in foreign policy, as in all affairs of state, were made by the tsar. And the tsar, although the professed champion of conservatism in Europe, often appeared willing to adopt a foreign policy of extreme radicalism.

When he first ascended the throne in December 1825, Nicholas I had certainly seemed prepared to pursue a radical policy in the Near East. Unlike his brother Alexander I, who for all his vagaries had generally cooperated with the other powers in defending the international order established after the Napoleonic Wars, Nicholas initially conducted a foreign policy designed to promote the exclusive interests of Russia as he understood them. He intervened frequently in the affairs of the Ottoman Empire, and in 1828 he went to war with Turkey because of Turkey's repudiation of previous treaty agreements. In the course of that war, however, a number of the tsar's ministers, foremost among them Count Nesselrode, expressed increasing alarm about the possibility of foreign intervention and warned of the dangers to Russia of weakening the Ottoman Empire still further. In response to these concerns, the tsar set up a special commission to consider further Russian policy toward the Ottoman Empire.

The tsar's commission, in whose deliberations Nesselrode played a leading role, recommended that Russia make peace with Turkey as quickly as possible and henceforth observe a policy of restraint in the Near East. Any further Russian advance risked the danger of provoking foreign intervention and war with one or more of the European great powers, or the participation of those powers in a partition of the Ottoman Empire with the result that Russia would have powerful and dangerous rivals along its frontiers instead of the hapless Turks. The interests of Russia would be best served, the tsar's advisers believed, by preserving the Ottoman Empire, which formed an enormous buffer zone along Russia's southwestern flank—an empire too weak to threaten Russian security in any way but that through its very existence shielded Russia from more dangerous powers. Meanwhile the decline of Turkey should be allowed to continue unhindered, leaving Russia in a position to absorb the entire Ottoman Empire when its rivals were occupied elsewhere or when some propitious opportunity should arise.[10]

The tsar accepted this advice, and for the next two decades Russia refrained from further advances at the expense of the Ottoman Empire and cooperated with other concerned powers to prevent the encroachments of anyone else. This was still the policy of the Russian government when Napoleon laid down his challenge to Russia in the Near East in the spring of 1850. In his reaction to this challenge, however, the tsar's flaw of exaggerated pride was glaringly revealed. Under intense pressure from France, the Ottoman government made concessions to France that conflicted with previous concessions to Russia. To compensate for what he regarded as the indignities suffered by Russia as a result of these concessions, the tsar was to submit demands to the Ottoman government that were to alarm Europe and provide all the evidence his enemies needed of Russia's aggressive intentions.

Chapter 2

The Initiation of the Crisis

The Dispute over the Holy Places

Napoleon's selection of the Near East as a location in which to provoke a crisis with Russia was a brilliant choice, for it was here that Russia posed the most serious threat to the interests of two other European great powers, Britain and Austria, and a threat to the very existence of the major non-European power involved, the Ottoman Empire. Moreover, the Ottoman Empire had not been included in the treaties concluded after the Napoleonic Wars, so that in making demands on that empire Napoleon was not violating or even challenging existing international agreements. The issue Napoleon selected for the provocation of that crisis was the right to protect the Christian Holy Places in the Ottoman Empire.

The dispute among political and religious bodies over the possession and control of the Christian Holy Places in the Near East (the scenes of the life and death of Christ) is as old as the history of the Christian church itself. The dispute entered a new phase with the conquest of the entire Near East by the Ottoman Turks and their capture of Constantinople in 1453. Since that time the two principal branches of the Christian faith—the Roman Catholic or Latin church and the Orthodox or Greek church—had vied with each other to secure permission from the Ottoman government to be allowed access to the Holy Places, to build churches and sanctuaries there, and to serve as their owners and guardians. Since the seventeenth century the principal foreign champion of the Latins in the Near East had been France, while for the Orthodox that role had been assumed by Russia since the days of Peter the Great, whose successors came to take it for granted that they exercised a sort of guardianship over the entire Orthodox church and its membership, including the Orthodox population of the Ottoman Empire.[1]

The issue of the Holy Places and the status of the Christian churches in the Ottoman Empire was of far greater importance to Russia than to France. There were approximately thirteen million Orthodox Christians in the Ottoman Empire, well over one-third of the entire population. Large numbers of Orthodox pilgrims from within the empire and from abroad (mostly from Russia), visited the Holy Places annually and contributed substantially to their support. The size of the Latin population of the Ottoman Empire, on the other hand, was comparatively small, as was the number of Latin pilgrims in relation to their Orthodox counterparts.[2]

The significance of the Orthodox church in the Ottoman Empire far exceeded its religious functions. All the larger confessional groups in the empire, including the Moslems, were organized in communities, or *millets*. These *millets* did not embrace a unified territory, and, although they were later to be identified with national groups within the empire, their membership differed widely in their ethnic as well as in their social, economic, and cultural composition. Despite their geographical dispersion and heterogeneous character, these *millets* were used by the Ottoman government as vehicles of secular administration. They had their own courts and prisons, schools, hospitals, and homes for the aged and infirm; they collected taxes on behalf of the Ottoman government; and they had the right to levy taxes for their own support.[3]

Foremost among the officials of the Orthodox church in the Ottoman Empire was the patriarch of Constantinople. Regarded by his fellow patriarchs (of Antioch, Jerusalem, and Alexandria) as only the first among equals, he was recognized by the Ottoman government as the leader of the entire Orthodox church. His election by the synod (council) of the church had to be confirmed by the sultan, and he was ceremoniously installed in office

by officials of the Ottoman government. In his capacity as head
of the Orthodox millet, the patriarch of Constantinople was thus
the civil as well as spiritual leader of the Orthodox church and
in theory exercised almost absolute jurisdiction over the entire
Orthodox population of the Ottoman Empire.[4]

The political authority of the Orthodox church and its hierarchy derived from the Ottoman government and had nothing
whatsoever to do with Russia, but it is easy to understand how
the tsar, as de facto head of the Orthodox church in Russia,
should resent any threat to the rights or influence of that church
in Turkey. It is easier still to understand how any Russian claim
to a protectorate over the Orthodox church in the Ottoman Empire would be feared as a move to establish Russian control over
the entire Orthodox population of that empire. The dispute over
the Holy Places was thus no empty issue of national prestige or
a mere church wardens' quarrel, as some historians have described it, but a question of power and influence in the Near
East.

Napoleon's III's intervention on behalf of the Latin church in
the Ottoman Empire has been interpreted as an effort to curry
favor with influential clerical groups in France, and there can be
no doubt that this consideration entered into his calculations. But
for the French emperor neither the issue of the Holy Places nor
any advantages he might have gained in Turkey or in France itself by acquiring protectorate rights over them were the main
issue. As noted earlier, his primary objective was the breakup of
the existing international system and the disruption of the alliances designed to defend that system, an objective described
with complete candor by Drouyn de Lhuys, Napoleon's foreign
minister since July 1852: "The question of the Holy Places and
everything affecting them was of no importance whatever to
France," he confided to a friend shortly after the beginning of the
war. "All this Eastern Question* which provoked so much noise

* The term *Eastern Question* was used by statesmen of the nineteenth
century to refer to problems in the Balkans and the Near East. There was
no uniform definition of the geographical area covered by the Eastern Ques-

was nothing more for the imperial government than a means of dislocating the continental alliance which had tended to paralyze France for almost half a century. When finally an opportunity presented itself to provoke discord within this powerful coalition, the Emperor Napoleon immediately seized it." Napoleon himself was equally candid. During the final negotiations for peace in March 1856, he informed his ministers that in order to destroy the effect of the treaties concluded after the Napoleonic Wars it had been necessary to separate Austria and Russia "which were always ready to menace us with the European coalition and which deprived us of all our liberty. That was the great objective of the war; to separate the two powers and to regain for France . . . its liberty of action abroad."[5]

Napoleon III launched his campaign in the Near East in May of 1850, and in successive representations to the Ottoman government over the next two and a half years he demanded the restoration of the rights of the Latin church over the Holy Places in the Ottoman Empire which had been allowed to lapse in the previous century. These French demands were based on a long line of treaties dating back to 1528, the most important of them a treaty of 1740.[6] As both Napoleon and the Turks were well aware, any concessions to France over the Holy Places were certain to generate conflict with Russia, because over the past century many rights previously conceded to France on behalf of the Latin church had been taken over by default by the Orthodox church, which the tsars had come to regard as being under their special protection.[7]

The French government set forth its claims in violent and intimidating language, and backed them up with impressive displays of French military power and threats to use it if the Turks

---

tion, but there was general agreement that it embraced the Balkan and Black Sea regions, Asia Minor as far as the Caucasus Mountains in the east and the Red Sea in the west, and the eastern part of North Africa, Egypt in particular. Politically, most of this area had been part of the Ottoman Empire at the beginning of the nineteenth century, but by the time of the Crimean War the Greeks had obtained their independence through revolution.

refused to make the required concessions. Although the Turks professed to be indignant about French demands and threats, they may actually have welcomed France's challenge to Russia over the Holy Places, especially as the French accompanied their demands with assurances of military support in case any concessions made to France should involve the Turks in difficulties with Russia. Whether intimidated by French pressure or happy to seize the opportunity to play off France against Russia in the Near East, the Turks in December 1852 conceded everything the French government had demanded.[8]

Russian Plans for a Counteroffensive: Prelude to the Menshikov Mission

Ever since the government of Napoleon III first raised the issue of the Holy Places in the Near East, the Russians had protested against French claims and the sultan's concessions to the Latin church, which they denounced as violations of Turkish treaties with Russia confirming the traditional rights of the Orthodox church. In response to the Turkish concessions of December 1852, the tsar ordered the mobilization of two army corps in southern Russia and sent an alert to his garrisons and naval forces on the Black Sea. At the same time he jotted down notes about possible policies Russia might pursue to exact reparation from the Ottoman government for Turkey's treaty violations and to secure guarantees for the future. These jottings have been interpreted as plans for the conquest or partition of the Ottoman Empire, but if anything they reveal the tsar's awareness of the dangers for Russia of drastic action and his fears about the consequences of the collapse of that empire. After weighing the pros and cons of various courses of action, all of which he appears to have rejected as excessively dangerous or ineffective (*inconvénients*), he considered the possibility of a peaceful partition of the Ottoman Empire among the major European powers (Austria, Britain, France, and Russia), but he clearly disliked the prospect of partition, which he labeled significantly, "the least bad of all bad possibilities [*combinaisons*]."[9]

These notes of the tsar, or the ideas expressed in them, were communicated to his chancellor and foreign minister, Count Nesselrode, who begged his sovereign to abandon all suggestions of a partition of the Ottoman Empire. "Your Majesty has observed with infinite good reason that the maintenance of the Ottoman Empire is closely linked with the true interests of Russia. Ever since the Peace of Adrianople [1829] its preservation has been the object of his most lively concern and the goal of his constant efforts." In making concessions to the Latin church, the Ottoman government had violated a solemn promise to the tsar, an act of bad faith that clearly required reparation. But how was Russia to obtain it without compromising the existence of the Ottoman Empire?

For this purpose Nesselrode proposed, "as the least dangerous method" of securing the restoration of Russian rights, that a special envoy be sent to impress upon the sultan the dangers he was incurring owing to the faulty advice of his ministers and to remind him of his solemn promises to Russia. Nesselrode recommended that such a diplomatic mission be entrusted to a person of high rank who enjoyed the confidence of the tsar, that he should be supplied with detailed instructions, but that he should be given discretionary powers to adopt a threatening or conciliatory tone according to the circumstances of the moment. Nesselrode enclosed the draft of a treaty embodying Russia's demands on Turkey and thought there was every reason to hope that the Ottoman government would accept them, especially as the presentation of Russia's demands would be supported, as the French demands had been, by ostentatious displays of Russian military might. "It is fear which drove it [the Turkish government] into the arms of France; it is likewise fear which will bring it back to us."

In making these proposals, Nesselrode emphasized yet again that the tsarist government must constantly bear in mind that the fundamental interests of Russia lay in the preservation of peace and the status quo in the Near East. While expressing confidence in the diplomatic mission he had suggested, he warned that even this "least dangerous method" was fraught with peril. If the Russian diplomatic mission failed, Russia might be obliged to carry out its threats and go to war with Turkey. Before incurring a risk of this kind, the Russian government should consider carefully the conditions under which such a war would have to be fought and be under no illusions that this would merely be a war against Turkey. It would be a war against France as well, and one that Russia would have to fight without allies. France would be able to exploit the deep-seated suspicions in Europe—above all in England—about Russian ambitions in the Near East, but Russia would also have to reckon with similar suspicions and hostility on the part of Austria. There remained only Prussia, which might at most give Russia moral support.

If Russia should nevertheless find it necessary to adopt a threatening attitude toward Turkey, Nesselrode advised that the Russian government make every effort to reassure other powers of the purity of its intentions and to secure their support in persuading Turkey to yield to Russia's just demands. Even then, prejudiced and jealous minds would remain suspicious of Russia's ulterior designs. To avoid nourishing such suspicions, Nesselrode warned the tsar not to inform the British or other governments about his ideas concerning the partition of the Ottoman Empire. In the case of Britain such a communication would not only be dangerous but useless, for it had always been a fundamental principle of British policy to avoid diplomatic engagements about the future and to await events before deciding what course to pursue.[10]

It must have been some time in January 1853 that the tsar agreed to Nesselrode's plan to send a diplomatic mission to Constantinople and to the appointment of Prince Alexander Menshikov to lead the Russian delegation, but there is no record of the tsar's decision on this matter or of how Menshikov was chosen for this critical assignment. The only record of his appointment was included in the detailed instructions that Nesselrode and his staff prepared for the Menshikov mission, dated 9 February, in which Menshikov was informed that the tsar had named him ambassador-extraordinary to undertake a mission of great im-

portance to Constantinople "which must be of very short duration."[11]

Several months later, after the failure of the Menshikov mission, the tsar complained that he had agreed to it with great
reluctance because he was convinced of its futility, but existing
documents indicate neither his reluctance nor his premonitions of
failure. He took it for granted that France would be hostile, but
he was hopeful that a firm but courteous policy toward France
would make possible a peaceful settlement of whatever differences might arise from forceful Russian behavior in Constantinople. Unlike Nesselrode, he had no doubts that he could rely
completely on the loyalty and support of the conservative governments of Austria and Prussia—especially Austria, whose policies had consistently demonstrated that there was "a complete
conformity of views and interests in the Orient between ourselves and the Cabinet of Vienna." About the attitude of Britain,
too, he saw reason to be confident, especially since December
1852 when Lord Aberdeen, with whom he had had a most satisfactory exchange of views during his visit to England in 1844,
had taken over the leadership of the British government.[12]

The tsar was soon given further reason to feel hopeful about
the prospects of the Menshikov mission, for early in 1853 an almost identical Austrian mission to Constantinople was completely
successful and incurred no international complications.

The Leiningen Mission

The occasion for the Austrian mission to Constantinople was yet
another crisis in the Near East, this one over the tiny mountain
principality of Montenegro, legally part of the Ottoman Empire
although never effectively controlled by the Turkish government.

In 1852 Danilo, the prince-bishop of Montenegro, a protégé
of the tsar and the recipient of a Russian subsidy, had been encouraged by Russia to secularize his rule and proclaim himself
prince. Interpreting this act as a step toward the complete independence of Montenegro, the Turks sent an army into the coun-

try under one of their most competent generals. Danilo appealed to the governments of Austria and Russia for aid. Austria, with the approval and support of Russia, responded to this appeal by sending a diplomatic mission to Constantinople in January 1853 under Field Marshal Count Leiningen (in French, Linanges) to demand that Turkey immediately suspend hostilities and withdraw its army from Montenegro. If Turkey refused, Leiningen was to threaten the sultan with joint Austro-Russian intervention. Like the French in the previous year, the Austrians backed up their diplomatic mission with an impressive display of military might and placed their troops along the Turkish frontiers on a war footing. When the Turks attempted to procrastinate, Leiningen rejected their evasive replies, threatened to break off diplomatic relations, and prepared to sail for home.[13]

Incorrectly informed that the Leiningen mission had failed, the tsar wrote to Austrian Emperor Francis Joseph on 23 February to assure him that if Austria became involved in war with Turkey, he would act exactly as though Turkey had declared war on himself. He had instructed Prince Menshikov (who had by this time embarked on *his* mission) to make a declaration to this effect in Constantinople; meanwhile, he was putting two army corps as well as his Black Sea fleet on a war footing. Thus they would be ready for anything. The tsar emphasized, however, that he would deplore having to go to war, for war might very well bring about the collapse of the Ottoman Empire and the consequences of that collapse would be incalculable.[14]

The tsar's fears proved to be groundless, for at the end of February the Turks yielded to all of Austria's demands. With this striking diplomatic victory the Austrians demonstrated, as the French had done, that the Turks would yield to diplomatic pressure backed up by the threat of war.

The success of the Leiningen mission not only encouraged the tsar to expect that the Menshikov mission would be equally successful, but, perhaps even more important, it reinforced his belief that the Austrians, who were lavish with their expressions of gratitude for Russian support during the crisis, could be counted on to give him similar support in his own negotiations with the Turks. The Leiningen mission was thus an event of considerable importance in fostering the illusions of the tsar. It was not, however, the model or inspiration for the subsequent Menshikov mission, as some historians have assumed, for the Menshikov mission had been conceived earlier and the procedures proposed by the Russians may in fact have provided the inspiration for the Leiningen mission rather than the other way around.

Russian War Plans

At the height of the crisis over Montenegro, the tsar informed his military advisers in a memorandum of 19 January 1853 that he expected a rupture with Turkey at any moment. In that case, he said, the best course for Russia would be to launch a sudden and decisive surprise attack on the Ottoman Empire before the French were able to intervene. To anticipate this possibility, he and his military and naval experts prepared plans to move large military and naval forces from Sebastopol and Odessa to capture Constantinople and gain control of the Straits* so as to block their entry to foreign warships. Convinced by his advisers that an attack on Constantinople and the Straits would be difficult if not impossible—the Turks were already reinforcing their well-nigh impregnable strategic positions there—the tsar prepared a set of alternative plans for attacking the Ottoman Empire, some of which were worked out by his military and naval staffs in considerable detail.[15]

The tsar's memorandum of 19 January and the detailed military plans subsequently drawn up by himself and his advisers provide even stronger support than his jottings of the previous December for the interpretation that the tsar intended to exploit the existing crises and go to war with Turkey in order to assure Russia's predominant position in the Near East. Once again, however, we seem to be dealing with a set of contingency plans.

---

* The Turkish Straits between the Black Sea and the Mediterranean, including the Dardanelles, the Sea of Marmara, and the Bosporus.

In sending a copy of his military plans to Field Marshal Paskevich in Warsaw, the tsar expressed the hope that the crisis
would still be resolved without war. "I shall decide on this only
in extreme circumstances," he said; it was easy enough to start a
war, but only God knew how it would end.[16]

The fact remains that the tsar did not go to war with Turkey at
this time or do anything else to implement his military plans; that
he agreed to Nesselrode's proposal to send a diplomatic mission
to Constantinople; and that he demonstrated remarkable restraint
in reacting to the numerous provocative incidents that took place
during the course of that mission. Following the failure of the
Menshikov mission, he sent a proposal for military action in the
Balkans to General Gorchakov, his commander in the Balkan region, to anticipate the renewed possibility of a rupture with Turkey. Far from being a plan to avenge Russia's diplomatic defeat,
the tsar's proposal stressed his continued desire to avoid war with
Turkey because of his concern for the welfare of his troops and
because of the ill-defined nature of Russia's goals in the event of
the collapse of the Ottoman Empire. He therefore intended to
keep up his military and diplomatic pressure on Turkey and if
necessary carry out his threat to recognize the independence of
Turkey's Danubian Principalities,* but he would undertake no
further action to undermine the Ottoman Empire for only Al-
mighty God would be able to determine what the consequences
of that might be.[17]

The Seymour Conversations

Although he had previously expressed confidence about the
friendly attitude of the British government toward the forthcoming Menshikov mission, the tsar nevertheless thought it ad-

---

* The Danubian Principalities were Moldavia and Wallachia, at this time
still under Turkish suzerainty, which in 1859 became the state of Rumania.
By agreements with the Ottoman government, Russia had sent an army into
the principalities in September 1848 to suppress a revolution there against
Turkish rule. Russian occupation forces remained in the principalities until
1851.

visable to make certain of Britain's understanding and support for Russian policy in the Near East.

Early in 1853, shortly after Aberdeen took office, the tsar had a series of conversations with the British ambassador to St. Petersburg, Sir George Hamilton Seymour. In the course of these conversations he expressed views about the Eastern Question similar to those he had expressed to Aberdeen in 1844, which Aberdeen, at that time British foreign secretary, appeared to have accepted and approved.[18] The tsar assured Seymour that he was still convinced that it was in the best interests of Russia to preserve the Ottoman Empire but noted that he was confronted daily with fresh evidence that the collapse of that empire was imminent. Because of the international dangers that would arise from its collapse, he thought it more urgent than ever that Britain and Russia come to an understanding prior to such a catastrophe so as to avoid the chaos, confusion, and likelihood of a general European war if no such preparations were made. The tsar did not ask for a formal treaty but only a general understanding—"that between gentlemen is sufficient."

The tsar emphasized that his desire for a preliminary agreement to anticipate the collapse of the Ottoman Empire did not imply any desire on the part of Russia to expand at the expense of that empire. On the contrary, he believed it would be positively dangerous for Russia to extend an empire that was already too large, and he specifically repudiated the expansionist ambitions attributed to Catherine the Great.[19]

Shortly after his first conversation with the tsar about the problems of the Ottoman Empire, Seymour sent a shrewd and on the whole sympathetic appraisal of the tsar's character to the British foreign secretary, Lord John Russell. "Although the Emperor walks about in a helmet, sleeps on a camp-bed, and occasionally talks gunpowder, he is not more keen on war than his neighbors," Seymour said. "He occasionally takes a precipitate step; but as reflection arrives, reason and Count Nesselrode make themselves heard. He is not sorry to recede if he can do so without a loss of dignity. He cannot, however, give up his pretentions as to the

Holy Places; his case is too clear, and the question is one which is very interesting to the feelings of the Church of which he is in some measure the head."[20] Seymour was also impressed by the tsar's desire for an agreement with Britain that might prevent a scramble for the inheritance of the Ottoman Empire. "A noble triumph would be obtained by the civilization of the nineteenth century," he concluded in his report of his first long conversation with the tsar, "if the void left by the extinction of Mahommedan rule in Europe could be filled up without an interruption of the general peace, in consequence of the precautions adopted by the two principal Governments the most interested in the destinies of Turkey."[21]

Had the tsar been content with a reaffirmation of his desire to preserve the Ottoman Empire and a clear-cut denial of all Russian ambitions to extend its territory or influence at the expense of that empire, he might have succeeded in reassuring the British about his intentions. Instead, in a subsequent conversation with Seymour on 21 February, he embarked on a discussion of his ideas about a partition of the Ottoman Empire, ideas that Nesselrode had so strongly warned him not to reveal because they would be certain to arouse suspicion about Russian motives. In the event of the dissolution of the Ottoman Empire, the tsar told Seymour, it might be less difficult to arrive at a satisfactory territorial arrangement than was commonly believed. The Danubian Principalities were in fact already an independent state under the tsar's protection, and he saw no reason why Serbia and Bulgaria might not be conceded a similar status. As for Egypt, he quite understood its importance to England and would not object if the British took possession of Egypt upon the collapse of the Ottoman Empire, and of Crete, too, if this suited their purposes.

The tsar's partition ideas seemed to contradict all his pious renunciations of further Russian territorial ambitions, for he was in effect claiming a Russian protectorate over the greater part of the Balkans—and seemed to be offering Britain a bribe to participate in or at least condone his nefarious schemes. No less alarming were the tsar's remarks about the attitude of Austria. When Seymour sounded him as to whether there was any understanding between the cabinets of St. Petersburg and Vienna, the tsar replied, "greatly to my [Seymour's] surprise:" "Oh! . . . but you must understand that when I speak of Russia, I speak of Austria as well; what suits the one suits the other; our interests as regards Turkey are perfectly identical."[22]

Nesselrode did his best to cover up his sovereign's indiscretions by drawing up a memorandum for the British government that purported to be a written summary of the tsar's "true" views. In discussing informally with the British ambassador the possibility of the imminent collapse of the Ottoman Empire, Nesselrode said, it had not entered the tsar's mind to propose an Anglo-Russian contingency plan for the disposal of the provinces ruled by the sultan, much less a formal treaty between the two cabinets. Although it was true, as the British consistently maintained, that the collapse of the Ottoman Empire was an uncertain future eventuality, the fact remained that such a catastrophe might take place, and very unexpectedly at that. This possibility was the reason why the tsar had so ardently desired an informal exchange of views on the subject.[23]

Nesselrode's memorandum was skillfully conceived, but as he must have feared it did not dissipate the suspicions aroused in Britain by the tsar's indiscretions. The tsar's views offered matter for the most anxious reflection, Seymour told Russell. If a sovereign insisted with such pertinacity upon the impending fall of a neighboring state, he must have settled in his own mind that the hour of its dissolution was at hand. Seymour suspected that an intimate understanding existed between Russia and Austria, and that the tsar's object in raising the question of the partition of the Ottoman Empire was to engage Britain as well as Austria in some partition scheme so as to exclude France from the arrangement. When the tsar went so far as to set forth specific partition proposals, Seymour became thoroughly alarmed and thought it might be necessary to go to war with Russia to thwart the tsar's ambitions. Lord John Russell, who relinquished the post of foreign secretary in February 1853 but remained a member of the

Aberdeen cabinet, was convinced that the tsar was "clearly bent on accomplishing the destruction of Turkey, and *he must be resisted.*"[24]

In studies of the origins of the Crimean War, the Seymour conversations are generally treated in some detail and have even been considered a turning point in Britain's relations with Russia, for they seemed to provide confirmation of British suspicions of the tsar and thus contributed significantly to the anti-Russian direction of British policy.

There can be no question that the tsar bungled badly in making his indiscreet revelations to the British envoy, yet there is reason to doubt whether the Seymour conversations were in fact as significant as they are often considered to be. The British press had already stirred up passionate hostility to Russia among the British public, and the British statesmen who were to take the lead in conducting an anti-Russian policy were already firmly convinced about Russian duplicity and did not need Seymour's reports to confirm their suspicions. The leaders of the British government at the time of the Seymour conversations—Lord Aberdeen, the prime minister, and Lord Clarendon, who had taken Russell's place at the foreign office—were as yet little affected by the anti-Russian clamor of the British press, nor do they appear to have been seriously disturbed by the Seymour conversations.[25] Aberdeen, in fact, assured Baron Brunnow, the Russian ambassador to London, of Britain's support for the forthcoming Menshikov mission. "Whether right or wrong, we advise the Turks to yield." With the receipt of this assurance, Brunnow was convinced that the prospects for the success of the Menshikov mission were excellent.[26]

They might have remained excellent if Aberdeen had remained in firm control of his own government, but in the following weeks his influence was undermined and usurped by more determined and passionate opponents of Russia in the British government. Foremost among them was Lord Palmerston, who had been compelled to resign as foreign secretary from a previous cabinet as a result of a controversy with the Crown and who presently held the post of home secretary in the Aberdeen government.

Unaware of or unconcerned by the widespread hostility that existed against him in Britain and blithely confident that he could count on the support of Austria and Prussia, the tsar went ahead with his plan to send an emissary to Constantinople to put pressure on the Ottoman government. Still anxious to reassure the British government, the tsar explained that this action had been provoked by the policies of France, which had employed tactics of intimidation and threats to extort concessions from the sultan in violation of solemn promises previously made to Russia. The Russian government had therefore regretfully decided that it must adopt similar measures and appealed to the British government for understanding and support.

Chapter 3

The Menshikov Mission

In proposing to send a mission of intimidation to Constantinople, Nesselrode had recommended that its leadership be entrusted to a person of high rank who enjoyed the confidence of the tsar and who would be capable of impressing upon the Turkish government Russia's determination to exact reparations for Turkey's violation of existing treaties and to secure guaranties for the future.[1]

Prince Alexander Menshikov possessed all these qualifications. A personal aide of the tsar, a former minister of the Russian navy, governor of Finland, and a cavalry general, he was one of the highest-ranking dignitaries of the realm and heir to an immense private fortune. In appearance he was tall and dignified, in manner overbearing and arrogant. People who knew him well described him as a man of wit and charm, but it was obviously his high rank and his less agreeable personal qualities that determined his selection to lead the Russian mission to Constantinople. To reinforce the impression of the Russian government's seriousness of purpose, Menshikov was accompanied by an imposing suite, including a glittering array of military and naval officers. The Russian government has been much criticized for selecting the arrogant Menshikov, a professional soldier, for so delicate a mission, instead of an experienced diplomat. The object of the mission, however, was not to conduct delicate diplomatic negotiations but, rather, to impress and intimidate. For this purpose, Menshikov seemed an ideal choice. It is ironic that a major reason for the failure of his mission was that he was not forceful and brutal enough in dealing with the Turks, and that his mission, which Nesselrode had insisted should be of "very short duration," dragged on for almost three months.[2]

Menshikov's Instructions:
The Demand for a Formal Treaty

Menshikov was supplied with a set of careful and detailed instructions, all of them dated 9 February 1853.[3] These instructions were ostensibly drawn up by Nesselrode and his foreign ministry staff in consultation with the tsar, but the German biographer of Nicholas I, Theodor Schiemann, believes they represent the unvarnished views of Nicholas himself. And indeed they seem to reflect the political thinking of the tsar far more than that of his chancellor, although the latter's cautious hand is occasionally apparent.[4]

According to these instructions, the objective of the Menshikov mission was to restore Russia's position of strength in Constantinople by securing a confirmation of Russian rights in the Ottoman Empire and a rectification of the situation created by recent Turkish concessions to other Christian sects under pressure from France at the expense of the Orthodox church and the dignity of Russia. Menshikov was to state categorically from the start that Russia wanted no new concessions, but he was to demand that the rights and privileges Russia had enjoyed for centuries should be properly promulgated and fully enforced. Menshikov was not to be satisfied with a mere repetition of promises but must insist that all previous rights and privileges be set forth in a formal convention (*sened*) that would have the force and validity of a treaty.

In case the Turks refused to agree to Russia's demands, Menshikov was to warn them that he was instructed to break off diplomatic relations and to present them with an official note summarizing Russia's grievances. Three days after the presentation of this note (presumably if the Turks had not yet agreed to Russia's conditions) he was to leave Constantinople and to give orders that he be followed by the entire Russian diplomatic staff.

Menshikov was repeatedly reminded, however, that Russia desired above all to avoid any sort of imbroglio with the Ottoman Empire. The first clash of arms would result in its inevitable dissolution, and the tsar had no desire to further such a catastrophe. But he did intend to protect the interests of the Orthodox religion in the Ottoman Empire, not only against the Turks "but against certain Christian powers." If the Turks seemed worried about the threat of French retaliation in the event they yielded to Russia's demands, Menshikov was empowered to offer them a treaty of alliance that would come into effect if France attacked the Ottoman Empire.

Menshikov was informed that the tsar's political goal in dealing with France was to inflict a moral defeat on the new Napoleonic government so as to lessen its influence over weak states such as Turkey. Napoleon needed an international complication at any cost to pursue his own ambitions, and, finding the risks too great in Belgium or on the Rhine, he had selected the Near East as the region to foment his crisis, completely indifferent to the fate of the Ottoman Empire. The present policy of the French government was designed to acquire an exclusive protectorate over the Latins in the Near East and to establish France's preponderant position there at the expense of Russia. In standing up to France in the Near East, Menshikov could count on the support of Austria, for between St. Petersburg and Vienna there was a complete conformity of views with regard to the problems of this area. Menshikov could also count on the benevolent attitude of Britain, where the Aberdeen government provided a guarantee of prudence and moderation.

The most important document included in Menshikov's set of instructions of 9 February was the draft of the formal convention with the Ottoman Empire demanded by Russia. Menshikov was informed that all the provisions of the proposed Russo-Turkish convention were based on previous engagements and involved no new concessions of any kind. Russia was demanding nothing to embarrass the Ottoman government or expose it to the com-

plaints of other Christian communities and their European protectors, which were seeking any means to destroy Russia's *secular* (my emphasis) influence over the Christian population of the
Ottoman Empire. The Russian government expressed the hope
that Menshikov could persuade the Turks to agree to Russia's
terms, but at the same time he was authorized to modify them
as he considered necessary to secure their acceptance—a most
important qualification, for Menshikov was indeed to modify
them substantially in the course of the crisis engendered by his
mission.

The purpose of the convention desired by Russia, as described
in the text of the Russian draft, was to remove all disagreement
and misunderstanding on the subject of "the immunities, rights,
and liberties accorded and assured *ab antiquo* by the Ottoman
emperors in their states to the Greek-Russian-Orthodox religion."
The convention stipulated that the "Christian Orthodox religion
would be constantly protected in all its churches, and that the
ministers of the Imperial Court of Russia will have, as in the past,
the right to make representation on behalf of the churches of
Constantinople and of other places and cities as well as on behalf of the clergy." The convention provided further that the four
patriarchs, the metropolitans, bishops, and other ecclesiastical
leaders, freely elected and ordained, should not be hindered in
fulfilling their functions, that the patriarchs should be appointed
for life, and that they should not be removed from office except
for offences against their religious community.[5]

Because of the nature of the *millet* system in the Ottoman Empire, which gave the leaders of the Orthodox church political as
well as religious authority over their membership, the convention
demanded by Russia would in effect have given the Russian government the right to make representations on behalf of all Orthodox Christians in the empire, about one-third of the entire population. The opponents of Russia were therefore perfectly justified
in maintaining that if the Turks agreed to the terms of the Russian treaty, the Ottoman Empire would be reduced to the status
of a Russian protectorate.

The Russian case was made even worse by the fact that their claims could not be justified on the basis of previous engagements with Turkey at all, but were instead the product of extravagantly broad interpretations of those engagements and longstanding Russian assumptions of protectorate rights that had no legal basis. In referring back to previous treaties, the Russians mentioned specifically only certain clauses in the Treaty of Kutchuk-Kainardji of 1774 and the Treaty of Adrianople of 1829.[6] The Treaty of Adrianople, however, said nothing whatever about Russian rights to protect the Christian religion in the Ottoman Empire except to confirm previous treaties. And of the articles of Kutchuk-Kainardji only one, Article 7, dealt with the protection of the Christian religion in the Ottoman Empire as a whole. In that article, the Ottoman government promised to provide constant protection to the Christian religion and the churches of that religion. Beyond that, however, it provided only that the Ottoman government permit a minister of the Imperial Court of Russia to make representations on all occasions on behalf of a *single* church in Constantinople—a new Orthodox church that was yet to be built—and on behalf of the clergy of that `one` church. The other provisions of the Treaty of Kutchuk-Kainardji dealing with the protection of the rights of Christians in the Ottoman Empire (Article 16) referred *only* to the populations of Turkey's Danubian Principalities of Moldavia and Wallachia.[7] These same rights were later extended to the population of Serbia (also still part of the Ottoman Empire) by the Treaty of Bucharest of 12 May 1812.[8] There was no mention of the rights of Christians or the Orthodox church in any subsequent treaties, and no previous treaties had contained specific provisions on behalf of the Orthodox patriarchs or their lifetime appointments.

Russian rights based on previous treaty provisions were thus extremely limited. The tsar and Nesselrode appear to have been completely unaware of these limitations, for they obviously assumed the existence of such rights and would have turned over the task of examining the precise terms of previous treaties to a government archivist or some other subordinate official.[9] The most likely explanation for the Russian government's crucial error in making such gross misrepresentations of previous treaty rights is that the government official entrusted with the examination of the treaties, either in an excess of patriotic zeal or more probably through sheer incompetence, made excessively liberal translations or interpretations of the pertinent clauses of Kutchuk-Kainardji. For what the Russians had done was to transform the treaty rights accorded to Christians in the Danubian Principalities into rights for Christians in the entire Ottoman Empire, and Russian rights to make representations on behalf of a *single* Orthodox church in Constantinople (yet to be built) and its clergy, into Russian rights to make representations on behalf of *all* Orthodox churches in the empire and their clergy, including the patriarch of Constantinople.[10]

Whatever the reasons for Russia's exaggerated claims, the Russian government's move to demand the formal recognition of any such claims, which not only went so far beyond the issue of the Holy Places but seemed to ignore that issue altogether, must be regarded as an egregious error of judgment. Yet that error was not necessarily irremediable. The Russians were to drop their demand for a formal treaty altogether and to modify their original claims so substantially that any remaining objections to them could have been resolved easily through negotiation. As the crisis developed, however, it became evident that the opponents of Russia were not really concerned about the terms of Russia's original claims at all, or about the fact that they were based on exaggerated interpretations of previous treaty rights. They objected to *any* Russo-Turkish agreement over the status of the Orthodox Christians in the Ottoman Empire on the grounds that any agreement would provide Russia with an excuse to intervene at will in the internal affairs of that empire and thereby deal a fatal blow to its sovereignty and independence. Thus the actual terms of the original agreement desired by Russia, significant as they seem in retrospect as justifying the rejection of Menshikov's original demands, were in themselves virtually disregarded at the time. Russia's demand for an agreement, not the terms of that agreement, was the crucial and indeed the only issue.

The objections that the opponents of Russia expressed to such an agreement, however, insofar as the agreement itself was concerned, were not only invalid but patently dishonest. As these opponents knew very well, Russia was bound by formal conventions with all five of the European great powers to respect the sovereignty and independence of the Ottoman Empire and the inviolable rights of the sultan. What the opponents of Russia feared as a threat to the Ottoman Empire was not a separate Russo-Turkish agreement; it was Russia itself, and the preponderance of Russian power in the Near East.

All the fears and apprehensions about Russia on the part of Russia's opponents were well summarized by the Duke of Argyll, a member of the Aberdeen cabinet.

By geographical position, by hereditary ambitions, by recent wars and extraordinary means and opportunities of access, Russia was the natural enemy of Turkey. It was Russia alone that was always overhanging the flanks of Turkey with her enormous mass and weight. . . . There was in the mind of all of us one unspoken but indelible opinion—that the absorption by Russia of Turkey in Europe, and the seating of the Russian Emperor on the throne of Constantinople, would give to Russia an overbearing weight in Europe, dangerous to all the other Powers and to the liberties of the world. . . . If this imperial dominion were to be added to what Russia already has, the Black Sea would be a Russian lake, the Danube would be a Russian river, and some of the richest provinces of Eastern Europe and of Western Asia would give to Russia inexhaustible resources in men, in money, and in ships. With these, together with a unique position of geographical advantage, she would possess inordinate power over the rest of Europe. . . . Men do not discuss opinions which are considered axiomatic. But it [this potential increase of Russian power] underlay every motive to action and every thought of policy. Moreover, the absorption of Turkey by Russia was not regarded by us at this time as so difficult as to be at all necessarily a very remote contingency. Russia had very recently advanced to Adrianople, and a later experience has shown us how surely she can always repeat the process. There was still another correlative assumption in our minds, and that was this: that Russia might proceed by sap and mine, and not by open conquest. By treaties, or diplomatic "notes," equivalent to treaties, giving to Russia special and exclusive rights of protectorate over the Christian subjects of the Porte, the Turkish Empire might be so politically mortgaged to Russia, that a foreclosure could be put in force at any convenient opportunity. We considered it our duty so to act and provide as to checkmate this method of deglutition as well as any other.[11]

The Conduct of Menshikov

Menshikov arrived in Constantinople on 28 February 1853, on board the steamship *Thunderer* from Odessa. He and his large entourage were immediately surrounded by immense and enthusiastic crowds of Orthodox Christians, who hailed him as their champion and savior. On his first ceremonial visit to the sultan and his government, he behaved with deliberate insolence. Violating traditional custom, he refused to call on the Turkish minister for foreign affairs, Fuad Effendi, whom the Russians blamed for earlier Turkish concessions to the French, an offensive gesture that provoked Fuad's immediate resignation.[12]

Menshikov's behavior successfully alarmed the Turks, as he had intended it should. What he failed to do was to exploit that alarm and use all the resources at his command to coerce them into accepting Russia's demands so as to bring about a speedy resolution of the crisis. Instead he allowed the Turks to procrastinate, a game at which they were supremely skillful, and in so doing he gave the anti-Russian forces in Constantinople and the cabinets of Europe the time and opportunity to mobilize their own resources to oppose the Russian demands.

After his first ceremonial visit to the sultan early in March, Menshikov did not communicate again with the Turkish government until 16 March, at which time he presented Russia's demands for a formal convention concerning Russia's rights in the Ottoman Empire.[13] But not until six days later, on 22 March, did he present the Russian draft for such a convention and demand that the Turks enter into negotiations with him immediately.[14] The Turks professed consternation and amazement over Russia's conditions. They appealed to Menshikov to be moderate. "Do not push us to extremes," Rifaat Pasha, the new Turkish foreign minister pleaded, "or you will compel us to throw ourselves into the arms of others."[15] Menshikov evidently decided to heed this warning. Instead of keeping the pressure on, he allowed himself to be diverted into negotiating over minor issues, and it was not until 10 April, seventeen days after he had first presented Russia's draft convention to the Turks, that he asked for further instructions from his own government as to whether he should persist with Russia's demands.[16]

While Menshikov procrastinated, the Turks were hard at work seeking the support of other powers against Russia. In appealing to the representatives of Britain and France, they did not show them the actual text of the Russian draft treaty but only hinted at the dire and extreme nature of the Russian demands which threatened Turkey's sovereignty and independence. Rejection of those demands, they predicted, would be followed by a Russian attack on Constantinople; if Turkey were not to fall under Russian dominion, the British and French governments would have to send their fleets to the Near East to protect the Ottoman Empire.[17]

French Fleet Sent to Salamis, March 1853

Napoleon responded to this Turkish appeal, not so much, it would appear, because he actually feared a Russian attack on Constantinople, as because he hoped the British would join in this naval action, and that such joint action would lead to closer Anglo-French cooperation in international affairs in general, one of his foremost foreign policy objectives. On 19 March 1853, he convened an extraordinary council to ask his advisers whether they thought it opportune to send a French fleet into the waters near Turkey, to the Greek anchorage of Salamis, for example. All but one of the members of the council opposed such a move, fearing that France would not find support among the other European powers, especially England. The sole supporter of the emperor's initiative was Persigny, the minister of the interior. If there was one country in the world where public opinion would be unanimous about the need to prevent Russia from acquiring Constantinople, Persigny said, it would be England. The moment the British were convinced that France was determined to halt Russia's march towards Constantinople, the British, far from resenting the attitude of the French, would jubilantly hasten to join them. Napoleon agreed. "Persigny is certainly right," he said. "If we send our fleet to Salamis, England will do the same and the union of our two fleets will initiate [*entraînera*] the union of our two peoples against Russia." He thereupon gave the order for the French fleet to proceed from Toulon to Salamis.[18]

Contrary to the expectations of Napoleon and Persigny, the British government, still dominated by Aberdeen and Clarendon, did not join in the French action. Clarendon even expressed regret that the French had made such a move without previous consultation with Britain, for he feared it might make the task of resolving the crisis in the Near East more difficult.[19]

The Return of Stratford de Redcliffe

The dispatch of the French Mediterranean fleet to Salamis clearly encouraged Turkish opposition to Russian demands. Even more encouraging was the return in April 1853 of the experienced, influential, and intensely anti-Russian British ambassador to Constantinople, Stratford Canning, who since 1852 had borne the title Viscount Stratford de Redcliffe.[20]

Stratford had been sent back to Constantinople after a lengthy leave of absence with special instructions to do everything in his power to prevent a crisis in the Near East. There is some question as to why Stratford, with his well-known anti-Russian bias and headstrong character, was selected for this delicate assignment, and in fact both Aberdeen and Clarendon had grave misgivings about his appointment. During his many years as representative of Britain in Constantinople, however, Stratford was generally believed to have acquired enormous prestige and influence among leaders of the Turkish government, and the British ministers may have hoped he would use this influence for conciliatory purposes. An even more telling motive may have been their desire to remove his influence from London.[21]

According to the instructions Stratford himself drew up for his mission to Constantinople that were subsequently approved by Aberdeen and Clarendon, he was to advise the Porte* to be prudent and urge the European powers to exercise restraint in dealing with the Ottoman government. "You are instructed to use every effort to ward off a Turkish war and to persuade the powers interested to look to an amicable termination of existing disputes." Stratford was to inform the French that the British government believed their interests in the Near East were identical and that there was nothing to prevent them from cooperating to maintain the integrity and independence of the Ottoman Empire. He was to bear in mind, however, the superior claims of Russia both with respect to the treaty obligations of Turkey and the loss of prestige the tsar would experience if, as ecclesiastical head of his church, he were to yield privileges to the Latin church previously held by the Orthodox church. In the event of an imminent threat to the existence of the Turkish government, Stratford was authorized to instruct the admiral of the British fleet at Malta to hold himself in readiness, but he was not to direct him to approach the Dardanelles without specific instructions from London.[22]

A few days before the arrival of Stratford in Constantinople, the French fleet appeared off Salamis. Clarendon, who had feared that this hasty dispatch of the French fleet would make the task of reconciliation between France and Russia more difficult, hastened to assure the Russians that Britain was making every effort to restrain France and to persuade the Turks to recognize the just demands of Russia, and that he had instructed Stratford to support the "superior claims" of Russia in Constantinople.[23] Thus Nicholas was once again allowed to believe that he could count on Britain's friendship and support. So far as Aberdeen and Clarendon were concerned, this belief was as yet thoroughly justified, but Lord Stratford de Redcliffe was quite another matter.

* The Porte: the Ottoman court; the government of the Ottoman Empire. Officially called the Sublime Porte, from the gate or portal of the sultan's palace at which justice was administered.

The Conduct of Stratford

Over the years, Stratford has had strong defenders who maintain that his conduct of policy in Constantinople was honorable and justified. Honorable it certainly was not, but it was justified if one accepts Stratford's view that Russia represented a menace to the independence of the Ottoman Empire and a threat to the interests of Britain in the Near East, and that any means were justified to halt and if possible turn back the Russian menace.

Stratford reached Constantinople on 4 April 1853. Before disembarking he wrote to his wife that Mohammed Ali, the Turkish grand vizier, had informed him of the Turkish negotiations with Menshikov, but that the Turks intended to await Stratford's arrival before making a decision. At the same time Stratford received another report from Constantinople, presumably from the acting British representative in the capital, Colonel Rose, who had been so alarmed by the Menshikov mission that he had sought to call up the British fleet when Menshikov first arrived. "We seem positively threatened at this moment by a *grand coup de main* on the part of Russia," Stratford was told. The Turks were terrified and looked upon Stratford's arrival as the signal as to whether they would live or die. "The *immediate* apparition of our fleet towards the Dardanelles would, no doubt, operate very favourably and efficiently in our sense; and it would, perhaps, be the only means of checking the Russian torrent."[24]

Stratford did not immediately call up the fleet, but he did consult immediately with leaders of the Turkish government and in general interpreted the instructions of his own government to act as mediator in Constantinople by acting as mentor to the Turks.

In advising the Turks, Stratford proposed tactics the Turks themselves had already decided to adopt. They should separate the issue of the Holy Places from all other problems and agree to a settlement of this question that would satisfy both France and Russia. But they should reject all Russian demands that would increase Russian influence over the Orthodox Christians in the Ottoman Empire. According to Stratford, the Turks had refused to show the British the actual text of the convention demanded by Russia, but they assured Stephen Pisani, the first dragoman (interpreter) at the British Embassy, that it would give Russia the right to intervene in all matters connected with the Orthodox religion in the Ottoman Empire and *"an exclusive protectorate over those who profess it."* Stratford himself concluded: "The effect of such a Convention would infallibly be the surrender to Russian influence, management, and authority, of the Greek Churches and clergy throughout Turkey, and eventually therefore of the whole Greek population dependent on the priests."[25]

Given this interpretation of the Russian demands, it was only natural that Stratford should advise the Turks to reject them and should urge them to concentrate instead on negotiations over the Holy Places. On 8 April Stratford was informed that the Turkish Grand Council had decided that Menshikov's demands were unacceptable, but for the time being they would simply tell Menshikov that until the question of the Holy Places was settled they could not enter into a discussion of other problems.[26]

In dealing with Menshikov himself, Stratford was generous with assurances that he was doing everything in his power to persuade the Turks to reach a settlement satisfactory to Russia. Menshikov nevertheless noted a marked stiffening in the attitude of the Turkish government after Stratford's arrival. He told Nesselrode that he had positive information that Stratford had been fully informed by the Turkish ministers about their negotiations on every issue.[27]

The Russian Reaction

Although suspicious that Stratford might be encouraging resistance to Russia's demands, Menshikov fell in with Stratford's tactic of negotiating on minor issues. It will be recalled that it was not until 10 April that he asked his own government about whether he should continue to insist that the Turks meet the Russian demand for a formal treaty. The Porte had accepted the substance of his proposals on the Holy Places, he told Nesselrode, and he hoped these would also prove satisfactory to the French. But the formal treaty was a far more difficult and dangerous matter. Should he press his demands to the extent of severing diplomatic relations with Turkey and in so doing threaten them with war? On the margin of Menshikov's request for instructions, the tsar wrote: "Yes. I will permit myself to add here that without a crisis of coercion it may be difficult for the Imperial Mission to regain the degree of influence that it formerly exercised over the Divan [the Turkish government]." Menshikov was therefore ordered to adhere to his original instructions: to demand a formal Turkish guarantee of existing rights and privileges of the Orthodox church in the Ottoman Empire, and to sever diplomatic relations if the Turks failed to agree within a specified period of time. The tsar could no longer tolerate having his intentions constantly called into question or having his representatives put off (*éconduits*) by promises that were not fulfilled or by uselessly prolonged negotiations that produced no satisfactory results of any kind.[28]

Nesselrode was far more impressed by the seriousness of the difficulties Menshikov was encountering in Constantinople and the possibility of dangerous international complications if the Porte did indeed reject Russia's demands. Ignoring the imperial outbursts calling for a crisis of coercion, Nesselrode sounded a cautionary note in his response to Menshikov's request for instructions. Realizing the extent of foreign suspicions of Russia's ulterior political motives in the Near East, Nesselrode emphasized that Russia was *not* seeking a new form of protectorate over the Christian population of the Ottoman Empire but simply a formal engagement from the Porte to respect existing rights. Whether this engagement was called a convention, an explanatory decree, or put in the form of a protocol or obligatory note, the tsar would make no difficulties about accepting it. But, angered by Turkish procrastination and deceit, the tsar was once again authorizing Menshikov to demand that the Turks give him a definitive reply by a specific date. It was his fervent hope, however, that the Turks would agree to Russian demands—so just, so easy for them to concede, so much in the interests of their own government—and thereby avoid the necessity for Russia to sever diplomatic relations.[29]

Before receiving these reactions to his 10 April request for instructions from St. Petersburg, Menshikov on 19 April again presented Russia's demands to the Porte. Once again he emphasized that Russia was not seeking political concessions of any kind but wanted only "to calm religious consciences by the certainty of maintaining what is and always has been practiced up to now." He did not present these demands as an ultimatum with a specific time limit but asked only for a speedy reply.[30]

Stratford was immediately informed by the Turks about what he described to his own government as Russia's new and "secret" demands, although they were neither new nor secret. As before, he advised the Turks to yield to Russian demands on inconsequential matters but to reject all demands that might allow any increase of Russian influence in the Ottoman Empire. Stratford wrote to his wife on 27 April that he was in constant touch with leaders of the Turkish government and was using all his considerable influence to block Russian demands. "If the Russians are in the wrong, as I believe they are, my business is to make the wrong appear, and to stand by the Porte, or rather make the P. stand by me."[31]

Menshikov was also accurately informed about Stratford's activity. He told Nesselrode that the foreign ambassadors, with Stratford in the lead, were encouraging Turkey's resistance to Russia while pressing for agreement over the Holy Places in order "to reduce to meaninglessness" the demands of Russia. The theme constantly reiterated by the opponents of Russia was that *any* agreement equivalent to a treaty would be dangerous to the independence and security of Turkey.[32]

In accordance with Stratford's advice, the Turks continued to negotiate about the Holy Places with Russia, and by the end of April they had reached an agreement with Russia that was also satisfactory to the French. The terms of this agreement were to be incorporated in two formal decrees (*firmans*) that would be promulgated by the Turkish government. Copies of these two Turkish decrees were sent to Menshikov on 5 May, together with an official note from the sultan indicating that these three documents constituted the Turkish reply to the Russian demands presented by Menshikov on 19 April.[33]

The Russian Ultimatum of 5 May 1853

Menshikov replied on that same day, 5 May, that the Turkish decrees had indeed met Russia's demands with regard to the Holy Places, but they said nothing whatever about Russia's most important demands about guarantees for the future. He was therefore sending another communication to the Turkish foreign minister setting forth Russia's claims "within the final limits of his instructions." These claims were yet another restatement of Russia's demands that the Orthodox religion, its clergy, churches, and possessions should continue to enjoy in the future, under the aegis of the sultan, the privileges and immunities guaranteed them *ab antiquo,* and that on the basis of the principle of equality the Orthodox Christians should also participate in any additional advantages accorded to other Christian sects. The Turkish guarantees to this effect, together with the promised decrees on the Holy Places, should be incorporated in a formal treaty (*sened*). Menshikov enclosed the draft of such a treaty that would be acceptable to Russia and requested the Turkish government to reply within five days since a longer delay would be considered a lack of respect to his own government and would impose on him "most painful obligations." As in all previous Russian draft treaties submitted to the Porte, this one stated that it contained no provisions for changes in the status of the Orthodox church but was based strictly on rights and privileges already granted.[34]

The ultimatum of 5 May is noteworthy because it represented the first move on the part of Menshikov to make use of his discretionary powers to modify the treaty provisions demanded by Russia. There was nothing in Menshikov's draft of 5 May about the rights of Russian ministers to make representations on behalf of Orthodox churches and their clergy, nothing about the rights of the four patriarchs and other high dignitaries of the church or their lifetime appointments.

Significantly, it was Stratford rather than an official of the Turkish government who replied first to Menshikov's note. He objected to the Russian demand for a formal *sened*, which he declared would restrict "for the benefit of foreign influences" the sultan's sovereign control over the Greek clergy of the Ottoman Empire with their wide authority "and affect the interests—and especially the sympathies—of . . . more than ten million of subjects."

Following the receipt of Menshikov's ultimatum, Stratford prepared a detailed memorandum for the leaders of the Turkish government analyzing his reasons for rejecting the Russian demands, which he declared would reduce the Ottoman Empire to the status of a Russian protectorate. He also had long talks with the leading Turkish ministers, and on 9 May he informed the sultan "in solemn private audience" that "in case of danger he was instructed to request the commander of H. M.'s forces in the Mediterranean to hold his squadron in readiness." Thus encouraged, the Turks rejected Menshikov's ultimatum in a note of 10 May. The Turkish reply had been carefully drafted after long consultations between Stratford and the Turkish ministers. The gist of their objection to Russia's demands was that the treaty desired by Russia threatened the sovereignty and independence of the Ottoman Empire.[35]

In a report to Nesselrode, Menshikov confessed that in view of Stratford's violent and passionate opposition to Russia's just demands and his constant efforts to stir up opposition to Russia among members of the Turkish government, he had not expected a satisfactory reply, but the actual Turkish note was even worse than he had anticipated. It contained nothing but vague assurances of friendship and goodwill, and did not respond clearly to a single one of Russia's demands. He had therefore immediately informed the Turks that their note of 10 May was unacceptable.[36]

Menshikov did not give up. On the day after receiving the

Turkish reply, he addressed a note to Rifaat Pasha, the Turkish foreign minister, disclaiming any Russian intention to impinge on Turkish sovereignty. Again using the discretionary powers given him by his government, he withdrew his demand for a formal *sened,* treaty, or convention, and said he would be satisfied with "an act emanating from the sovereign will of the sultan, a free but solemn engagement." He appealed to the Turks to reconsider their decision and extended his ultimatum three days (to 14 May) in the hope that this would give them the necessary time for reflection as required by the gravity of the situation.[37]

Menshikov's Appeal to Reshid

By this time Menshikov had abandoned all hope that the present leaders of the Turkish government would respond positively to his appeal. He had received a steady flow of information about the bellicose and hostile attitude of Rifaat Pasha and of Mohammed Ali, the grand vizier, he knew that they consulted regularly with the British ambassador and believed that they were absolutely under his influence. He therefore resolved to appeal directly to the sultan, who was reported to be much alarmed by the crisis and dissatisfied with the way his ministers were handling it. In seeking an audience with the sultan, Menshikov selected as his intermediary Reshid Pasha, a Turkish statesman who had held numerous high-level positions in the government but was now out of office, despite Reshid's own well-known ties with Stratford and his reputation of hostility toward Russia. "It may seem strange to Your Excellency to receive a letter from the ambassador of a power which one supposes has never had your sympathies," Menshikov wrote Reshid on 10 May. "But it is to a man of experience and ability to whom I am addressing myself," and he appealed to Reshid to present to the sultan a clear picture of the existing situation and the consequences of the failure of his mission.[38]

The unfortunate Menshikov now found himself caught up in a Levantine intrigue so complex that it is impossible to reconstruct the exact course of events or the motives of the characters involved. The principal dupe in the whole affair was Menshikov. How he came to select Reshid as his intermediary is not known, but in doing so he made a terrible blunder, for Reshid was still staunchly anti-Russian and had remained in close touch with Stratford even while out of office. Following Menshikov's appeal for his mediation with the sultan, he somehow managed to secure his reinstatement in office (perhaps through the influence of Stratford) and cooperated with Stratford in frustrating Menshikov's final efforts to secure an agreement satisfactory to Russia.

Menshikov saw the sultan on the morning of Friday, 13 May, and was much encouraged by the sultan's promise to respond promptly to the Russian demands. He would have done so immediately, the sultan said, but he had just acceded to the request of his grand vizier, Mohammed Ali, to be relieved of his post, and he proposed to take this opportunity to dismiss Rifaat Pasha as well and to replace him as foreign minister by Reshid Pasha. The sultan would thus be deprived of his principal advisers at this critical moment and would need an additional two or three days to consult with his new ministers before giving his reply to Russia.

Menshikov originally assumed that the sultan's acceptance of Mohammed Ali's resignation and his decision to get rid of Rifaat had been sudden and spontaneous, motivated by a desire to remove these bellicose ministers in favor of more conciliatory spirits. It was only later that he discovered that Mohammed Ali had not resigned voluntarily but had been dismissed, and that the sultan had ordered his dismissal *after* Menshikov's audience.

Menshikov had mixed feelings about the personnel changes in the Turkish government. Mustafa Pasha, who had been selected to succeed Mohammed Ali as grand vizier, had impressed Menshikov favorably and had assured him of his desire for a satisfactory settlement with Russia. Less satisfactory was the retention of Mohammed Ali in the critical position of minister of war (*seraskier*), where he would remain an obstacle to a peaceful solution. Reshid's appointment as foreign minister, on the other hand, was interpreted by Menshikov as a conciliatory gesture toward Russia. He was complacently amused that the public and the diplomatic corps, not knowing the facts of the case and believing Reshid to be a tool of British interests, had attributed his appointment as foreign minister to the influence of Stratford. But the latter, ordinarily so well-informed, did not hear of the dismissal of the grand vizier until late in the evening and, as Menshikov later learned, the news had provoked him to an insane outburst of fury.[39]

It was Menshikov, however, who proved to be ill-informed. Unknown to him, Stratford had sent Reshid written advice about how he was to reply to Russia's latest demands immediately after Reshid's appointment as foreign minister. When Menshikov visited Reshid at his house on Sunday, 15 May, the day he had been led to expect the Turkish reply, Reshid pleaded that he was unable to comply with Russia's wishes because of the inexorable opposition of the Turkish Grand Council—an assembly composed of the highest dignitaries and scholars of the realm, whose official function was to prepare laws for the sanction of the sultan and deliberate over possible declarations of war. Menshikov now resorted to severe language: he had exhausted all means of conciliation, he could make no further concessions, and he demanded a clear and precise reply in the shortest possible time.

After Menshikov's departure Reshid had a visit from Stratford, who stayed with him for two hours. That same evening Reshid sent Menshikov the reply he had requested, which proved to be nothing more than an explanation of the need for further delay. The sultan could not make a final decision about the Russian ultimatum, Menshikov was informed, without consulting the Grand Council, which he had ordered to convene on 17 May.

Although Menshikov had learned of Stratford's visit to Reshid on 15 May and was infuriated by Reshid's renewed appeal for a delay, he still did not carry out his threat to sever diplomatic relations with Turkey. He told Nesselrode that he remained convinced of Reshid's good faith with regard to Russia "in so far as a Turk is capable of such sentiments," and had therefore yielded

to Reshid's plea to relax his pressure for a few more days to give
him time to modify the hostile feelings among members of the
council in the hope that he might yet arrange a satisfactory settlement.[40]

Gradually, however, Menshikov was beginning to see just how
badly he was being duped. He learned that Stratford had been
busy trying to influence the members of the Grand Council by
sending memoranda to its members setting forth reasons for rejecting Russia's demands and that shortly before the meeting of
the council Stratford had called on the majority of its members
to persuade them to vote against the Russian demands and to
agree to a reply to Russia drafted in the British embassy. The
Turks were obviously prepared to be persuaded, for at the meeting of the Grand Council on 17 May they rejected Russia's proposal by a vote of 42 to 3.

On the day following the vote of the Grand Council (18 May),
Reshid called on Menshikov and, according to Menshikov, was
visibly embarrassed to discuss its decisions. He avoided all mention of its overwhelming rejection of the Russian proposals and
concentrated instead on the concessions it was prepared to make.
The council had agreed to issue a proclamation guaranteeing the
maintenance of the status quo of the Holy Places in Jerusalem
and promising that no changes would be made without a prior
understanding with the cabinets of Russia and France; to issue a
decree on behalf of the patriarch of Constantinople guaranteeing
the preservation of his religion; to send Menshikov an explanatory note at the conclusion of the negotiations; and to propose a
sened having the force of a treaty to provide land for the con-
struction of a Russian church and hospice in Jerusalem.

These insignificant and meaningless concessions have the quality of a calculated insult and may well have been designed to
provoke Menshikov or the Russian government into making statements or taking action that would reveal to all Europe the sinister nature of Russian intentions and how wise the Turks had
been to reject their demands. Menshikov noted that Reshid had
seemed ashamed in presenting these Turkish proposals, and he

had explained that he had been powerless to modify them. But Menshikov was at last thoroughly disillusioned with Reshid. He angrily rejected the Turkish proposals, and informed Reshid that he was breaking off diplomatic relations with the Porte and would leave Constantinople with his entire mission.

Menshikov learned later that before his own meeting with Reshid on 18 May, Stratford had called on the Turkish foreign minister, and that during the entire course of Reshid's talk with Menshikov, Stratford had sat in a caïque in the Bosporus below waiting to be informed of the results. Stratford had seen Reshid yet a third time that day after another meeting of the Grand Council, where an English dragoman had been monitoring the debates. "There, my dear Count," he wrote to Nesselrode, "is what the British agents have the effrontery to call the independence of the Turkish government."[41]

Menshikov's Final Proposal, 20 May 1853

Following the break in diplomatic relations between Russia and Turkey, Stratford moved quickly to secure the support of the representatives of the other European great powers for the Turkish position by convincing them that the Russian demands were a threat to Turkish sovereignty and independence and that the Porte was therefore justified in rejecting them. For this purpose he assembled a conference of the representatives of Austria, France, and Prussia at his house, where they agreed that the Austrian representative should address a collective appeal to Menshikov to reconsider his decision, delay his departure, and moderate Russian demands. At the same time, Reshid, possibly also at the instigation of Stratford, addressed a similar appeal to Menshikov to revive their negotiations.[42] As Menshikov had already boarded a Russian vessel that was to take him from Constantinople, Stratford may have hoped that he would disregard both the collective appeal and that of Reshid, and thereby provide another display of Russian intransigence for the benefit of his diplomatic colleagues and European public opinion. If this was indeed Stratford's intention he was to be disappointed, for Menshikov responded positively to the joint appeals.

Menshikov's motives in doing so can only be surmised. It may be that he saw the need to demonstrate that Russia was willing to go to extreme lengths to arrange a compromise agreement or that he was determined at all costs to salvage something from his mission. Whatever his reasons, Menshikov sent another note to Reshid on 20 May 1853 that he said would satisfy the demands of Russia. He complained to Nesselrode that Reshid no longer dared make a move or say a word without the consent of Stratford, but he had learned from a confidential source that Reshid had sent a fervent appeal to Stratford to allow him to accept the Russian note because he dreaded the consequences of a refusal. So Menshikov still saw reason to hope.[43]

In his note of 20 May Menshikov once again made use of his discretionary powers to modify Russia's demands. His note omitted any mention of a formal treaty, *sened,* or convention. It simply called for a Turkish note containing the most solemn assurances of the sultan's solicitude for the Orthodox church in his states. To remove all past misunderstandings and ambiguities, the note was to declare that "the Eastern Orthodox Church, its clergy, churches, and possessions, as well as its religious establishments, shall enjoy in the future, without any restriction whatsoever, under the aegis of His Majesty the Sultan, the privileges and immunities which have been assured them *ab antiquo* or that had been granted to them on various occasions by Imperial favor," and that they should also enjoy all rights conceded to other Christian sects.[44]

Menshikov had thus scaled down Russia's demands so appreciably that it is impossible to find in the demands themselves any threat to the sovereignty and independence of the sultan.[45] Stratford thought otherwise. As soon as he received the text of Menshikov's note, which was sent to him immediately by Reshid, he convened another meeting of the representatives of the powers at the British embassy and sought to secure their unanimous agreement in advising the Turks to reject the Russian note. In this endeavor he was unsuccessful. They agreed only to communicate to the Porte their opinion that "in a matter which touched so closely upon the freedom of action and sovereignty of the Sultan, Reshid Pasha was the best judge of the line to be pursued."[46]

Such ambiguous advice was not good enough for Stratford. He followed up the joint communication of the European ambassadors with a personal memorandum to Reshid setting forth in detail his objections to these latest Russian demands. Although the phrase "having the force of a treaty" had been expunged, Stratford said, the note still had the meaning and spirit of a treaty, with "all the characteristics of an engagement binding solemnly the Porte for its strict execution in perpetuity to Russia." Its immediate result would be "the introduction of Russian influence, to be exercised with all the force of acknowledged right, into a department of internal administration affecting the religious sentiments and worldly interests of more than ten millions of the Sultan's subjects."[47]

At three o'clock in the afternoon of 20 May, Menshikov received from a confidential source a detailed and accurate report of Stratford's memorandum to Reshid advising against the acceptance of the Russian note, and on the following day he was officially informed of the Turkish rejection, which the Turks attempted to disguise under a flurry of counterproposals. Menshikov's last hope was now extinguished, and on 21 May, immediately after the receipt of the Turkish rejection, he finally left Constantinople and sailed across the Black Sea to Odessa, his mission a failure.[48]

Russia's Policy of Confrontation Reconsidered

In a dispatch to the Austrian ambassadors in Paris and London, Buol, the Austrian foreign minister, offered a penetrating analysis of Russia's policy of confrontation in dealing with the Ottoman Empire. The fundamental error of the policy, he said, was that it was unnecessary. The community of faith that existed between the Orthodox population of the Ottoman Empire and the Russian people already gave the Russians an enormously advantageous position in the Near East and constituted a political fact of life about which Europe could do nothing. Given this situation, the Russians should have remained content to exploit their advantageous position at their leisure instead of parading it before the world and insisting on having it officially confirmed through the kind of convention Menshikov had attempted to impose on the Porte in a manner as rude as it was imperious. The Menshikov mission had merely drawn the attention of the powers to the Russian threat to their interests in the Near East and had given the Turks an opportunity to rally those powers to their defense.[49]

Brunnow, the Russian ambassador to Britain, struck even more directly at the heart of the problem. Writing to Nesselrode early in April 1853, he had warned that Russia should not draw the cord too tight in presenting its demands to the Ottoman government, otherwise it might either strangle the sultan (that is, bring about the collapse of the Ottoman Empire) or risk having the cord break in its hands (that is, face a war against a European coalition that Russia might very well lose). As the Russian government did not desire either alternative, it should keep its demands modest and be satisfied with a compromise treaty with the Ottoman government. A harsh treaty would contribute nothing whatever to the reality of Russian influence in Turkey. *"This was determined by the facts of the situation, not by words. Russia is strong, Turkey is weak, there is the preamble to all our treaties. . . . This epitaph is already inscribed on the tomb of the Ottoman Empire."*[50]

Here was a brutal description of the political facts of life in the Near East, but Brunnow himself had missed the point so far as Russia's real interests were concerned. For those interests were not served in writing the epitaph of the Ottoman Empire but, rather, in working for its preservation. As the tsar's advisory commission had recognized in the course of Russia's war with Turkey in 1828–29, the empire formed an enormous buffer zone along

Russia's southwestern flank that was too weak to threaten Russian security but that, through its very existence, shielded Russia from more dangerous powers. For if Turkey was weak, Britain and France were not, and the establishment of these powers in the Near East was a far greater potential danger for Russia than any advantages Russia might gain through the collapse of the Ottoman Empire. This was another political fact of life, of which the tsar and his government remained fully aware. Hence the dismay of that government when it found it had lost control of the situation.

Chapter 4

To the Brink of War

British Reaction to the Failure
of the Menshikov Mission

Stratford was delighted with the failure of the Menshikov mission. Menshikov's "untoward negotiations," as he called them, had at last come to an end. The British emissary took some pride in the part he had played in undermining the recent negotiations and bringing about the diplomatic defeat of Russia. In a letter to his wife of 29 May, he said he thought he had been of some use in settling the issue of the Holy Places. "I would have settled the other, but it could not be. The Russians were determined to have the whole, and it was necessary to prevent them. The consequences of their defeat may certainly be very serious, but it was my duty to support the Turks in withstanding them, and *there* I have succeeded." There would be people in England who would wish him to the devil because he would not keep the peace by giving way, Stratford continued. "All now depends upon our Cabinet at home. Will they look the crisis fairly in the face and be wise enough as well as great enough, now that it has unavoidably occurred, to meet it fairly and settle it for ever? *Shilly-shally* will spoil all. France it seems has come to a stout resolution: should Russia invade, the Emperor will come to the rescue. Such the private message conveyed yesterday to Reshid."[1]

Stratford did his best to see that Britain too came to a stout resolution. On the day following Turkey's rejection of the Russian note and Menshikov's departure from Constantinople, he wrote what has been called a "grim" dispatch to Clarendon, the British foreign secretary, explaining that the Turks had no choice but to reject the Russian demands. "It was not the amputation of a limb, but the infusion of poison into the system that they are summoned to accept." It was now up to Britain to decide how far it was prepared to support the Turks, but Stratford warned that unless Turkey received help it was certain to succumb to Russian domination sooner or later.[2]

In the British cabinet, Stratford's call for a hard line against Russia was supported most enthusiastically by Palmerston. Even before receiving news of the failure of the Menshikov mission and Stratford's dire warnings, Palmerston wrote to Clarendon: "The policy and practice of the Russian Government has always been to push forward its encroachments as fast and as far as the apathy or want of firmness of other Governments would allow it to go, but always to stop and retire when it was met with decided resistance, and then to wait for the next favourable opportunity to make another spring on its intended victim."[3]

The Russian Ultimatum of 31 May 1853

In Russia, the tsar's reaction to the news of the failure of the Menshikov mission was one of frustrated fury. "I feel the five fingers of the Sultan on my face," he said. To show the Turks he could not be trifled with and to secure acceptance of his demands, he proposed to occupy the Danubian Principalities of Moldavia and Wallachia. Again it was Nesselrode who advised caution. He persuaded the tsar not to resort immediately to extreme measures but to send the Turks a final ultimatum specifying the measures he proposed to take if they persisted in their rejection of Russian demands. This Russian ultimatum was embodied in a note from Nesselrode to Reshid dated 31 May. It demanded that the Turkish government agree to the proposals that Menshikov had presented to them before his departure (in his note of 20 May) within eight days. Otherwise Russian troops would be ordered to cross the borders of the Ottoman Empire—

not to wage war against the sultan but to obtain those material guarantees of Russian rights that the Russian government had attempted in vain to obtain through peaceful means.[4]

As at moments of previous frustration with the Turks, the tsar indulged in talk about the drastic measures he would take to wreak vengeance on them if they persisted in defying him. If the Turks rejected his latest ultimatum, he told one of his generals, his first step would be to occupy the principalities. If they remained stubborn, his next step would be to blockade the Bosporus, seize all Turkish shipping on the Black Sea, and encourage the Austrians to occupy Herzegovina and Serbia. If even then the Turks refused to yield, he would propose a joint Austro-Russian recognition of the independence of the Danubian Principalities, Serbia, and Herzegovina, and thus initiate the disintegration of the Ottoman Empire, for granting independence to these Balkan states would ignite revolts among all its subject peoples.[5]

The tsar sounded a similarly belligerent note in writing to Emperor Francis Joseph of Austria. If the Turks rejected his ultimatum and remained defiant after his occupation of the Danubian Principalities, he would go to war no matter what the consequences, and in that event he would urge the Austrians to occupy Serbia and Herzegovina. But even in his fury and frustration, the tsar bore in mind that the interests of Russia were best served through the preservation of the Ottoman Empire, and in this same letter to Francis Joseph he proposed a far more sober policy. "Let us combine our efforts to maintain this miserable empire so long as this is feasible," he said, "but if it should begin to crumble, let us work together to forestall the dangers which might confront us."[6]

Far more consistent in their attitude toward the Ottoman Empire were the tsar's civilian advisers. Although they had yielded to the tsar's demand to threaten the Turks with the occupation of the principalities, they remained convinced of the desirability for Russia of preserving that empire and resolutely opposed war that might result in its destruction.

The most telling arguments against war and the destruction of the Ottoman Empire came from Brunnow, the Russian ambassador in London. Out of the debris of the empire would come all sorts of new states, which would be as ungrateful to Russia for their independence as Greece had been, and as troublesome as the principalities. In all of them the influence of Russia would be contested by Britain, France, and Austria. A war could be of no possible benefit to Russia, which would only be spending its blood and treasure so that Greece might acquire Thessaly, England could pick up a few more islands, and France could share in the spoils. As for the new states that would be formed, they would be for Russia either onerous protectorates or hostile neighbors.[7]

British and French Fleets Dispatched to the Near East

The decision for war or peace, however, was not the exclusive prerogative of the Russians. In London the Aberdeen government, which had allowed the tsar to believe that it understood and supported Russia's efforts to secure Turkish recognition of Orthodox rights in Constantinople, had grown increasingly apprehensive about Russian intentions, bombarded as it was by the alarmist reports of Stratford and British journalists in the Near East. Members of the Aberdeen government were also acutely aware of the rising tide of anti-Russian sentiment among the British electorate, stirred up by political demagogues and the press, and of the increasing popular support enjoyed by their colleagues, with Palmerston in the lead, who shared these anti-Russian feelings, and did not hesitate to stimulate and exploit them to their own political advantage. Aberdeen himself remained relatively unaffected by this mounting popular hysteria, but his colleagues were not so immune. Gradually it became evident that he was losing control of his cabinet, and that even Lord Clarendon, his foreign secretary, was swinging over to the side of Palmerston into the anti-Russian camp.

Upon receiving news of the failure of the Menshikov mission, together with reports of massive Russian military preparations on the Turkish frontier, Clarendon believed that it was now im-

perative to take exceptional measures for the protection of the
Ottoman Empire. Accordingly, on 31 May, in the name of the
queen, he authorized Stratford to summon the British fleet at
Malta to any place where he considered the presence of the
British force essential to the safety of the Turks. Two days later
Clarendon took the lead in persuading the cabinet of the need for
a dramatic gesture of support on behalf of the Turks, and on 2
June the British fleet at Malta was ordered to Besika Bay, just
outside the Dardanelles.[8] Clarendon assured Aberdeen that this
was "the least measure that *will satisfy public opinion* and save
the government from shame hereafter, if, as I firmly believe, the
Russian hordes pour into Turkey from every side."[9] Palmerston
immediately and unofficially communicated these decisions of
the British government to Musurus, the Turkish ambassador in
London, who needless to say immediately passed this information on to his own government.[10]

The French, who had been playing a very cautious game because they were uncertain about the attitude of the British government, were enthusiastic about the dispatch of the British fleet
to Besika Bay and immediately ordered their own fleet at Salamis
to join forces with the British. Walewski, Napoleon's ambassador to London, wrote to Thouvenel, head of the political section
of the French foreign ministry, that this union of the French and
British fleets was "the most happy event that could happen for
France today: a general war in which we would have been alone
was the greatest danger for the new government; a war with
England against Russia with the rest of Europe remaining neutral
can only be considered as an unexpected favor of Providence
which is so clearly protecting the imperial dynasty."[11]

Turkish Rejection of the Russian Ultimatum, 16 June 1853

On 16 June 1853, after the arrival of the British and French
fleets at Besika Bay, the Turkish government at last replied to
the Russian ultimatum of 31 May. The Turks maintained that the
document demanded by Russia still contained the sense of a

diplomatic engagement that would not be in accordance with the independence of the Ottoman government or the rights of its sovereign authority. It was therefore impossible for the Turks to agree to the Russian demands. But, the note said, because their inability to agree was the result of a genuine impossibility, their reply should not be given the title of a refusal and transformed into a question of honor for the tsar.[12]

Russia Occupies the Danubian Principalities, July 1853

The sophistry of the Turkish reply, and the mere suggestion that their refusal should not be transformed into a question of honor, ensured that the tsar would have to regard it as such and carry out his threat to occupy the principalities. The tsar was now caught in that most invidious of political traps, the need to save face, a trap which he himself had set and which his opponents believed they could afford to spring. The tsar was well aware that the occupation of the principalities might lead to war with the Ottoman Empire and might well expand into a war with Britain and France as well. He was still convinced that he could count on the support or at least friendly neutrality of Austria and Prussia, but realized that the true interests of Russia required the avoidance of war altogether.[13]

Unable to escape from this predicament without loss of face, the tsar announced in the last week of June that his troops would shortly move into the principalities. Early in July 1853 Russian forces crossed the Pruth River.[14]

The crisis in the Near East had now reached a volatile stage. The Russian army in the principalities was poised at the Danube, the British and French fleets were lying at Besika Bay, and the British and French ambassadors were empowered to summon them into Turkish waters to protect the Ottoman Empire. The Turks for their part had been given every reason to hope that if they chose to become involved in hostilities with Russia, they could count on active British and French support.

Chapter 5

Final Efforts to Preserve Peace, June–October 1853

The Background of the Vienna Note

The failure of the Menshikov mission, the tsar's occupation of the principalities, and the dispatch of the British and French fleets to Besika Bay represented a combination of circumstances that impressed upon the leaders of all the European powers the realization that a major war was imminent unless they took immediate and energetic steps to avoid it. And they did take such steps.

The tsar, although he had made wild statements in fits of anger and was still determined to save face, nevertheless was well aware of the dangers to Russia posed by a major war and the collapse of the Ottoman Empire. In Britain, Aberdeen desperately desired to avoid war altogether, while Clarendon and other more moderate members of the cabinet, though fearful about Russian intentions, definitely favored mediation and compromise if some formula could be worked out to protect the sovereignty of the Ottoman Empire and British interests. Napoleon too, always nervous when faced with the possibility of drastic measures and anxious above all to preserve good relations with Britain, appeared willing to cooperate or even take the lead in finding a compromise solution to the crisis if this seemed necessary in order to stay on good terms with Britain.

But the statesmen who worked hardest and most persistently for peace were the Austrians, for they had most reason to fear a general war in which they would be exposed to extreme dangers no matter which side they joined or even if they remained neutral. If the Austrians sided with Russia they would disrupt the balance of power in the east and be reduced to the status of a Russian satellite, for they would then be dependent on Russian support against the hostility of Britain and France (both powers were already threatening to undermine the Austrian position in Germany and especially in Italy, where the Austrians were particularly vulnerable). If the Austrians sided with Britain and France, they would be compelled to bear the brunt of the fighting because of their geographical position and, even if victorious, would be permanently obliged to stand guard against a vengeful neighbor. And if they remained neutral, they would be exposed to the pressure, threats, and animosity of both sides. As Buol, the Austrian foreign minister, described Austrian policy at the time: "We are seeking to pacify on every side and above all to avoid a European complication, which would be particularly detrimental to us."[1]

Even before the Turkish rejection of the Russian ultimatum and the Russian occupation of the principalities, which had brought the crisis in the Near East to its present acute stage, leaders of the European powers who sought to avoid war had initiated negotiations to work out a compromise solution. The most promising of these solutions was a document that became known as the Vienna Note. It was the product of the efforts of the representatives of all the great powers, and it might very well have prevented war had it not been sabotaged by statesmen who were obsessed by personal animosity toward Russia and the tsar, who were convinced that Russia could never be trusted to honor its engagements, or who had come to believe that their various political goals could only be fulfilled through war.

A detailed analysis of the profusion of proposals, counterproposals, and compromise proposals made during this period is not only difficult but tedious.[2] Fortunately it is also unnecessary, for all proposals that represented sincere efforts to mediate the crisis had essentially the same substance: their basic idea was that the representatives of the neutral great powers—Austria, Britain, France, and Prussia—should employ their individual or joint efforts to persuade the Russian and Ottoman governments to agree to an exchange of notes that they had not been able to arrange between themselves and that should satisfy the interests, safeguard the security, and preserve the honor of both sides. The assumption behind them all was that neither Russia nor Turkey would risk rejecting proposals submitted in the name of one or, preferably, a union of the four neutral European great powers.[3]

It is significant but hardly surprising in view of the dilemma in which the Russian government found itself that the initial appeal for the mediation of neutral powers that culminated in the Vienna Note came from the tsar.

Following the dispatch of the Russian ultimatum of 31 May 1853, the Russian monarch, justifiably apprehensive about the machinations of the British and French representatives in Constantinople and their influence over the Porte, approached Castelbajac, the French ambassador to St. Petersburg, on 4 June and requested him to write to Napoleon directly—directly because the tsar did not trust Napoleon's advisers—to solicit his intervention in Constantinople. He counted on the high intelligence and sense of justice of the French ruler to persuade the sultan to accede to his reasonable and rightful demands and thereby avoid for himself, for Europe, and for everyone the dire consequences that might result from a final Turkish refusal. Because only revolutionaries would profit from discord among the great powers, it would be criminally foolish if these powers failed to cooperate with one another to maintain peace and order. The tsar gave Napoleon his word of honor that if a final refusal of the Porte forced him to occupy the principalities, he would not attack the Turks unless the Turks first attacked Russia; he would not tolerate any kind of revolt against the authority of the sultan; he desired the preservation of the Ottoman Empire, and under no circumstances would he take an inch of its territory; he wanted no increase of Russian influence (*puissance*) in the Near East or elsewhere, but simply the honor and prosperity of his empire, respect for treaties, and a general strengthening of the moral and political order. He blamed the Porte's rejection of his latest proposals on the personal animosity of Stratford, with his violent and splenetic character, and it was above all to counteract the influence of Stratford in Constantinople that he appealed for Napoleon's support and cooperation.[4]

A few days after the tsar had addressed this appeal to Napoleon, Nesselrode, who did not trust the French emperor *or* his advisers, persuaded his sovereign to send a similar appeal to the government of Austria.[5] The Austrians, with greater reason to fear a general European war than any other European power, responded far more quickly to the Russian appeal than did the French (indeed the French did not respond for almost a month), and almost immediately they sent instructions to Bruck, their new ambassador to Constantinople, who was still on his way to the Turkish capital, to urge the Turks to accept the latest Russian note (of 20 May), but with several revisions and deletions.[6]

Buol's instructions for Bruck on the Russian note were actually part of an overall Austrian mediation proposal: the Turkish government should use the Russian note of 20 May as the basis for a note of its own, which should amend the Russian note so as to exclude any suggestion of a Russian protectorate over the Orthodox church; this Turkish note should then be submitted to the Russian government as the Turkish reply to the Russian ultimatum, and Austria would engage to secure its acceptance in St. Petersburg. Bruck was to use his own judgment as to how much he should seek the association of the British and French ambassadors in Constantinople in this mediation effort.[7]

The moment was hardly propitious for such a diplomatic initiative. On 16 June, two days after Bruck's arrival in Constantinople, the Turks rejected the Russian ultimatum, and a succession of Turkish domestic crises prevented Bruck from initiating direct negotiations with the Turks for some time. Even then the Turks were in no mood for mediation and compromise, their bellicosity stimulated by the presence of the Anglo-French fleets at Besika Bay. But the greatest of Bruck's difficulties was the obstructionist strategy of Stratford, who guessed correctly that the Austrian mediation proposal had not been sent to Constantinople without previous consultation with Russia, and who assumed that if it was satisfactory to the Russians it must automatically be unsatisfactory to the Turks.[8]

The Constantinople Note, or Turkish Ultimatum

Stratford now took the lead in conducting negotiations, which culminated in what has been called the Constantinople Note, or Turkish Ultimatum. Upon hearing of the Austrian mediation proposal, Stratford at once took steps to prevent any unilateral Austrian negotiations in Constantinople and to ensure his own supervision of any negotiations that might take place. He convened a conference of the representatives of the four neutral European great powers at his residence, where they agreed on a joint memorandum recommending the Austrian proposal to the Porte.[9] Stratford informed Clarendon that Bruck was not pleased to find the initiative taken from his hand, and with considerable self-satisfaction he pointed out that by this simple expedient the exclusive mediation of Austria was skillfully quashed.[10] From this meeting of 24 June, writes Stratford's admiring biographer, "dates the collective action of Europe which, properly directed, might have averted the misery and futility of the Crimean War."

Stratford's only use of this collective action, however, was to invoke the authority of Europe to encourage the Turks to reject any mediation proposals satisfactory to Russia. He assured Clarendon that he thought it right "to catch at any chance of peace which is not attended with a sacrifice of principle." Since the diplomatic engagement required by Russia would represent such a sacrifice, he refused to grant it, and he hoped the tsar would change his mind about his demands when he found himself faced with the opposition of all Europe. The Austrian mediation plan, which Stratford himself had persuaded his diplomatic colleagues to recommend to the Porte, was dismissed by Stratford as hopeless. He promised to do his best with this "most meagre proposition," while warning Clarendon not to be persuaded to support this or any other unilateral scheme.[11]

On 24 June, the day Stratford convened his conference of ambassadors at his residence to take charge of the Austrian mediation proposal, the news of Turkey's rejection of the Russian ultimatum was received in St. Petersburg; on 26 June the tsar issued a manifesto to the Russian people announcing the imminent occupation of the principalities and explaining Russia's reason for doing so; in the first days of July Russian forces crossed the Pruth River.[12]

When the news of the Russian occupation of the principalities reached Constantinople, Reshid, the Turkish foreign minister, drew up a note of protest that was subsequently amended by Stratford in a manner Reshid found very gratifying. At the recommendation of Stratford, the Turkish government also rejected a renewed effort on the part of Bruck to persuade the Turks to accept the Austrian suggestions for a note to be addressed to Russia and sought Stratford's advice in drawing up a note of its own.[13]

The Austrian proposal, Stratford wrote to Clarendon on 9 July, was a complete surrender of the principle at stake. Stratford thought that whatever one might hope to accomplish through further negotiations should be tried at once, but he was clearly not sanguine about their prospects of success. If the next attempt should fail, he said, there would no longer be room for half measures. "If the object be, as I presume, to get the Russians out of the Principalities without surrendering the main point in dispute, it is difficult to conceive how that object can have a chance of being accomplished without hard knocks on a large scale." Stratford insisted he was as much for peace as any man but argued that there should be a limit to attempts "which can only prove nugatory in the end and turn to the benefit of uncompromising Russia." To his wife he was even more frank. He did not see how they could get the Russians out of the principalities

without a major war and thought that only a miracle could avoid
it. He had written oceans urging the people at home to make up
their minds and to equal Russia in foresight and consistency.
"Now is the time for decision—one more attempt if possible at
negotiation, and then war."[14]

What Stratford meant by negotiation certainly did not augur
well for peace. After helping Reshid draw up a note protesting
Russia's occupation of the principalities and a second note that
Reshid proposed to send to Nesselrode as Turkey's reply to the
Russian ultimatum, Stratford convened another conference of the
ambassadors at his residence on 17 July. At this conference they
agreed that the Turkish government should address a communication to Russia consisting of three documents: the Turkish note
protesting Russia's occupation of the principalities, Reshid's letter to Nesselrode, and the text of the latest Turkish government
decrees confirming the spiritual (but no other) privileges of the
non-Moslem subjects of the sultan. Together these three documents came to be called the Constantinople Note, or Turkish
Ultimatum.[15]

In persuading Bruck to drop the Austrian mediation proposal
and agree to the Turkish Ultimatum, Stratford appears to have
done a masterful job of taking advantage of the Austrian emissary's vanity and diplomatic inexperience, for he managed to
convince Bruck that the entire Turkish Ultimatum scheme was
Bruck's own idea and that it was due to Bruck's persuasive skill
that the plan had been accepted without argument by his diplomatic colleagues.[16]

Even so it is difficult to understand how Bruck could have
agreed to this extraordinary proposal, for it contained nothing
that could be regarded even as a gesture toward compromise or
that might provide a basis for negotiation. Far from being an
attempt at mediation, the Turkish Ultimatum was nothing less
than a challenge to Russia, and Stratford's colleagues must have
been much misled or ill-informed not to recognize it as such.

It is easier to understand the behavior of the Turkish Grand
Council, which endorsed the ultimatum enthusiastically on 24

July. The Turkish Ultimatum was then dispatched to Vienna with the request that it be transmitted to St. Petersburg as the Turkish reply to the Russian ultimatum. "An *ultimatum* and a condition may sound harsh to Russian ears," Stratford wrote to Seymour in St. Petersburg, "but I really do not see how the Porte can possibly, with justice to itself, take any other course."[17] The documents constituting the Turkish Ultimatum reached Vienna on 29 July, just as the representatives of the powers in Vienna had formulated a note of their own to be sent to St. Petersburg.

The Vienna Note

While negotiations, if one can call them that, were going on in Constantinople, negotiations were also being conducted in the capitals of Europe. Late in June 1853, with some hesitation and after anxious consultations to make sure of the approval of the government in London, Napoleon decided to respond to the tsar's appeal of 4 June (see p. 68) for French mediation in Constantinople and ordered the preparation of a French mediation proposal that would be acceptable to both Russia and Turkey. The draft of such a proposal, dated 1 July, was sent to Britain for approval and, at the advice of the British, was also communicated to the government of Austria. Upon receiving the endorsement of both Britain and Austria, Napoleon instructed Castelbajac to present the French proposal to the tsar personally, which he did on 8 July.[18]

The tsar liked the French proposal and believed it could be accepted with minor modifications. He would not give France a definite answer immediately, however, for he had meanwhile also appealed to the good offices of Austria (see p. 69) and would have to await the results of Austrian mediation efforts in Constantinople.[19]

The Austrian government was also awaiting the results of the the deliberations in Constantinople, and with considerable impatience. As no news arrived to suggest that any progress was being made in the Turkish capital, Buol resolved to wait no longer, and

on 24 July he convened a conference of the ambassadors of the
four neutral great powers in Vienna to work out a settlement of
the Russo-Turkish dispute. Knowing that the tsar had already
seen and approved the French government's mediation proposal
and that it had previously been approved by the British government as well as his own, Buol decided to use the French proposal
as a basis for negotiation. His strategy worked exceptionally well.
After a few modifications by the British and himself, the French
proposal, henceforth known as the Vienna Note, was adopted by
the representatives of the four neutral great powers in Vienna on
28 July, the day before the Turkish Ultimatum reached the Austrian capital.[20]

Buol was appalled by the documents embodied in the Turkish
Ultimatum. Reshid's letter to Nesselrode, he said, was far more
calculated to intensify than to resolve the crisis. He therefore
never considered sending the Turkish Ultimatum to St. Petersburg and even refused to acknowledge officially its reception in
Vienna.[21]

The Vienna Note now became the exclusive basis for negotiation among the European powers. Following its adoption in
Vienna, it was ratified by the governments of the four powers,
signed by their representatives in Vienna on 31 July, and immediately transmitted to St. Petersburg. It was accepted by the
Russian government four days later on condition that the Turkish
government also accept it without modifications of any kind.[22]
Following acceptance of the Vienna Note by Russia, the governments of the four powers instructed their representatives in
Constantinople to secure its acceptance by the government of
Turkey.[23]

Turkish Rejection of the Vienna Note

The agreement among the four powers on the Vienna Note and
its acceptance by Russia should have ended the Near Eastern
crisis, for it is inconceivable that the Turks, no matter how
fanatic or bellicose, should have rejected a mediation proposal

agreed upon by all the European great powers, thereby running the risk of engaging in war with Russia without support of any kind and, indeed, contrary to the advice and wishes of this union of the European powers. The Turks, however, were obviously convinced that the European powers were not united and that they would receive powerful support even if they provoked a break with Russia. This Turkish confidence was based on reports the Turkish government was receiving from London about the pro-Turkish attitude of British public opinion and among certain leading British statesmen. Such reports must have been powerfully reinforced by the conduct of Stratford, who was infuriated that the Turkish Ultimatum, drawn up in such close consultation with himself, had not been sent to St. Petersburg as the basis for negotiation.

Stratford reported to Clarendon that he had supported the Vienna Note *officially*, in accordance with his instructions, but unofficially he denounced it in the most violent terms.[24] Lacour, the French ambassador in Constantinople, reported to his government what he termed the strange conduct of Stratford, which he believed had much to do with the recalcitrant attitude of the Porte. "Publicly and officially . . . Lord Stratford has obeyed his instructions, and called upon the Ottoman government to accept the Vienna Note; but he lets it be seen at the same time that his private opinion is at variance with his official language, and he does not bring that personal influence to bear which would have been so useful at the present moment." Further, the French ambassador continued, "to his *intimes*, Lord Stratford uses the most violent language, that he disapproves all the proceedings at Vienna, declares war preferable to such a solution" and that a change must take place in the government of England "which will bring into power the friends and supporters of his policy in Turkey." Lacour's information was communicated to Cowley, the British ambassador to Paris, who passed it along to Clarendon.[25] Bruck described Stratford's behavior in similar fashion. Both he and Lacour had found the British ambassador in a passionate rage. After a long discussion, however, Stratford had declared that he would "perhaps" support the Vienna drafts if he did not receive other instructions.[26]

Lacour himself does not seem to have behaved altogether correctly, for while carrying out his own government's instructions to advise the Porte to accept the Vienna Note, he indulged in many brave words about the ulterior and active measures that France was prepared to take in support of the Ottoman Empire. He as well as Stratford now helped Reshid draw up amendments to the Vienna Note, although they both knew of the tsar's stipulation that the note be accepted unaltered.[27]

In addition to the unofficial diplomatic encouragement the Turks received from Stratford and Lacour to resist the pressure of the European powers, they received substantial material encouragement with the arrival of an Egyptian fleet at Constantinople on 12 August.[28] Their most compelling encouragement, however, must have derived from the reports of Musurus, the Turkish ambassador to London, who informed his government in glowing terms of the rising tide of popular feeling in England on behalf of the Turks. Musurus was in close touch with Palmerston, the most pro-Turkish and bellicose member of the British government, and each day the British press seemed to grow more vehement in urging the British government to take a firm stand at the side of the Ottoman Empire. The impression Musurus conveyed to his government was that if it persisted in its resistance, the British would send their fleet to Constantinople—not to put pressure on the Turks to accept the Vienna Note but to support a Turkish war effort.[29]

In stormy meetings of the Turkish Grand Council, a majority of its members advocated outright rejection of the Vienna Note. Reshid informed Stratford that he saw no hope of securing its acceptance by the council and that he himself would refuse to sign it without modifications. He was very bitter about the British government's acceptance of the "compromising" arrangement worked out in Vienna. It would have been better for Turkey, he told Stratford, to have yielded at first, than *after so much support from the powers* (my emphasis) to be now unreasonably abandoned. Stratford reported to Clarendon that he had "abstained from making any admissions calculated to encourage the Porte in its resistance," but as it was certain the note would not be accepted as it stood, he had felt compelled to suggest a reply that would present the character of acceptance and yet leave room for adjustments. When Reshid showed Stratford the text of the amendments he had drawn up, Stratford had been obliged to conceal how impressed he had been by the validity of Reshid's arguments justifying Turkish resistance to the Vienna Note. Reshid had kissed Stratford's hand and implored him with tears in his eyes not to forsake his country in the midst of such dangers and distresses. Stratford assured Clarendon that he had made yet another effort to secure Turkish acceptance, but on 20 August the Turkish Grand Council had decided to reject the Vienna Note unless it were amended substantially.[30]

In rejecting the Vienna Note, the Turks used the familiar arguments so often recommended to them by Stratford—namely, that the note conceded the principle of a Russian protectorate over the Orthodox church in the Ottoman Empire—and they refused to accept it without amendments making clear that the privileges of the Orthodox church derived exclusively from voluntary concessions of the sultan and not from agreements with Russia.[31]

Buol was infuriated by the Turkish response to the Vienna Note. He dismissed their requested amendments as "contemptible," and sent renewed instructions to Bruck to put pressure on the Porte to accept the Vienna Note *pure et simple*.[32]

In England, Aberdeen was also very critical of Turkish behavior. "The Turkish modifications, although not absolutely altering the sense of the Note, are not insignificant," he wrote to Clarendon on 26 August. "I cannot say what the Emperor [of Russia] may be disposed to do for the sake of peace; but I am sure that we have no right to ask him to agree to further alterations, after what he has already done . . . I should not think it probable that he would submit to have the work of the Four Powers altered by the Porte. Indeed, he made an express stipulation to this effect. The conduct of the Porte is suicidal, and some fatal influence must be at work. It can only be explained by a desire that the affair should end in war."[33] He clearly suspected that this fatal influence was Stratford and was impatient to learn how Stratford would explain the conduct of the Turks and whether the ambassador himself had sanctioned it.[34]

Clarendon expressed substantial agreement with the views of his prime minister. He thought that the fresh conditions demanded by the Turks showed clearly that they were determined to oppose any kind of settlement. "I have read the [Vienna] Note again and again and can discover nothing in it derogatory to the dignity or the independence of the Sultan, and all the important parts are taken verbatim from Reshid's own note to Menshikoff."[35] Clarendon believed that Stratford had deliberately sabotaged the Vienna Note and that his personal hatred of the tsar and temper "have made him take a part directly contrary to the wishes and instructions of his Government."[36] Stratford "thinks that now or never is the time for putting an end to Russia." It was to Stratford's *amour propre froissé* that the present obstacles to peace had to be attributed.[37]

The "Violent" Interpretation of the Vienna Note

The tsar's reaction to Turkey's rejection of the Vienna Note and demand for amendments was more moderate than might have been expected. Although his government had insisted on unconditional Turkish acceptance of the Vienna Note, he was inclined to agree to amendments but was evidently persuaded by Nesselrode that the modifications desired by Turkey should be carefully examined by chancellery experts. Even then, Nesselrode warned, any Russian concession to Turkey's demands for modifications in the Vienna Note would constitute a humiliation for Russia and be contrary to the honor and dignity of the tsar.[38]

Nesselrode's actual reply to the powers in response to Turkey's demand for modifications was itself moderate. In a dispatch of 7 September sent to the Russian representatives in Vienna,

Paris, London, and Berlin, Nesselrode instructed them to remind
the governments to which they were accredited that Russia had
accepted the Vienna Note on the condition that there be no
modifications which would compel Russia to examine and discuss projects inspired by the bellicose influences that seemed to
surround the sultan and his ministers at the present time. He
would not discuss the modifications desired by the Porte—this
would be the subject of another dispatch—but he counted on the
powers to bring their united pressure to bear on the Porte to
secure the acceptance of the Vienna Note without modification.
For, either the modifications were important, in which case Russia would be obliged to reject them; or they were insignificant,
in which case there was no reason for the Turks to demand them.
In any case, it was up to the powers to secure the acceptance of
the note they had drawn up and agreed upon, and to bring the
present crisis to an end. The moment the Turkish ambassador
arrived in St. Petersburg with the signed note, orders would go
out to Russian troops to evacuate the principalities.[39]

In addition to this dispatch, Nesselrode sent his ambassadors
a copy of a document prepared by his chancellery officials analyzing the modifications of the Vienna Note desired by the Porte,
with instructions to communicate it to the governments of the
four powers.[40] There was no mysterious "leak" of this document
as many writers have stated, but the document became known
to the general public when a translation was published in a Berlin newspaper.

This Russian examination of the Turkish amendments was to
be labeled the "violent" interpretation of the Vienna Note, and
its authors have been described as bellicose extremists whose influence triumphed over the more moderate Nesselrode, just as
extremists in Britain were asserting their influence over Aberdeen.[41] Yet Nesselrode saw nothing violent or extreme in this
analysis by his officials, otherwise he certainly would not have
authorized its communication to the governments of the neutral
great powers. The British and French governments, however,
perceived sinister implications in the Russian analysis and be-

lieved that the "violent" interpretation obliged them to abandon the Vienna Note and to support the Turks' rejection of it unless it were substantially amended.

Since the "violent" interpretation critically altered the course of British and French policy, or was used as the justification for doing so, the document deserves careful scrutiny. The Russian analysis pointed out, quite correctly, that the modifications desired by the Turks reduced the Vienna Note to a farce. The Turks wanted the statement about the tsar's solicitude for the rights of the Orthodox church in the Ottoman Empire changed to eliminate "in the Ottoman Empire," which deprived the statement of all meaning since no one contested the solicitude of the tsar for the Orthodox church in general. More important, the Turks wanted this statement altered to read that not the tsar but the sultan had always guarded the privileges of the Orthodox church, which meant that Russia had no legitimate complaints about the Ottoman treatment of that church and that all Russian demands for guarantees were unjustified and the Vienna Note itself superfluous. Finally, the Russians objected that the Turks failed to mention that the protection of the Christian religion was a promise, a treaty engagement on the part of the sultan, and that the desired amendments seemed to cast doubt on the right of Russia to watch over (*veiller*) the strict execution of that promise. This last point was the only part of the Russian examination that could be interpreted as "violent," for it seemed to suggest that Russia was claiming the right to intervene in the internal affairs of the Ottoman Empire and that all suspicions about Russia's true motives throughout the crisis—to reduce the Ottoman Empire to the status of a Russian protectorate—were justified.

This interpretation of the Russian examination, however, is far more violent than anything in the Russian document itself and suggests that the statesmen of Britain and France either neglected to study the document carefully or willfully chose to read into it an interpretation that would give them an excuse to withdraw from their commitment to support the Vienna Note and coerce the Turks into accepting it.

The Austrian government at least saw nothing sinister or prejudicial to Turkish interests in the Russian explanations for refusing to accept Turkey's amendments to the Vienna Note. After receiving these explanations, Buol sent renewed instructions to his ambassador in Constantinople to insist that the Porte sign the Vienna Note unaltered and without further delay.[42]

Entirely different was the reaction of Clarendon in London. Upon receiving the Russian interpretation of the Vienna Note on 16 September, he professed to see in it a Russian claim to a de facto protectorate over the Ottoman Empire. It was he who described the Russian interpretation as "violent," and he immediately informed the French ambassador to London that in view of this distortion of the meaning of the Vienna Note, the British government could no longer recommend it to the Porte.[43]

The Russians were taken aback by the British reaction. A Russian diplomat described it as an obvious pretext, seized upon by the British cabinet in its weakness, to evade its obligation to put pressure on the Turks, thereby escaping the criticism of British public opinion and a confrontation with its irresponsible agent in Constantinople, who could not be trusted to obey its orders.[44]

This Russian interpretation of British policy was absolutely accurate. Aberdeen was unable to stand up to the more bellicose members of his cabinet; Clarendon had begun to waver toward the war party; and both seemed strangely blind to the consequences of policies they themselves were to pursue or condone. Even before learning of the "violent" interpretation of the Vienna Note, Clarendon had decided that the British government could not risk coercing the Turks into accepting the unamended note because British and French public opinion would not stand for it.[45] He had also joined Palmerston and Russell in urging that the Anglo-French fleets be sent through the Turkish Straits to Constantinople in violation of the Straits Convention of 1841 (see chap. 5, n. 28). "They can't remain much longer in the open Bay of Besika," he had told Aberdeen on 28 July, "and however bold you may be in the cause of peace, I don't think you would have the courage to order the British fleet back to Malta, before the Russians have re-crossed the Pruth."[46] To Cowley, the British ambassador to Paris, Clarendon acknowledged that the British government was now in a position of having to support the present Turkish government, right or wrong. Painful and serious as it was to violate a treaty (namely, the 1841 Straits Convention), "that is far preferable to anything like a retreat."[47] On 15 September, still before having learned of the "violent" interpretation, Aberdeen and Clarendon joined Palmerston in agreeing "to propose at Vienna that the four powers should declare that they adopted the Turkish modifications as their own interpretation of the note"—a proposal that they should have realized had no chance whatever of acceptance and was nothing less than an insult to Russia.[48]

The French government followed the lead of Britain in denouncing the Russian interpretation of the Vienna Note and abandoning its efforts to impose it on the Porte. Buol was convinced that the French professed to agree with the British because their real concern was to keep their policy in line with that of Britain. He informed the French government that after a minute examination of the Russian interpretation of the Vienna Note, he found nothing in it to justify the apprehension of the British and French governments or to prevent them from carrying out the policy toward Turkey on which they had all agreed.[49] Buol's arguments, however, had no effect on the policies of Britain and France, and with the refusal of these powers to join Austria and Prussia in coercing the Turks into accepting the Vienna Note, the negotiations to mediate the dispute based on that note ended in failure.

The Anglo-French Fleets Ordered to Constantinople

In Turkey meanwhile, the bellicosity of the Turks had been growing steadily since their rejection of the Vienna Note and their demand for amendments. In late August and early September there was a succession of demonstrations in Constantinople demanding a holy war against Russia. These and other domestic disturbances gave the leaders of the Turkish government a pretext for appealing to the British and French ambassadors to summon the Anglo-French fleets from Besika Bay to Constantinople to protect the lives and property of foreigners as well as the Turkish government itself. In view of the dangerously inflamed state of Turkish public opinion, the Turkish government could not count on the reliability of its own security forces, which were entirely controlled by the prowar party.[50]

Stratford opposed summoning all the ships of the Anglo-French squadrons on the grounds that it was important to avoid the appearance of intimidating the Turkish government, but the real reason for his conduct appears to have been his desire to avoid an excessively flagrant violation of the Straits Convention of 1841. He suggested bringing up only a few additional steamers "under cover of the steam-communications continually plying between the squadrons and the capital." These would be sufficient to "protect us from any immediate attack, and enable us to assist the government in case of an outbreak threatening its existence, without attracting any unusual attention." In accordance with Stratford's recommendations, he and Lacour brought up only two warships from each of their fleets. Stratford had previously been assured by a senior British naval officer that these would be sufficient to block the Straits in the event of a Russian surprise attack.[51]

In France, Napoleon seemed to have been as eager as the Turks to exploit the possibility of riots in Constantinople as an excuse to bring up the Anglo-French fleets, and on 19 September he instructed his ambassador in London to propose to the British government the simultaneous and immediate entry of their fleets into the Dardanelles.[52] Three days later Aberdeen and Clarendon, without waiting to consult their colleagues in the cabinet, acceded to the French proposal and sent orders to Stratford to summon the British fleet to Constantinople.[53] The British government had long been under intense pressure from British public opinion and the press to take action on behalf of the Turks, but for Aberdeen the chief consideration in making this decision appears to have been a genuine concern about the danger of unrest in Constantinople. "Our main object in going to Constantinople is for the protection of British life and property, and if necessary, of the person of the Sultan," he wrote to Clarendon on 23 September. ". . . I think it very essential that information should forthwith be given to Russia, through Seymour, of our proceeding; with an explanation that [it] is not intended as a menace, or hostile movement directed against Russia."⁵⁴ Clarendon, however, was by now convinced of Russian perfidy and of the need for action. "All hope of negotiation appears now to be at an end," he wrote to Stratford on 24 September. ". . . The only real likelihood however now is war."⁵⁵

The Olmütz Mediation Proposal, or Buol Project

The Russians were seriously alarmed by the Anglo-French reaction to the "violent" interpretation. Fearful that the Turks might feel sufficiently encouraged actually to risk war with Russia and that they might be joined by Britain and France, the Russians made another determined effort to resolve the crisis by negotiation and to calm the suspicions of the British and French governments.

In the last week of September, the tsar and Nesselrode journeyed to Olmütz to attend Austrian army maneuvers and to meet with Emperor Francis Joseph, Buol, and representatives of the British, French, and Prussian governments. The Russians went out of their way to be friendly to the British and French representatives. Nesselrode assured them yet again that the tsar desired no new rights or increase of his influence in Turkey. The tsar went further and told the British emissary that he was willing "to meet every legitimate wish" the European powers had expressed to him. He insisted only on two points: the maintenance of existing treaties and the status quo in religious matters. "His Majesty asks only for a general guarantee of the immunities already granted to the Greek Church," Westmorland, the British ambassador, reported from Olmütz, "and for nothing which could in any way prejudice the independence or rights of the

Sultan, or which would imply a desire to interfere with the internal affairs of the Porte."[56]

After further discussion of the issues involved, the tsar requested the Austrian foreign minister to draw up a new proposal whereby the powers would again submit the unaltered Vienna Note to the Turks but accompanied by an unequivocal interpretation of that note to which all the European powers, including Russia, should adhere. As soon as the Turks had signed, Russia would begin the evacuation of the principalities. Buol, concerned as ever to prevent a war that he was convinced would be disastrous for Austria, responded eagerly to the tsar's request and drew up a proposal embodying the tsar's ideas that was subsequently known as the Olmütz Proposal or Buol Project.[57]

Napoleon was impressed by the tsar's moderation, but as usual his primary concern was to remain in step with England—and England remained obdurate. In response to a French communication of 4 October expressing willingness to accept the Olmütz Proposal if the British government concurred, Clarendon replied that the British cabinet had not yet considered it but that he was certain the cabinet would not approve a measure it knew to be useless and unjustifiable in any case.[58]

Clarendon's prediction proved to be correct. The cabinet did not approve the proposal. It did not even debate the measure or give the Olmütz Proposal any serious consideration. "Of course the proposition from Olmütz is intended only to deceive," Russell wrote to Clarendon on 5 October, and this was the attitude that prevailed in the British cabinet when it met three days later.[59] Clarendon's reply to the Olmütz Proposal reads as though he had not even bothered to read it, much less pay any attention to the tsar's solemn assurances. In view of Nesselrode's interpretation of the Vienna Note, Clarendon said in his dispatch to Vienna of 8 October, the Turks could not be expected to accept it; the Buol Project appeared to agree with the Russian interpretation of previous treaties giving Russia "a protectorate over the Greek subjects of the Sultan." Clarendon acknowledged that the tsar had disclaimed "all desire of acquiring any new right" in the Ottoman Empire and found it "impossible therefore to comprehend why a point that could so easily be made clear should so perseveringly be left in doubt."[60]

The Turkish Declaration of War

The Buol Project was already doomed in any case, for by this time Britain and France as well as the Turks had taken critical steps that eventually frustrated all attempts at negotiation. On 23 September, the British and French governments had ordered their fleets to enter the Dardanelles; on 26 September the Turkish Grand Council voted for war with Russia; and on 4 October the Turkish government officially declared war. Included in the Turkish declaration of war was an ultimatum to Russia to evacuate the principalities; if within fifteen days the Turkish government did not receive a positive reply to this ultimatum, Turkey would commence hostilities.[61]

The order to send the Anglo-French fleets to Constantinople did not have a decisive influence on the subsequent actions of the Turkish government as is often supposed, for news of this order arrived after the crucial decisions of the Turkish government had already been made. Formal notification of Russia's rejection of Turkey's demands for amendments to the Vienna Note was received in Constantinople on 25 September. On the following day the Turkish Grand Council resolved unanimously to refuse to accept the unamended note on any terms and to declare war on Russia rather than continue fruitless negotiations.[62]

In making this decision, which proved to be the prelude to their actual declaration of war, the Turks were undoubtedly encouraged by the action of the British and French ambassadors in bringing additional warships to Constantinople. But even greater encouragement came from Musurus, the Turkish ambassador in London, who for months had been sending his government a steady stream of information about the passionate support of British public opinion, the British press, and influential British leaders for the Turkish cause. Through Musurus the sultan had addressed a personal appeal to Palmerston telling him that the Turkish government was counting on his aid to persuade the British cabinet to come to the support of the Ottoman Empire. On 7 September Musurus informed Constantinople that Palmerston had authorized him "to give [the Turkish government] on his part the assurance of an aid all the more efficacious because the present Cabinet counts in its numbers influential members, equally devoted to the cause of the Ottoman Empire, such as Lord John Russell, Lord Lansdowne, Lord Clarendon, and others."[63]

In Constantinople, Stratford continued to pursue his own policies. Before the fateful meeting of the Turkish Grand Council on 26 September, he again joined his diplomatic colleagues in vain attempts to persuade the Porte to accept the unamended Vienna Note in return for a joint guarantee of the four neutral powers. In view of the advice and support Stratford had given them earlier, however, the Turks had little reason to take his appeal to accept the Vienna Note seriously. After the meeting of the Grand Council, Stratford suggested a course of action to the Turks that was anything but pacific. In fact, it was only concerned with making sure that the Turks placed themselves in the strongest possible moral position before issuing their declaration of war. Stratford's advice was that the Turks should address an ultimatum to the Russians to evacuate the principalities; Russia would refuse; Turkey would therewith have a justification for declaring war. "On that supposition it may fairly be alleged that the provocation would lie as much to the charge of Russia as if she had been the first to declare war."[64]

Stratford informed Clarendon that he had advised the Turks to delay sending their ultimatum as long as possible because any precipitate action "would not only diminish the Porte's chances of carrying the main point without the dangers of war, but increase the difficulty of looking with confidence to foreign sympathy and eventual assistance."[65] As Stratford knew full well that the Turks could not carry the main point without the dangers of war, he was clearly most concerned about the latter consideration—the ability of the Turks to win foreign sympathy and support.

He need not have worried. The Turkish declaration of war was greeted with enthusiasm in England. That fervent Christian and humanitarian, Charles Kingsley, declared that the Turks were "fighting on God's side," and Karl Marx announced that the British and French ruling classes were being driven by the inexorable force of history to take sides with the enemy of the tsar.[66]

On 18 October the Turks received a reply to their ultimatum from the Russian commander in the principalities, who said he had no authority to treat of peace or war or the evacuation of the provinces. The Turks chose to regard this evasive reply as negative and assumed that they were now officially at war with Russia. On that same day, the Turkish government sent orders to its military commanders in the Balkans and the Caucasus regions to attack Russian positions—the precipitate action Stratford had urged them to avoid because it gave the Turks the appearance of being the aggressors. The tsar delayed until 1 November to issue the Russian equivalent of a declaration of war. "Russia is challenged to the fight; she has therefore no other course left her than putting her trust in God, to have recourse to arms in order to compel the Ottoman Government to respect Treaties, and to obtain reparation for the insults with which it has responded to our most moderate demands, and to our legitimate solicitude for the defense of the Orthodox faith in the East which is equally professed by the Russian people." The Russian government assured all foreign powers that Russia would stand strictly on the defensive; it therefore depended entirely on other powers not to extend the limits of war.[67]

Chapter 6

Britain and France Enter
the Conflict

Britain's Partisan Neutrality

On 7 October 1853, after the Olmütz Proposal had been sent to London for consideration by the British government, the British cabinet met for the first time since the dissolution of Parliament six weeks earlier. As we have seen, the cabinet rejected this latest mediation proposal without serious discussion or debate.

Instead of discussing the Olmütz Proposal at this cabinet meeting of 7 October, Aberdeen found it necessary to confront proposals from Palmerston and Russell that the British fleet, which had been ordered to enter the Straits, should now be sent into the Black Sea in order to detain all Russian ships found cruising there. Aberdeen's own account of that meeting shows how he was allowing himself to be swept along by his colleagues and reveals at the same time an incredible self-delusion or confusion about the implications of the policies to which he was agreeing. "We came at last to a sort of compromise," he reported to Graham, the first lord of the admiralty,

our great difficulty being how to deal with the question of entering the Black Sea. I consented to this being done, provided it was strictly in defense of some point of attack on Turkish territory. I have no fear that this will take place; as long as we abstain from entering the Black Sea, peace may be possible between us and Russia. We have thus assumed a strictly defensive position, which for the moment may be sufficient, and will enable us to carry on negotiations; but this cannot last long. Under the character of a defensive war we should inevitably become extensively engaged. Should the Turks be at all worsted, which is probable, of course we must increase our assistance. We should have a French Army, and put up English money,—all for defence.[1]

The queen and Prince Albert saw far more clearly than Aberdeen the probable consequences of the cabinet's decisions. After a long discussion with Graham, Prince Albert told him that Aberdeen's letter had made the royal couple very uneasy. "It was evident that Lord Aberdeen was, against his better judgment, consenting to a course of policy which he inwardly condemned, that his desire to maintain unanimity at the Cabinet led to concessions which by degrees altered the whole character of the policy, while he held out no hope of being able permanently to secure agreement."[2]

The queen was angered that dispatches based on the latest cabinet decisions had been sent off without her sanction. The instructions to Stratford in particular appeared to her very vague and entrusted to him enormous powers and a latitude of discretion that could hardly be called safe. "As matters have now been arranged," she wrote to Clarendon on 11 October, "it appears to the Queen, moreover, that we have taken on ourselves in conjunction with France all the risks of a European war without having bound Turkey to any conditions with respect to provoking it. The hundred and twenty fanatical Turks constituting the Divan at Constantinople are left sole judges of the line of policy to be pursued, and made cognisant at the same time of the fact that England and France have bound themselves to defend the Turkish territory!"[3]

Prince Albert also sought to alert the cabinet to the dangers it was incurring. "It is evident that the Turks have every inducement not to let this opportunity to slip in going to war with Russia, as they will probably never find so advantageous a one again, as the whole of Christendom has declared them in the right, and they would fight with England and France actively on their side!"[4]

By mid-October Aberdeen himself had come to recognize the hopeless dilemma in which the British government had placed itself, at least so far as the preservation of the peace of Europe was concerned. On 17 October he wrote to Gladstone, the chancellor of the exchequer and one of the few members of his cabinet still sincerely anxious for peace: "The Turks, with all their barbarism, are cunning enough, and see clearly the advantages of their situation. Step by step they have drawn us into a position in which we are more or less committed to their support. It would be absurd to suppose that, with the hopes of active assistance from England and France, they should not be desirous of engaging in a conflict with their formidable neighbor. They never had such a favorable opportunity before, and may never have again. They will therefore contrive to elude our proposals and keep us in our present state, from which it will be difficult to escape."[5]

The champions of Stratford insist that the British ambassador was still doing everything possible in Constantinople to restore peace and keep the conflict localized, but, although he continued to draft mediation proposals and professed to be doing everything in his power to secure the agreement of the Porte to proposals made by his own government, his efforts met with a conspicuous lack of success.

The queen was certainly not convinced about Stratford's desire for peace. On the contrary, after reading his private letters, which were communicated to her by Clarendon, she wrote to Aberdeen on 5 November: "They exhibit clearly on his part a *desire* for war, and to drag us into it. When he speaks of the sword which will not only have to be drawn, but the scabbard thrown away, and says, the war to be successful must be a *'very comprehensive one'* on the part of England and France, the intention is unmistakable, and it becomes a serious question whether we are justified in allowing Lord Stratford any longer to remain in a situation which gives him the means of frustrating all our efforts for peace."[6]

Aberdeen and Clarendon shared the queen's fears. To Cowley, the British ambassador in Paris, Clarendon wrote on 10 November:

It is a misfortune and complication that we cannot feel sure of Stratford acting with us for a peaceful solution. He pretends to do so, and
writes notes and gets promises and appears to carry out his instructions; but it is impossible to believe, if he put his heart into it and set
about the work *as he knows how to do there,* that everything in our
view should fail as it does . . . He is *bent on war,* and on playing
the first part in settling the great Eastern question, as Lady S. de R.
admitted to me two days ago he now considered it to be—that the time
was come and *the man was there* for curbing the insolence of Russia
and resettling the balance of power in Europe. In short, he seems just
as wild as the Turks themselves, and together they may, and will, defeat every combination coming from the West, however well devised
it may be.[7]

While Aberdeen and Clarendon vacillated, complaining about
the conduct of Stratford and the Turks but lacking the moral
courage or determination to oppose them, Palmerston took a firm
line that fully supported the policies Stratford seemed to be pursuing. He wrote to Aberdeen on 1 November saying that Russia
had attacked the independence and violated the integrity of the
Ottoman Empire and that Russia must "by fair means or foul" be
brought to give up its pretensions and withdraw its aggression.
Far from regretting the position in which his country now found
itself, he expressed satisfaction that the British government could
now no longer change course. "We passed the Rubicon when we
first took part with Turkey and sent our squadrons to support
her," he said. Scoffing at the prime minister's qualms about encouraging Moslem oppression of Christians and his vague ideas
about reform of the Ottoman Empire, Palmerston declared that
any moves for the reconstruction of Turkey would mean nothing
less than its subjection to Russia. "It seems to me, then, that our
course is plain, simple, and straight: that we must help Turkey
out of her difficulties by negotiation, if possible; and that if negotiation fails, we must, by force of arms, carry her safely through
her dangers."[8]

The hapless Aberdeen did not see the British course as either
plain or simple, but when forced by the Russians to confront the
implications of British policy squarely, he found himself taking
the same line as Palmerston. This confrontation took place shortly

after the entry of the Anglo-French fleets into the Straits on 14 October. At the instructions of the tsar, Brunnow, the Russian ambassador to London, asked Aberdeen what Britain would do in the event of a serious conflict on land or sea between Russia and Turkey. Aberdeen replied that Britain would do nothing if Russia remained on the left bank of the Danube and the war was not extended to the right bank, implying that Britain would do nothing if *Russia* did not take the offensive. (Marginal note of the tsar: "and the Turks may unexpectedly cross over to the left bank! There is a paradox worthy of the English!") Nor did Britain consider itself obliged to give material assistance to the Porte unless Russia attacked a Turkish seaboard on the Black Sea. In that case, however, the English squadron would cover Turkish ports against a Russian offensive. By adopting this policy, the British government would still be able to claim that it was not at war with Russia (the tsar: "this is infamous!"), but Aberdeen thought it necessary to add that Britain could not abandon the Turks to their fate because that would mean the certain destruction of the Ottoman Empire, a catastrophe that England wanted to prevent as long as possible. (The tsar: "Thus it's to be war! So be it!")[9]

The Tsar's Reaction

To this candid acknowledgment of the British government's thoroughly unneutral stance, the tsar responded with a typical outburst of rage and grandiose plans to counteract further British perfidy.

He suspected that the British, by spurring the Turks into war, in fact intended to hasten the collapse of the Turkish Empire in Europe, and were preparing to exploit the ensuing chaos at the expense of Russia by taking the lead in the emancipation of the Christians of Europe and organizing them in a manner directly contrary to Russian interests. It was therefore imperative for Russia to anticipate this infamous policy by declaring that Russia, while remaining faithful to the principle of renouncing all conquests, recognized that the moment had come to restore the independence of the Christian states of Europe which for centuries had been under the Ottoman yoke. In taking the initiative in this holy cause, Russia would appeal to all Christian nations to aid in the realization of this sacred goal. Russia would declare its desire to restore the true independence of the Moldo-Wallachians, the Serbs, the Bulgars, the Bosnians, and the Greeks. Each of these nations should once again enjoy the lands they had inhabited for centuries; each should be governed by leaders of their own choice elected by themselves from members of their own nationality. By a declaration of this kind, the tsar thought it would be possible to gain the support of Christian Europe and put an end to British ill will, because after such a declaration they surely could not join the Turks in a war against the Christians.[10]

Nesselrode hastened to reply to these incredibly naïve ideas. He thought the Russian government should bear in mind that, although hostilities had begun, it should not yet abandon all hope of a diplomatic solution to the crisis. Nor did he think that Britain and France, which had loudly proclaimed their desire to maintain the Ottoman Empire, would dare compromise their honor by calling for the emancipation of the Christian peoples and therewith bring about its collapse. If Russia issued an emancipation proclamation, on the other hand, they could say that Russia had finally dropped its mask; that they had been right all along to distrust Russian assurances; that Russia really wanted the disintegration of the Ottoman Empire and the formation of nominally independent small states that it would dominate and control. Nesselrode pointed out that Russia had always resolutely protested against all encouragement of revolutionary movements, whether Polish, Hungarian, Italian, Caucasian, or even that of the so-called Daco-Rumanian nationality in the principalities. How could Russia now violate the doctrines it had professed by appealing to the European states to support revolution in the Christian provinces of the Ottoman Empire? How could Prussia or Austria, which Russia had supported during domestic as well as national revolutions, join in such an enterprise? If revolutions should break out in the Ottoman Empire in the course of its war with Russia and if they were successful, Russia might recognize the independence of any new states that were formed, for in that case Russian recognition would appear as a generous and disinterested act. But until the Ottoman Empire was clearly on the verge of disintegration, Russia should not attempt to anticipate their adversaries' plans to exploit the Christians in the Ottoman Empire. For the moment, Russia should restrict its efforts to dealing with existing dangers and strengthening its military position.[11]

The Collective Note of 5 December 1853

Nesselrode's belief that there was still reason to hope for a diplomatic solution to the crisis despite the commencement of hostilities was based on another Austrian diplomatic initiative. Immediately after the Turkish declaration of war, Buol informed Nesselrode that he was willing to continue his mediation efforts, but he wanted a signal from Russia that such efforts would be welcome.[12] Nesselrode sent the desired signal on 17 October, and on the twenty-fifth Buol once again convened a conference of ambassadors in Vienna to draft yet another mediation proposal.[13]

The formula was familiar. The four neutral powers were to address a Collective Note to the Porte containing all the assurances previously agreed upon by Russia and the other European powers with respect to the sovereignty and independence of the sultan, and all assurances previously accepted by the sultan with respect to the rights of the Orthodox church in the Ottoman Empire.

Clarendon was not impressed. There was little new in Buol's latest proposal, he wrote to Westmorland in Vienna. Besides, the British government could not support any proposals to the Porte without the previous concurrence of the Turkish government—in other words, Britain would only support a four-power effort to secure Turkish agreement to a mediation proposal if Turkey had already agreed to that proposal. Nevertheless, in view of the Russian government's readiness to accept the mediation of the

four powers, the British government was prepared to participate
in a four-power Collective Note to the Porte, and he promised to
send Buol the draft of such a note, which was to be drawn up in
agreement with the French.[14]

Anxious to get negotiations going on virtually any conditions,
Buol agreed to Clarendon's proposal and used the Anglo-French
note Clarendon sent him as the basis for a Collective Note and
Protocol that was accepted by the representatives of the four
powers in Vienna on 5 December and forwarded to Constantinople. The four powers had every reason to believe that this note
would be accepted by the Turks, for it turned over to them the
right to stipulate *their* conditions for making peace.[15] Whether
the Russians would have agreed to such conditions was another
matter. It was already too late, however, for this particular mediation to have any chance of success.

The Battle of Sinope and Its Repercussions

Very shortly after the Turkish declaration of war on 4 October
1853, the Turkish government sent orders to its military commanders to begin offensive operations against the Russians on
both the Balkan and Caucasus fronts, and to its naval commanders to undertake sorties in the Black Sea. Meanwhile the Russians, still awaiting the results of the four-power Collective Note,
adhered to the promise they had made on 1 November in what
was the equivalent of a declaration of war and remained strictly
on the defensive.

On 30 November, however, before the Collective Note had
been received in Constantinople, a division of the Russian fleet
pursued a Turkish fleet into the Turkish Black Sea harbor of
Sinope (in Turkish, *Sinoub*), where the Turks had sought refuge.
Maintaining that the Turkish fleet had been transporting men
and supplies to the Caucasus front, the Russians abandoned their
defensive posture and engaged the Turks in battle.[16] Within
hours the Russian ships, equipped with shell-firing guns, had
destroyed the Turkish fleet, which still consisted entirely of

wooden vessels, and in their bombardment of Turkish coastal batteries the Russian destroyed much of the city of Sinope as well.[17]

Accounts differ widely as to why Turkish naval vessels had been ordered to make sorties into the Black Sea in the face of vastly superior Russian sea power, and why the Turkish fleet destroyed at Sinope had been allowed to expose itself to the risk of such destruction. It was strongly suspected at the time, however, that these sorties of the Turkish fleet were deliberately provocative acts to lure the Russians out of their defensive posture and therewith provoke Anglo-French intervention. Upon learning that Turkish vessels had been ordered to cruise past the Russian naval fortress of Sebastopol in the Crimea, Queen Victoria inquired of Aberdeen three days before the incident at Sinope: "Wherefore should three poor Turkish steamers go to the Crimea, but to beard the Russian fleet and tempt it to come out of Sebastopol, which would thus constitute the much desired contingency for our combined Fleets to attack it, and so engage us irretrievably!"[18]

Whatever the true reason for the Turkish sortie, it had the effect the queen predicted. The Russian naval victory at Sinope was greeted with jubilation in Russia, but the most important result of that victory was its effect on the British and French governments and public opinion. The governments denounced the Russian naval action as a violation of the tsar's pledge that Russia would remain on the defensive, and the reaction of public opinion in Britain toward the "massacre of Sinope" was an outburst of emotional outrage against the brutal and inhuman Russians.[19]

The response of French public opinion appears to have been far less violent, but the official French press was full of sound and fury, and Napoleon took advantage of the situation to call for the British and French fleets to "sweep the Russian flag off the Black Sea"—if the British failed to support him he would act alone.[20] In Britain, Palmerston resigned from the cabinet, ostensibly over a franchise reform bill, but his resignation was generally interpreted as a gesture of protest over his government's failure to conduct a more forceful policy in the Near East.[21] By now, however, thanks to Sinope, a majority of the cabinet had swung over to Palmerston's point of view. Graham, the first lord of the admiralty, confessed that heretofore he had been one of the staunchest advocates of peace, "but the Sinope attack and recent events have changed entirely the aspect of affairs."[22] Clarendon wrote to Aberdeen, who still hesitated: "You think I care too much for public opinion, but really when the frightful carnage of Sinope comes to be known we shall be *utterly disgraced* if, on the mere score of humanity, we don't take active measures to prevent any more such outrages."[23]

On 22 December the Aberdeen government succumbed to the pressure of British public opinion and Napoleon's threat to act alone. After a debate of five and a half hours, the cabinet, which Palmerston had now rejoined, decided to order the British fleet to join the French in the Black Sea and to inform the Russians that any Russian ship caught out of harbor would be seized or sunk.[24]

Already at the time of the initial order to the British fleet to enter the Black Sea, an action that British leaders realized would very likely lead to war, the British had fixed on the most promising objective of British naval action. "Should any such opportunity present itself," Graham wrote to Dundas, the commander of the British Mediterranean fleet, "I conclude that you will have your eye on Sebastopol. That is a place where a blow might be struck which would be memorable in Europe, and which would settle the affairs of the East for some time to come." Clarendon wrote much the same thing to Cowley, the British ambassador in Paris. He expected and hoped that the tsar would declare war as soon as he learned of the orders to the Allied admirals. The Allies could then attack Sebastopol and "*finish up* Russia as a naval power in the East" as well as wipe out the Russian Baltic fleet. Such great blows "would be very gratifying to our respective *publics* and might have incalculable consequences for the future."[25] When war at last seemed certain, Graham became even more emphatic. "*The* operation, which will be ever memorable and decisive," he told Clarendon on 1 March, "is the capture and destruction of Sebastopol. On this my heart is set: the eye-tooth of the Bear must be drawn; and till his fleet and naval arsenal in the Black Sea are destroyed, there is no safety for Constantinople—no security for the peace of Europe."[26]

Post-Sinope Diplomacy

The tsar did not respond as Clarendon had expected and hoped. Fully aware of his danger, he continued his efforts to resolve the conflict by diplomacy or at least to persuade the other European powers to remain neutral and cease their encouragement and support of the Turks. In mid-October he had authorized his government to accept the mediation offer of Austria;[27] in late October and November he addressed personal appeals to Queen Victoria of England[28] and Emperor Francis Joseph of Austria;[29] in December he addressed a second personal appeal to Victoria and Francis Joseph[30] and another, through Castelbajac, the French ambassador to St. Petersburg, to Napoleon. Castelbajac joined his own appeal to that of the tsar. He was convinced that the tsar had never wanted to dominate Turkey, that he really desired peace and would seize any opportunity to negotiate.[31] Victoria, however, simply turned the tsar's letters over to her government to answer, while Napoleon was determine to preserve his alliance with Britain at all costs. When the French foreign minister, Drouyn de Lhuys, warned his sovereign about committing France too closely to the policies of Britain, Napoleon replied: "When we sent our fleet to Salamis, we had only one wish, to draw a cool and hesitant England into an alliance with ourselves." Now that this goal had been achieved, he warned, the French government should not jeopardize the fruits of its efforts. "The interest of France today is perfectly clear. It consists first of all in making common and close cause with England at Constantinople, then to attract Austria and Prussia into our alliance."[32]

The tsar for his part was seeking to draw Austria and Prussia into an alliance with him, although by the time the Anglo-French fleets had entered the Black Sea he had given up all hope of securing their active support and sought only to ensure their neutrality. He was dismayed that Austria had endorsed the four-power Collective Note that gave the Porte the right to stipulate conditions for making peace and ascribed Austria's adherence to such a document to fear of French threats. To counter the effects of French intimidation, the tsar promised Francis Joseph full Russian support to defend his empire on every front. At the same time he proposed a defensive alliance between Austria, Prussia, and Russia, the three conservative powers that had so long safe-guarded the welfare of Europe.[33]

The tsar need not have worried about the four-power Collective Note. That document, sent to Constantinople on 5 December, had not reached the Turkish capital until 16 December, well after the Battle of Sinope. There the representatives of the four neutral great powers, with Stratford in the lead, took the position that the Collective Note from Vienna was now no longer applicable and therefore they never even bothered to present it to the Porte. Instead they drew up a note of their own, worked out in close consultation with the Turkish government, which they sent to Vienna to be forwarded to Russia. Thus it would be left up to Russia to agree to what was essentially a Turkish note or bear responsibility for the continuation of the crisis and its probable eruption into a general war.[34] This substitution of notes in Con-stantinople is hard to understand, unless it was a product of Stratford's insistence on playing the principal role in any diplo-matic initiative or his revenge for Buol's refusal to forward the Turkish Ultimatum to St. Petersburg in the previous July. For, as we have seen, the Collective Note too was essentially a Turkish document and a statement of Turkish conditions.

Buol was infuriated by this disregard of his orders on the part of Bruck, the Austrian emissary to Constantinople, but confessed that he was unable to understand anything that was going on in the Turkish capital at this time except the behavior of Stratford.

"He hates Russia, does not love his own ministry, pays no attention to the instructions he receives, and has limitless conceit. He wants either the humiliation of Russia or to draw Turkey and the other powers through violence into his operations."[35]

Despite his anger, Buol, anxious as always to take advantage of any foothold to resume negotiations, reconvened a conference of the ambassadors in Vienna to consider the mediation proposal formulated in Constantinople. On 13 January 1854, this latest Vienna conference agreed to endorse the Constantinople Note in place of the Collective Note of 5 December, and to forward it to St. Petersburg.[36]

The Orlov Mission to Vienna

Toward the end of January 1854, in a major effort to secure some kind of commitment from Austria, the tsar sent Count Orlov, one of his most experienced and trusted officials, to Vienna with two personal letters to Emperor Francis Joseph: the first, a request for an assurance of Austrian armed neutrality in the present war; the second, a reply to both four-power Collective Notes, the one of 5 December as well as that of 13 January.[37] Although the Russian counterproposals had been formulated before the receipt of the latter communication, Orlov informed the Austrians that they were intended to serve as a response to that document as well.[38]

The Austrians were caught in a difficult dilemma. They were desperately anxious to bring the war to an end or at least prevent its expansion. An Austrian declaration of neutrality, however, might encourage the tsar to abandon his own efforts to prevent an extension of the conflict. As the tsar himself had foreseen, a successful Russian advance might lead to revolutions of the Christian populations in the Balkans, which would stir up the forces of revolution among subject nationalities everywhere, most notably in the Habsburg Empire. In response to the tsar's request for an Austrian declaration of armed neutrality, Francis Joseph replied that he could not provide such a declaration unless the tsar gave him a "formal guarantee" to maintain the existing Otto-

man Empire and the present status of the populations in the territories adjacent to Austria.

The Russians were generous with their assurances. Orlov promised that Russia would permit no changes in the Ottoman Empire without Austria's consent. The tsar went further and offered
to share with Austria all protectorate rights he might exercise in
Ottoman territories in the Balkans. This was a mistake. Francis
Joseph was doubtful whether the Russians could prevent changes
even if they honestly attempted to do so, and the Russian offer to
share protectorate rights with Austria in the Balkans was more
alarming than tempting. The religious sympathies that linked the
Balkan peoples with Russia gave Russia such preponderant influence in these areas that any Austrian protectorate rights would
be nominal at best, and a situation would be created that would
lead to constant tension between Austria and Russia.

Orlov thought Austrian expressions of alarm about changes in
the Balkans were exaggerated and that the real reason for their
negative reaction to Russian proposals was fear of France. "The
declaration you are asking us to make," Buol had told him,
"would bring France into Italy, and it is this we want to avoid."
Whatever the Austrians' major motives may have been, they rejected the tsar's request for a declaration of armed neutrality.
Francis Joseph promised only to maintain a status of "expectant
neutrality"—and placed an army corps on his Balkan frontier to
observe developments. At the same time both Austria and Prussia rejected a Russian proposal that they join Russia in a new
triple alliance of the northern conservative powers.[39]

Orlov also failed to secure Austrian support for the Russian
reply to the four-power Collective Notes of 5 December and 13
January. Although Buol convened yet another conference of the
ambassadors in Vienna to consider the Russian counterproposals,
he informed the Russians before the conference met that because
their counterproposals did not correspond in any way to the conditions set forth in the note of 13 January, he did not feel justified in supporting them and would confine himself to submitting
them to the consideration of the conference. When this conference convened on 2 February, it decided that the Russian coun-

terproposals were not sufficiently satisfactory to warrant their communication to Constantinople.[40]

Napoleon's Letter to the Tsar, 29 January 1854

While Orlov was in Vienna, Napoleon III finally replied to the tsar's repeated appeals for French mediation. In a letter of 29 January he reviewed the development of the entire crisis, emphasizing Russia's responsibility for the failure of diplomatic efforts to resolve it peacefully and singling out Sinope as a turning point in the attitude of France, for Russia's attack on the Turkish fleet had been a blow to French honor and prestige. To restore peace and prevent an extension of the conflict, Napoleon proposed that the Russians evacuate the principalities and that the Anglo-French squadrons leave the Black Sea. Russia should then negotiate a peace treaty directly with Turkey that should be submitted to a conference of the four neutral powers. If the tsar refused to accept this procedure, France and Britain would be obliged to leave the resolution of the crisis to the hazards of war.[41]

Napoleon's letter has been subjected to many interpretations. Was the French emperor making a sincere effort to avoid war with Russia now that his own major political aims appeared to have been realized, namely, the consolidation of his alliance with Britain and the destruction of the Concert of Europe? Or was his letter designed to goad Nicholas into making a declaration of war against France and Britain and thus establish Russia as the aggressor? The fact that Napoleon authorized the publication of his letter before the tsar even had a chance to reply suggests that it may have been intended primarily as a piece of propaganda to justify France's belligerent stance, and contemporary diplomatic observers as well as large segments of French public opinion tended to regard it as such. One of the emperor's domestic political opponents, at any rate, was in no doubt about his intentions. "This letter crowns the whole," he said, "it throws on him [Napoleon] the responsibility of the war, and that responsibility will crush him."[42]

The tsar himself seems to have been in some doubt about the

French emperor's intentions. His reply of 9 February was moderate, considering the accusatory tone of Napoleon's letter. He challenged Napoleon's interpretation of recent events and complained of the unneutral and one-sided behavior of the Anglo-French fleets. He was prepared at any time to negotiate a peace settlement directly with the Turks; they need only send an emissary; Russian conditions for peace were known in Vienna.[43]

Russia Severs Diplomatic Relations; the Anglo-French Ultimata

The possibility for avoiding a major extension of the war seemed to be slipping away rapidly, however. Since the beginning of the year the British and French fleets had been carrying out their instructions to sweep Russian shipping from the Black Sea and were protecting Turkish shipping as well as the coasts and seaboards of the Ottoman Empire. After protesting repeatedly and in vain against this de facto warfare against his empire, the tsar instructed his diplomatic representatives in London and Paris early in February 1854 to demand their passports and to break off diplomatic relations with Britain and France on 6 February.[44]

The British and French governments responded on 27 February with separate ultimata demanding that Russia refrain from all military activity in its conflict with Turkey, announce the withdrawal of Russian forces from the principalities, and complete their withdrawal by 15 April (the British date was 30 April). A refusal to comply with these demands, or silence, would be regarded as the equivalent of a Russian declaration of war.[45]

Final Efforts to Preserve Peace

Even after the Vienna conference's rejection of the Russian counterproposals to the four-power Collective Notes on 2 February 1854, Buol did not give up his efforts to arrange a peaceful settlement. Before Orlov left Vienna on 9 February, Buol persuaded him to attempt to secure a Russian formulation of new counterproposals that corresponded more closely to the conditions embodied in the four-power notes. If Russia did so, Buol promised,

Austria would support these new Russian proposals at another conference in Vienna, where a Russian emissary would be authorized to negotiate a final formulation of conditions with the other representatives to render them acceptable to the Porte. The conference would then engage to secure their acceptance in Constantinople and would at the same time be authorized by Russia to arrange a temporary cessation of hostilities. With the preliminaries of peace thus arranged, an exchange of documents between Russia and Turkey would follow. The tsar would then order the evacuation of the principalities, while the governments of Britain and France would order their fleets to leave the Black Sea and the Straits. Buol left it up to Orlov to secure the agreement of the tsar to these proposals, and Orlov asked Austria to lay the groundwork for a favorable reception of these arrangements by Britain and France if his own government agreed to them.[46]

The Russian government was understandably angered by these Austrian proposals, which amounted to a demand for a complete Russian surrender. The Russians nevertheless decided to reply, and did so on 26 February, the day before the dispatch of the Anglo-French ultimata.

With some dismay, Buol noted that the Russians' reply could hardly have come at a less favorable time. He was even more dismayed that it was addressed to Austria alone and ignored the conference, which had formulated the four-power Collective Notes, and that it still contained conditions that did not correspond with the terms of those notes. Authorized by the Russian ambassador in Vienna to communicate the Russian proposals to the representatives of the other great powers, Buol reconvened a conference of the ambassadors on 5 March and invited its members to render their judgment of the Russian proposal in writing. The representatives of Britain and France declared that the Russian proposals differed in several decisive ways from the conditions of the note of 13 January and were therefore unacceptable.[47] With that judgment, the last hope for preventing a major extension of the war was extinguished.

Lord Stanmore, the biographer of Sidney Herbert, the British secretary at war, points out that these latest Russian proposals did not constitute an ultimatum, that they were still open to negotiation, and that the remaining differences between the Western and Russian conditions were slight and "eminently such as might have been removed by negotiation and discussion." He concludes: "Few will now venture to assert that the negotiations came to an end on account of any irreconcilable deadlock in them. They came to an end because the Western Powers had already determined on war, in every case but that of absolute and unconditional submission on the part of Russia."[48]

The Anglo-French Declarations of War

On 14 March the British and French ultimata were presented to the Russian government by their representatives in St. Petersburg, who were informed by Nesselrode shortly afterwards that "the tsar did not think it proper to make any reply" to their communications.[49] Russia's refusal to reply was duly interpreted as the equivalent of a Russian declaration of war on Britain and France, and on 27–28 March 1854, the British and French governments declared war on Russia. On 12 March they had concluded a formal alliance treaty with the Ottoman government, "fully persuaded that the existence of the Ottoman Empire in its present Limits is essential to the maintenance of the Balance of Power among the States of Europe," and on 10 April they concluded an alliance with each other and invited all the other states of Europe to join their anti-Russian coalition.[50]

Lord John Russell explained to the House of Commons the reasons for the British government's decision for war. "Unless we are content to submit to the future aggrandizement of that Power and, possibly, to the destruction of Turkey—whose integrity and independence have been so often declared essential to the stability of the system of Europe—we have no choice left us but to interpose by arms." It was impossible to maintain Turkish integrity and independence "if Russia was allowed unchecked and uninterrupted to impose her own terms on Turkey."[51]

Chapter 7

War Aims and the Austrian Ultimatum to Russia

British and Russian War Aims

The clear-cut declaration of war after so many months of frustrating negotiation was greeted with enthusiasm and relief by many British and French statesmen and by the most vociferous elements of public opinion in both countries.[1]

In a speech before the House of Lords on 31 March 1854, Clarendon declared in response to a question about Britain's aims in the present conflict: "We enter upon the war for a definite object. It is to check and to repel the unjust aggression of Russia . . . and to secure a peace honourable to Turkey." Clarendon then took up the theme that by now governed his own thinking and that of so many of his colleagues and British public opinion. He was convinced, he said, that there was not a man in Russia who did not expect that Constantinople would ultimately belong to Russia.

It will be our duty as far as possible to see that that expectation shall be disappointed. Because, were it to succeed—were Russia to be in possession of Constantinople, commanding as she then would the Black Sea and the shores of the Mediterranean—being able then, as she would then be able, to subjugate Circassia and Georgia, and convert the resources of those countries to swell her mighty armaments—having access to and command of the Mediterranean, having a vast naval fleet in the Baltic, and determined, as she is now, to increase her naval power by all the facilities which steam and modern inventions give for the transport of troops—it is not too much to anticipate that more than one power would have to undergo the fate of Poland.

The present war was no longer a war over the Eastern Question. It was a war for the independence of Europe, a battle of civilization against barbarism, a war to liberate mankind, advance civilization, and at the same time "gain great and solid things of the future" for Britain.[2]

Palmerston's war aims, which he did not express in public, were more specific and considerably more ambitious. In a memorandum to the cabinet of 19 March commenting on proposals set forth by Lord John Russell, Palmerston said:

My beau ideal of the result of the war which is about to begin with Russia is as follows: Aland and Finland restored to Sweden. Some of the German provinces of Russia on the Baltic ceded to Prussia. A substantive Kingdom of Poland re-established as a barrier between Germany and Russia. Wallachia and Moldavia and the mouths of the Danube given to Austria. Lombardy and Venice set free from Austrian rule and either made independent States or incorporated with Piedmont. The Crimea, Circassia and Georgia wrested from Russia, the Crimea and Georgia given to Turkey, and Circassia either independent or connected with the Sultan as Suzerain. Such results it is true could be accomplished only by a combination of Sweden, Prussia and Austria, with England, France, and Turkey, and such results presuppose great defeats of Russia. But such results are not impossible and should not be wholly discarded from our thoughts.[3]

These views of Palmerston were no mere "beau ideal" of fanciful ideas thrown out in the heat and enthusiasm of the moment. He submitted an almost identical program to the British foreign secretary, Lord Clarendon, on 6 April, and believed Austria and Prussia could be persuaded to join in a great Continental war against Russia if promised sufficiently large territorial gains at Russia's expense. "Prussia might get the German Provinces on the Baltic in exchange for the Polish Part of the Duchy of Posen in the event of a Restoration of the Kingdom of Poland; and such a Restoration not under Russian rule, would probably be the best security for the future independence of Germany. . . . Austria to get the Principalities giving up in exchange her Italian Provinces, and Turkey being indemnified by the Crimea, the Eastern shores of the Black Sea and Georgia."[4]

Palmerston's war aims went far beyond anything previously proposed by Allied leaders and certainly far beyond anything that could have been achieved through negotiation. Aberdeen commented that the attempt to impose them on Russia would plunge Europe into another Thirty Years War, but Palmerston remained adamant. He thought the war would be pointless if it did no more than halt Russian expansion and failed to eliminate the menace of Russian aggression for the foreseeable future. He expressed these views very clearly in a letter to Lord John Russell of 26 May 1854. Merely to expel the Russians from the principalities and leave them in full strength "would be only like turning a burglar out of yr house, to break in again at a more fitting opportunity. The best & most effectual security for the future peace of Europe would be the severance from Russia of some of the frontier territories acquired by her in later times, Georgia, Circassia, the Crimea, Bessarabia, Poland & Finland . . . she wd still remain an enormous Power, but far less advantageously posted for aggression on her neighbours."[5]

Stratford expressed very similar views somewhat less clearly and at far greater length. Writing to Clarendon on 12 June, he quoted the Duke of Wellington's statement that a people who resorted to war must understand "that the sword, once drawn, cannot be sheathed again, until their object is *completely attained*." And what was that object? To curb the tyrannous will of a power opposed to the interests, the feelings, the convictions of millions. "But in order to curb it effectually, we must do more than check its present outbreak, we must paralyze its spring of action by bringing home to its inner sense a feeling of permanent restraint." This would be a difficult task, for the power of Russia was a natural growth, instinctively encroaching. Clipped, and it would shoot out with greater vigor. How could that power be effectively curbed? By making a peace which would leave Russia "separated from Turkey by a *cordon* of principalities, or states, no longer dependent upon her . . . Russia, such as Russia was before she proclaimed without shame or disguise her appetite for territorial expansion at the expense of every neighbor in turn, whether friend or foe." The Allies could therefore not afford to hasten peace and staunch the wounds of Europe by the moderation of their views. To realize their goals, Stratford suggested a settlement "by which the course of the Danube would be free, the Principalities extended to the Black Sea, and released from Russian protection, Circassia restored to independence under the *suzeraineté* of the Porte, the Crimea established in a similar manner, the Black Sea opened to foreign ships of war, and Poland restored in the limits recognized by the Congress of Vienna." With these objects in view, it would be indispensable to have the material cooperation of Austria. Britain and France would therefore be obliged to offer any guarantees Austria might require to safeguard its own interests. Stratford was uncertain what those would be, but feared they might come perilously close to a restoration of the status quo. As Stratford had insisted that such an outcome of the war must be avoided at all costs, one must surmise that Stratford was suggesting in a deliberately oblique manner that Austria be given any guarantee to bring it into the war against Russia but that the final conditions imposed on Russia would be those desired by Britain, France, and the Ottoman Empire.[6]

The aims formulated by Russian statesmen were considerably more restrained. "The aim of our war against Turkey," Gorchakov, the Russian ambassador to Vienna, wrote early in April 1854, "is to reaffirm on a solid basis the religious immunities of our brothers of the Orthodox Church." This goal had to be attained and in fact could be attained the moment the other great powers of Europe equally concerned with the religious and civil rights of Christians "will endeavor to obtain from the Porte not worthless words but effective guarantees." Once these were obtained, the tsar would allow nothing to stand in the way of making peace.[7]

Russian statements of this kind were designed to enlist the support of neutral powers, Austria in particular, but this does not mean that they were not genuine expressions of Russian intentions. In contrast to the Allies, however, the Russians could afford restraint because of their incomparably superior geographical position and the facts of power politics of which they were so well aware in their saner moments. Russia was strong, Turkey was weak. All Russia needed to do was sit still and await developments. Involvement in war with the Ottoman Empire was for Russia a great misfortune and a great mistake. Small wonder that the Russians should have been anxious to make peace or that their rivals, equally aware of the facts of power politics, should have desired radical amputations of Russian territory to render Russia's geographical position less advantageous and reduce Russia's overall strength.

The Changing Stance of Austria

In comparison with the radical war aims of the more extreme Western leaders, the aims of the Austrians in this crisis were essentially conservative. As Stratford had suspected, they wanted little more than the restoration of the prewar status quo. Like the British and the French, the Austrians desired to halt the expansion of Russian influence in the Balkans, but they indicated that this purpose would be achieved if Russia abandoned its occupation of the principalities. The conservative and moderate nature of this Austrian goal makes the subsequent conduct of Austrian policy all the more incomprehensible, for instead of seeking to attain this objective through tactful negotiation, they committed the fateful blunder of presenting Russia with an ultimatum demanding that Russia cease all offensive military operations south of the Danube and set an early date for the evacuation of the Danubian Principalities.[8]

The Austrian ultimatum was a blunder for the simple reason that it was certain to alienate Russia, and this was something that Austria could not afford to do. Like all great powers, the Habsburg Empire was faced with a multitude of foreign and domestic dangers, the two greatest of these being Russia itself and the threat of national revolution in the multinational Habsburg realm. By far the most certain and most economical way for Austria to cope with either danger was through the preservation of international peace, which in dealing with Russia required the avoidance of all policies likely to disturb good relations with that country. Peace with Russia meant safety from Russia, while the preservation of peace in general gave Austrian statesmen the time and opportunity to deal with the nationalities problem.

Peace in itself, of course, did not remove the Russian danger, but percipient Austrian statesmen had long recognized that this danger could never be eliminated and that they must learn to coexist with the Russian colossus. Since the Congress of Vienna, the Austrians had endeavored to control Russian ambitions by bringing Russia into the European Concert, and by convincing the tsar that the interests of his own government and country were best served through a policy of monarchical solidarity against the forces of change and revolution, by cooperating with other European governments to ensure the preservation of the existing domestic and international order, and by resisting the temptation to seek petty (or even substantial) gains for Russia at the risk of major wars that in the long run could only benefit the forces of revolution. It was a policy, as Castlereagh had called it, of keeping the tsar "grouped," and it had worked remarkably well. In the spring of 1854, however, the Austrian government abandoned its policy of grouping in favor of a policy of confrontation.

The most obvious and undoubtedly most important reason for this shift in Austrian policy was that the responsible directors of Austrian foreign policy, Buol in particular, lost their sense of balance and judgment. As the crisis in the Near East intensified and with the imminent entry of Britain and France into the war, they succumbed to fears of Russian intentions comparable to if not so extreme as those of the Russophobes of the West, and to the temptation to exploit this seemingly uniquely favorable opportunity to halt the extension of Russian influence on their eastern and southern flanks. The tsar's numerous irresponsible pronouncements about the liberation of subject nationalities in the Ottoman Empire, and the very real possibility that a Russian victory would allow Russia to assume protectorate rights over all the Balkan provinces and the Orthodox Christian population of the Ottoman Empire, had given them ample reason for fear and ample reason to believe that Austrian interests required adherence to the European coalition dedicated to the prevention of such developments.

In a memorandum to Emperor Francis Joseph of 21 March 1854, and in subsequent ministerial conferences, Buol reviewed the evidence of what he perceived as the increasingly menacing nature of Russian policies, which he believed were dedicated to the breakup of the Ottoman Empire and posed a mortal threat to the vital interests of Austria. In the preceding July Russia had actually occupied the Danubian Principalities, a violation of the territorial integrity of the Ottoman Empire and contrary to the rights of nations (*Völkerrecht*) and the interests of Europe. Since then Russian authorities had been taking measures in the principalities that clearly foreshadowed their incorporation into the Russian Empire. Since October the Russians had been engaged in military operations south of the Danube, which if successful would give them control over all of southeastern Europe, without considering themselves bound by any obligations whatever to Austria.

The question must now be asked, Buol said, whether Austria could afford to maintain its present passive attitude or whether it must act to safeguard its vital interests by entering the conflict on the side of Allies. Buol did not think there could be any doubt about the answer. Never in the history of the House of Austria had there been a more favorable opportunity to win a complete and desirable solution to the Eastern Question, which had always hung like a sword of Damocles over Austrian affairs, and to remove Russian control over the Danube, that artery vital to the welfare of all of Germany. Just to achieve this latter purpose, to ensure that Russia should not continue to press like an Alp on Austria and the rest of Germany, would in itself justify a policy of intervention. If Austria did not act now, when all of Europe was united in its opposition to Russia's arrogant behavior, this uniquely favorable opportunity would be lost forever.

There were additional important considerations that argued for Austria's entry into the war. Intervention would ensure Austria a voice in all future settlements of the Eastern Question, whereas adherence to a policy of strict neutrality would offend all the belligerent powers, which might subsequently arrange settlements detrimental to Austrian interests or even at Austria's expense. In return for intervention, Austria could demand that the Allies conduct their major military campaign against Russia through the Balkans, where it was most likely to safeguard and promote Austrian interests, and thereby fend off the possibility that their major campaign would be waged in the Crimea or on the Caucasus front, as the British seemed inclined to do. Finally, and most important, by siding with Britain and France on behalf of the preservation of the Ottoman Empire, Austria would also be enlisting the support of those powers on behalf of the preservation of the Habsburg Empire and against the forces of national revolution, that mortal enemy of both the Ottoman and Habsburg realms.

As Buol saw it, the only decisions the Austrian government would still have to make would be determining the right moment for intervention and specifying the guarantees Austria would require from Britain and France in return for Austria's entry into the war on their side. The most important of these, Buol believed, would be to make certain that Britain and France did not restrict themselves to mere naval expeditions but seriously intended to mount a major campaign in the principalities; otherwise Austria would be obliged to bear the entire burden of the conflict. The moment for intervention would have come, therefore, when British and French expeditionary forces actually stood at the Danube, united with the Turkish army, ready to attack the enemy or to repel an enemy attack. In addition Buol thought that Austria would have to agree with Britain and France about the following points: to provide mutual pledges to seek no territorial gains; to provide mutual pledges not to withdraw from the war or make a separate peace with Russia; to make specific commitments over the number and nature of the military forces that each power should provide; all three powers to use their influence with the Porte to guarantee the position of all Christian sects in the Ottoman Empire; Britain and France to use their influence with the Porte to entrust Austria instead of Russia with a protectorate over Serbia and the Danubian Principalities.

In anticipation of these agreements with the Western powers, Buol proposed that Emperor Francis Joseph address a summons to Russia in the name of the Habsburg Empire demanding Russia's evacuation of the Danubian Principalities. This summons could include the assurance that Austrian intentions were restricted to upholding the territorial integrity of the Ottoman Empire and defending the interests of Europe. If Russia saw in this demand a *casus belli* and declared war, it would have only itself to blame for the consequences. To meet that eventuality, Austria would have to be assured of the support of Prussia and the German Confederation. Buol confessed that he was unable to judge the state of Austria's military preparedness, but he pointed out that armed intervention in the principalities would not necessarily mean war with Russia. Austrian forces would halt at the Pruth River, at which time the Austrian government would call for new peace negotiations.[9]

It is easy to understand Buol's fears about recent Russian policies and his euphoria about the prospect of a major European coalition for the restraint and containment of Russia, but the same cannot be said of Buol's own policy recommendations—so unrealistic, confused, and contradictory, and so inconsistent with his previous conduct of affairs. There was no chance whatever that the British and French governments would agree to the conditions he proposed and very little chance that Prussia and the German Confederation would guarantee to support Austria in the event of war with Russia. The chance that an Austrian ultimatum would result in war with Russia, on the other hand, was very great indeed.

Even more astonishing was Buol's apparent failure to appreciate the probable consequences of his policies and his confusion over what they were intended to achieve. By his mere willingness to risk war with Russia, he was proposing a course in which means and ends were completely out of balance, and the ends he was suggesting were in themselves vague and contradictory. Allegedly he wanted nothing more than Russia's evacuation of the principalities, but he was prepared to threaten and if necessary proceed to armed intervention (and thus risk war with Russia) to achieve that goal. If Austria were actually compelled to conduct military operations in the principalities, he proposed that Austrian forces halt at the Pruth River to allow for renewed peace negotiations. Yet among his reasons for urging Austrian intervention was his belief that Austria must take advantage of the present anti-Russian coalition to achieve a desirable solution of the Eastern Question, remove Russian control over the Danube, and in general halt the march of Russian aggression, a program which called for war aims as extreme as those of Palmerston.

Buol's ministerial colleagues immediately perceived the flaws in his arguments and policy recommendations, and they unanimously opposed his interventionist program. The arguments of the opposition were expressed most vigorously and cogently by General Hess, the master general of ordnance. Hess had grave misgivings about a policy of cooperation with the Western powers, which he believed deserved Austria's mistrust far more than Russia. The governments of Britain and France had always been thoroughly unreliable and had consistently encouraged revolutionary movements, whereas Russia had always been conservative and had loyally supported the governments of Austria and Prussia against the forces of revolution.

Hess also opposed an Austrian ultimatum to Russia. Such a move, he was convinced, would certainly mean war with Russia, for the tsar would never accept the humiliation of submission. Had anyone seriously considered the consequences of such a war? The Austrian government should face the fact that war with Russia would be a major undertaking, requiring an enormous expansion of Austria's armed forces, and Austria was not prepared for such a war, either militarily or financially. Already the Habsburg Empire was burdened with immense debts. The cost of putting an army into the field capable of waging war against Russia would impose ruinous additional tax burdens on the empire's population, which would in turn fan the flame of domestic discontent. The idea of halting Austrian forces at the Pruth River was ludicrous. If forced to evacuate the principalities, the Russians would never agree to peace negotiations under such humiliating circumstances, and the Austrian armies would be compelled to advance deep into Russian territory if the fortunes of war allowed them to do so. Even a victorious advance into Russia would be fraught with peril for Austria, however, for it would be certain to set off a national uprising in Poland; Sweden would use the opportunity to conquer Finland; and meanwhile the Austrian armies would be deep in the vastness of Russia, unable to strike a decisive blow. In short, it would be a war of unforeseeable dimensions with unforeseeable consequences. And no matter what the fortunes of war, those consequences were likely to be disastrous for Austria. Any Austrian setback would encourage the forces of revolution; if Russia won, Austria would have to pay the reckoning; if Britain and France won, a major reorganization of Europe along revolutionary lines would take place. The foremost task of Austrian statecraft, therefore, should be to stay out of the present conflict and do everything possible to promote peace negotiations.

On one issue only did Buol's colleagues agree with the views of their foreign minister: the urgent need for an alliance with Prussia and the German Confederation to strengthen Austria's hand to meet any eventualities. Prussia had already indicated its desire for such an alliance, and at the end of March 1854 Hess was sent to Berlin to negotiate on behalf of the Austrian government.[10]

The negotiations with Prussia were successful, and on 20 April 1854, the governments of Austria and Prussia signed a defensive

alliance guaranteeing each other's territory and the joint defense
of German interests for the duration of the war and inviting
other German states to join the Austro-Prussian agreement. In
announcing their alliance, Austria and Prussia called for an end
to the war and expressed the belief that the possibility for a settlement had been considerably enhanced by a recent Russian
declaration indicating Russia's intention to withdraw from the
principalities. At the insistence of Buol, Austria secured Prussia's
acceptance of an additional article that authorized Austria to
submit an ultimatum to Russia demanding that Russia halt its offensive operations and evacuate the principalities; if the Russian
reply was unsatisfactory, Austria could intervene actively in the
principalities under the protection of the Austro-Prussian alliance. Prussia, however, would join in offensive action only if
Russia actually incorporated the principalities or if Russian forces
crossed the Balkan mountains and thus threatened to establish
Russian dominion over all of southeastern Europe.[11]

The Austrian Ultimatum to Russia, 3 June 1854

The Austro-Prussian defensive alliance bolstered Austria's ability
to maintain a position of strict neutrality, for Austria was thereby
assured support in warding off threats and pressures from all the
belligerent powers. There is no question that the Austrian government should have adhered to this position and followed the
advice of Hess to devote all its energies to the promotion of peace
negotiations. Buol, however, believed that more forceful diplomatic action was necessary, as his insistence on the additional article in the Austro-Prussian alliance treaty indicated.

Since the ministerial conferences at the end of March, Buol
was no longer urging Austria's outright intervention in the war.
He himself appears to have become aware of the dangers of such
a course, and the task of securing Anglo-French agreement to the
conditions he proposed for Austria's entry into the war was prov-
ing more difficult than he had anticipated. But Buol was still
convinced that Austrian interests required Russia's evacuation of

the principalities and that an Austrian ultimatum to Russia would be the most effective means of accomplishing this purpose. By the end of May he had obviously won over Emperor Francis Joseph to his point of view, for on 29 May the emperor convened another ministerial conference to discuss and give final approval to the text of the ultimatum that was to be submitted to Russia— a text that must have been drafted by Buol or under his direction.

At this conference, Hess continued to oppose an Austrian ultimatum, still convinced that the tsar would reject it and that it was therefore certain to lead to war with Russia. Hess believed that the only way the tsar could be persuaded to evacuate the principalities would be to offer him reciprocity on the part of the Allies. Instead of an ultimatum, Hess proposed that Austria persuade all the belligerents to agree to an armistice that would include a provision that Russia evacuate the principalities in return for an Allied promise to withdraw their fleets from the Black Sea.

With some annoyance Buol turned aside Hess's proposal, saying he could only regret the need to discuss questions that he believed had long ago been settled. The demand for the evacuation of the principalities was being made in the name of Austria alone and on behalf of Austrian national interests. Austria was therefore not in a position to offer the Russians the kind of reciprocity Hess had suggested because Austria could not presume to ask the Allies to make concessions to Russia on behalf of an exclusively Austrian diplomatic initiative.

Hess then urged that the submission of the ultimatum at least be postponed, again citing Austria's lack of military preparedness, but Buol did not consider this sufficient reason for further delay. Even if Russia rejected the Austrian ultimatum, he said, Austria was not *obliged* to intervene and would thus remain in a position to select the most favorable moment.

Because Buol clearly had the support of the emperor on this question, the ministerial council of 29 May approved the text of the Austrian ultimatum, and the emperor concluded the meeting by pointing out the necessity for an agreement with the Porte

sanctioning the future entry of Austrian troops into the principalities to guarantee their evacuation by the Russians.[12]

The Austrian ultimatum, sent to St. Petersburg on 3 June 1854,
demanded that Russia halt all military operations south of the
Danube and fix an early date for the evacuation of the principalities. The Russians were told that the Russian evacuation of
Turkish territory was not only a necessity for Austria but also an
essential condition to clear the way for a general peace settlement, and thus an urgent necessity for all of Europe.[13]

The Austrian ultimatum was an act of almost inconceivable
folly. Not only was it certain to do irreparable damage to Aus-
trian-Russian relations, but it exposed Austria to the very real
risk of war before Austria had even assured itself of specific
British, French, or Prussian-German support. The most charita-
ble explanation that can be made of Buol's policy was that he
believed Austrian interests required a speedy end to the war;
that the Russian evacuation of the principalities was an essential
precondition for peace; that further diplomatic pressure on Russia would only admit of further delays; and that only an Austrian
ultimatum and the threat of Austrian military intervention would
ensure the prompt Russian evacuation which Austria required.
Buol, however, had no way of knowing whether the tsar would
actually submit to the ultimatum—Hess for one was convinced
that he would not—so that even if Buol had indeed been acting
in the interests of peace, he had done so at the risk of a major
extension of the war. As it turned out, his policy was successful,
but the question remains whether he could have achieved this
success through further negotiation without subjecting Russia to
the humiliation of an ultimatum, which, by permanently alienating Russia, made his policy a disaster in the long run.

The American historian Paul Schroeder has kindly drawn my
attention to another possible interpretation of Buol's policy,
namely, that Buol thought Austria must secure Russia's prompt
evacuation of the principalities because if Russia continued to
occupy them the Allies would mount their major military campaign against Russia through the Balkans—the Turks and Rus-

sians had been fighting in this area since the beginning of the war, and in April 1854 a large Anglo-French army had landed at Varna, in Bulgaria. Thus the Austrians faced the danger of having the major theater of the war on their doorstep without being able to control events. By issuing their ultimatum the Austrians actually did secure Russia's evacuation of the principalities and therewith successfully avoided this danger at least.[14]

It is by no means certain, however, that Buol wished to avoid a major Allied campaign through the Balkans. On the contrary, one of his reasons for favoring intervention on the side of the Allies had been to secure the support of an Allied army in the Balkans and to minimize the danger that the Allies would mount their major campaign elsewhere, leaving Austria to face the Russians in the Balkans alone.

Whatever the explanation for Buol's policy, and in history few things are more difficult to explain than policies that in retrospect seem mistaken, the Austrian ultimatum had the effect on the tsar that might have been expected. The Russian monarch was infuriated, but he was even more shocked, for until this time he had continued to count on the friendly neutrality of Austria, though he had given up hope of securing Austria's active support.[15] To the Austrian ambassador in St. Petersburg he expressed his profound indignation about the conduct of his fellow monarch, Francis Joseph, who had forgotten how much the tsar had done for him. The good relations between them that had contributed so much to the well-being of both their empires had been shattred, never to be restored.[16]

Disillusioned and indignant over Austria's ingratitude for the selfless support Russia had given the Habsburg monarchy during its hours of trial, the tsar at first refused even to consider the Austrian ultimatum and declared he would prefer war with Austria rather than submit to such a humiliation, but he was eventually persuaded by his advisers and the urgent pleas of the king of Prussia to evacuate the principalities if Austria would guarantee to prevent the Allies from entering them.[17]

Austria gave the desired guarantee, and in August 1854 the

Russians withdrew. The principalities were now occupied by the Austrians, an action sanctioned by an Austrian treaty with Turkey of 14 June that provided for a joint Austro-Turkish occupation for the duration of the war.[18] It is difficult to see how else the Austrians could have fulfilled their pledge to Russia to prevent the occupation of the principalities by the Allies, yet their occupation by Austria was regarded by Russia as an additional affront that seemed to emphasize Russia's humiliation and loss of face.

By capitulating to Austria's demand to evacuate the principalities, the Russians had prevented or at any rate postponed Austria's active participation in the war against them. As for the Austrians, far from strengthening their position by siding with the anti-Russian coalition and their own occupation of the principalities, they had made it infinitely more precarious. They had gratuitously transformed a friendly and supportive power on their long eastern frontier into an infuriated and vengeful enemy, and through their occupation of the principalities they had aroused the suspicion of both sides that Austria intended to exploit the crisis for its own territorial aggrandizement.

In assessing Buol's policy during this critical period, Professor Schroeder, who takes a more sympathetic view of the Austrian foreign minister than do many of his colleagues, believes that the ultimatum to Russia must be seen as part of Buol's overall strategy and that throughout the crisis his fundamental purpose was the formation of a lasting partnership with the Western powers which would ensure the permanent containment of Russia—and of Prussia, the other restless power. I agree with this assessment, but I also agree with Professor Schroeder's further observation that this goal was a chimera based on totally false illusions about British and French conceptions of their own interests and the enduring reliability of an alliance with these powers.[19]

Even in his pursuit of such an alliance, however, Buol's policy was inconsistent and vacillating, for instead of continuing to press for Austria's full participation in the war on the side of Britain and France, he attempted to achieve his ends by diplomacy and to use the lure of Austrian participation (or in the case of Russia, the threat) as a bargaining counter to extract commitments from all the belligerents. His tactics were clever enough, and in view of the policies of the belligerent governments, especially Britain, it is difficult to see what else he could have done, but to all the belligerents his policies seemed devious and dishonest, and the final result for Austria was disaster on every front. In abandoning its position of strict neutrality, Austria made a permanent enemy of Russia, but in refusing full cooperation with Britain and France, it lost whatever chance may have existed to create an enduring anti-Russian coalition among the European powers, which would have been Austria's only safeguard against a vengeful Russia. The fact that the possibility for such a coalition was virtually nil reinforces the verdict that the shift in Austrian policy toward Russia which culminated in the ultimatum of 3 June was a terrible blunder.

In retrospect the ultimatum can also be seen as a turning point in European history, for it marked the end of the friendship and cooperation between the two Eastern European conservative powers and the beginning of a bitter hostility that was to culminate in war in 1914, the destruction of both imperial houses, and the liquidation of the Habsburg Empire.

Chapter 8

The Conduct of the War[1]

The Allied Decision for the Crimean Campaign

Russia's withdrawal from and Austria's occupation of the principalities is frequently considered to have changed the entire course of the war. The most obvious overland route for an Allied military offensive against Russia was through the Balkans, a route that was now cut off by the Austrian occupation of the principalities so long as Austria remained neutral.

The military significance of the Austrian occupation, however, was not so great as is often assumed. Already the Allies had probed the possibility of using their superior sea power to attack Russia in the Baltic, the White Sea, and even in the Pacific. They did in fact send a formidable naval force into the Baltic that in August 1854 succeeded in capturing Bomarsund, the principal fortress on the strategic Aaland Islands, but they did not follow up this victory by an attack on the Russian mainland because Russian fortifications seemed too formidable to offer solid prospects of success. There was no prospect whatever of striking a decisive or even crippling blow against Russia via the White Sea or the Pacific, although the Allies conducted naval operations in both areas.

But the Black Sea was different. Russia's most important waterways and arteries of commerce flowed into it. On it were located Russia's most important seaports and the great Russian naval base of Sebastopol. Since the Anglo-French entry into the war, their fleets had been in full control of the Black Sea and were therefore in a position to attack Russia anywhere along its extensive Black Sea coast, including the Crimean Peninsula where Sebastopol was located. The opportunity to attack and destroy Russian seaports and naval bases on the Black Sea was particularly attractive, because the destruction of Russian sea power there would accomplish three of the major Allied objectives in the war: it would facilitate renewed Allied intervention in the event of the future Russian threats to their interests in the Near East; it would significantly diminish Russia's ability to mount such threats; and it would make it easier for the Allies to ensure freedom of navigation in the Black Sea and Danube areas for their own shipping and commerce.

As we have seen, from the moment war with Russia seemed likely British leaders had advocated launching their principal strike against Sebastopol, so that even if a campaign through the Balkans had been feasible it might never have been more than a sideshow—at least until Sebastopol had fallen.[2] According to the Duke of Argyll, lord privy seal in the Aberdeen cabinet, the cabinet was unanimous about the desirability of launching the major Allied campaign in the Crimea even before it became apparent that a Balkan campaign was impossible.

One glance at the map of Europe and one moment's recollection of the great object we had in view, were enough to force upon us the conviction that the capture and destruction of Sebastopol and of its fleet would be the very summit of our desire. There were three conclusive reasons in favour of this course. In the first place, it would fulfil, as nothing else could, our avowed object of relieving the Turkish Empire from the most imminent danger to which it was exposed. In the second place, Sebastopol was the point in the Russian dominion most accessible to the assault of fleets, and affording the most secure naval base for military operations, however prolonged. In the third place, it was that point of Russian territory which, at the extremity of her dominions in Europe, would call for the greatest drain on her resources, both as to men and materials of war.[3]

The War: General Observations

In transporting an expeditionary force to the Black Sea area and keeping it supplied even under the most adverse climatic conditions, the Allied fleets and merchant navies, still composed primarily of sailing vessels, performed something of a miracle. It was, to be sure, a tarnished miracle, for the supply system, like Allied leadership and their conduct of the war in general, was marred by gross incompetence and inefficiency. Guns were shipped without the correct ammunition; supplies desperately needed by the troops on land and actually stored on ships lying off-shore were never delivered, or delivered too late, because the stores had never been properly labeled or identified.[4] Nevertheless, the fact that the Allies were able to land their armies on Russian soil and keep them supplied at all gave them their most important advantage, and was decisive in enabling them to win the war.

A further important Allied advantage was that their supplies themselves, inadequate though they frequently were, were still far superior to the supplies and military equipment of the Russians. The Minié rifle with which all the French and many of the British troops were equipped, had a range of up to 1,000 yards as compared to the 100-yard range of the smooth-bore muskets of the Russians, which even at that distance were hopelessly inaccurate. Although the Minié rifles themselves were not very accurate over 200 yards, they were nonetheless devastatingly effective in battles with the Russians, who kept their troops in closely packed formations. Because of the far greater range of Allied weaponry, the Russians were obliged to endure heavy casualties before they themselves came within effective range or could close with the enemy, with effects on Russian morale that help explain their failure to break through the Allied lines even when they enjoyed great numerical superiority. "The Minié is the king of weapons," wrote W. H. Russell, the famous *Times* correspondent in the Crimea. British troops still armed with the much-beloved Brown Bess musket could do nothing with their rolling volleys against the massive multitudes of the Muscovite infantry, "but the fire of the Minié smote them like the hand of the Destroying Angel."[5]

Allied artillery and shells were also generally supposed to have been superior to those of the Russians, but there were so many different varieties of artillery weapons and ammunition in all the armies that it is impossible to compare them with any authority.[6]

The quality of the military leadership of the various armies is also difficult to assess, but on the whole the judgment of contemporaries and historians alike has been sharply critical. Much of this criticism may be unduly harsh and downright unfair, for a good deal of the bungling for which military leaders have been blamed was a result of problems beyond their control, above all, the muddles created by the political leaders and bureaucrats of their home governments and the generally poor state of their various military organizations. Even when due allowance is made for difficulties for which they were not responsible, however, it must be said that the quality of military leaders overall was wretched and that the commanding generals on both sides were singularly lacking in enterprise and imagination.

The British commander in the Crimea, Lord Raglan, had fought at Waterloo but had spent most of his career as a military administrator and had never commanded a company, much less an army, in the field. He was an unassuming and kindly man of unfailing courtesy, a conscientious bureaucrat with an unselfish devotion to duty, loyal to his superiors in the government and his subordinates alike. But these estimable qualities were also his greatest handicaps as a military leader, for he found it impossible to take the tough line that was needed in dealing with government ministers and bureaucrats to remedy the deficiencies of the British military system (when he saw them at all) or to impose his will on his officers. A French general complained that he had never heard Lord Raglan express an opinion, and even on the battlefield his orders were unclear and imprecise when he took it upon himself to issue them at all, which was seldom. Raglan was later to be made the scapegoat for British military failures and the inadequacies of the British military system in general. He was certainly to blame for much, but responsibility was shared by most British government departments, and by many of the ministers and bureaucrats who joined in the chorus of criticism, for the entire British military establishment had been allowed to stagnate and decay since the Napoleonic Wars. Raglan died shortly after an unsuccessful and particularly costly attack on Sebastopol in June 1855, drained by overwork, discouragement stemming from this defeat, and the virulent criticisms of the British press. After his death Florence Nightingale lamented that he had not been a *very great* general but a *very good* man.[7]

Raglan was succeeded by General James Simpson, sixty-three years of age. Simpson had seen a good deal of active service in the Napoleonic Wars and in India, but in the words of the British military historian W. Baring Pemberton, years of experience had done nothing to improve his mediocre talents. He gave no orders, devised no plan, and left everything to his staff. An honest man and aware of his deficiencies, he is supposed to have said on the day of his appointment, "they must indeed be hard up when they appointed an old man like me."[8]

The French commanders in the Crimea were neither very great generals nor very good men. They all had the advantage over Raglan and most of the British officers of having had battlefield experience in the brutal Algerian wars, and the entire French military system, apart from the navy, was on the whole far more efficient and better organized than the British. Throughout much of the war, the French had twice as many troops in the Crimea as the British, and they were generally better supplied and fed. But the French commanders made poor use of these advantages. The first French commander, Marshal Saint-Arnaud, hardly had time to prove himself. He was a dying man when he arrived in the Crimea and succumbed to cholera after the first major battle. His successor, Canrobert, though a competent enough general, was irresolute and excessively cautious, without the self-confidence or moral authority to impose any kind of joint strategy on his British allies. He resigned his command in May 1855 partly as a result of differences with Lord Raglan, partly because of an unusually honest appreciation of his unfitness for the top command. General Pélissier, who succeeded Canrobert, had arrived from the Algerian wars with a reputation for energetic behavior and ruthlessness, and he evidently enjoyed living up to it, referring to himself as "that bastard Pélissier." As reckless as Canrobert had been cautious, he had no scruples about sacrificing the lives of his soldiers to attain his objectives. It was he who directed the final successful assault on the key fortress of Sebastopol, which resulted in a terrible (and according to some of his critics, unnecessary) cost in French dead.[9]

Fortunately for the Allies, the Russian military services were infinitely worse than their own and the Russian generals, if anything, more incompetent. Of Menshikov, the first Russian commander-in-chief in the Crimea (the same Menshikov who conducted the unfortunate Russian diplomatic mission to Constantinople), the British historian Albert Seaton writes that he was "completely unfitted for any military command," and he cites Count D. A. Miliutin, at that time a Russian staff officer in St. Petersburg, who described Menshikov as "a morbid character and a sick, disordered mind," who, among all those involved in the bloody Sebastopol drama, played the most contemptible part. The Soviet historian, E. V. Tarle, writing before the Stalinist historical rehabilitation of the old Imperial Army, denounced Menshikov's generalship (and that of all other Russian commanders) at the first major battle in the Crimea for its "total absence of leadership, the complete lack of even a vestige of intelligent and coherent command." Tarle had an equally low opinion of Menshikov's eventual successor, General M. D. Gorchakov, whom he described as prematurely aged, absent-minded, muddle-headed, and incoherent in thought and speech.[10] Tarle's views may have been colored by ideological prejudice, but his estimate of the capacities of Russia's military commanders is fully substantiated by the record of their conduct of the war. Russia's naval commanders did better. It was they who, after scuttling many of their vessels to close off the mouth of the harbor of Sebastopol, conducted the gallant defense of the city with tenacity and courage, inspiring the garrison and population with their own example. On the Russian side, however, the most celebrated figure to emerge from the war was a military engineer, the brilliant Colonel Todleben, whose organization of the defenses of Sebastopol has generally been considered a major factor in the garrison's ability to hold out as long as it did.[11]

Throughout the war, one of the most serious difficulties with which the governments and military leaders on both sides had to contend was disease, which killed far more soldiers in every army and in every theater of the war than enemy action. The armies of all the belligerents were stricken with severe epidemics of cholera and typhus, dysentery and malaria, and owing to the lack of sanitary facilities in military hospitals, even minor wounds suffered through accident or on the battlefield generally proved fatal.[12] Reports of the grim conditions in British field hospitals and the fearful mortality among the sick and wounded called forth the heroic efforts of the British nurse Florence Nightingale, who organized a corps of volunteer nurses and initiated a thoroughgoing reform of the British medical services.[13]

Well before the end of the war these reforms had proved their worth. Of the approximately 18,000 British soldiers who died of disease in the Crimea, roughly 16,000 died in the first nine months of the war, whereas only about 2,000 died of disease in the second nine months, the latter figure actually lower than comparable mortality rates in the barracks in England. Similar medical reforms did not take place in the French army, where mortality rates rose substantially in the final months of the war, primarily because of particularly virulent new outbreaks of cholera and typhus. This dismaying rise in French mortality rates appears to have had much to do with Napoleon III's decision early in 1856 to ignore appeals of his British allies to carry on with the war and to agree instead to peace negotiations.[14]

As a result of the deficiencies exposed by the Crimean War, there were reforms in the governments and armed services of all the belligerent countries, most notably, in Russia. These included not only reforms of the armed services, but reforms of the administrative and judicial systems, and above all, the emancipation (though only partial) of the serfs.

As in all modern wars, the Crimean War saw the introduction and use of improved weaponry, the products of the European technological and industrial revolutions. The most striking changes took place in naval warfare. The naval operations in the Black Sea demonstrated conclusively the superiority of steam over sail, and of steamships driven by the screw propeller over the side-wheeler. They also revealed the obsolescence of wooden war-ships, which were unable to withstand the firepower of rifled shell-firing cannon. To meet this deficiency, the French developed the first ironclad warships, which were used as floating batteries in the siege of Sebastopol.[15]

In land warfare, too, improved rifled artillery and infantry weapons were introduced, including the aforementioned Minié rifle, which was soon to be superseded by breech-loading weapons with an even greater range and far greater accuracy. A railroad of a sort was used for the first time for military purposes, though only on a very limited scale, to bring supplies and equipment from the harbor of Balaclava to the front lines before Sebastopol.[16] An attempt was made to employ another new invention, the telegraph, to direct military operations in the various theaters of the war, but the results of such long-distance leadership were sufficiently unfortunate to end this experiment quickly.

The telegraph was put to more significant use by British war correspondents, whose reports of the incompetence and inefficiency of the entire British military establishment and the consequent suffering of the soldiers aroused public opinion and led to notable reforms not only in the hospital services but in all branches of the British military organization. Less salutary for the Allied commanders and soldiers alike was the custom of British war correspondents to telegraph to London the condition and disposition of Allied troops and whatever they had learned about Allied war plans, so that the Russians received this information almost as quickly as British newspaper readers. "I ask you to consider whether the paid agent of the Emperor of Russia could better serve his master than does the correspondent of the paper that has the largest circulation in Europe [that is, W. H.

Russell of *The Times*]," Lord Raglan complained to the British
secretary at war, Lord Newcastle. "I am very doubtful whether
a British army can long be maintained in presence of a powerful
enemy, that enemy having at his command through the English
press and from London to his Headquarters by telegraph, every
detail that can be required of the numbers, condition and equipment of his opponent's force."[17]

The Crimean Campaign and the Siege of Sebastopol

The first landings of Allied troops in the Near East took place at
the end of March 1854 at Gallipoli, at the entrance to the Straits,
and at Scutari, opposite Constantinople, but toward the end of
April a large Allied force was transported to Varna, in Bulgaria,
to counter an expected Russian offensive through the Balkans.
On 29 June, however, even before the Russians had agreed to
evacuate the principalities and before their occupation by the
Austrians, the British government had issued the order for the
invasion of the Crimea.[18]

The Allied landings in the Crimea began on 14 September
1854 and were made at two points on Calamita Bay, some thirty-
three miles north of Sebastopol, sites chosen because of their
extensive sheltered beaches and because the area could be defended by a relatively small number of troops.[19] To the surprise
and relief of the Allies, the Russians made no attempt to hinder
their landings, although they might have seriously disrupted
Allied shipping and landing efforts by bold naval sorties. The
Russians had apparently decided, however, that such sorties
would have little more than nuisance value and that the only
way to inflict a decisive defeat on the Allies was to allow their
armies to land on Russian soil, where they might be destroyed
by Russian military might.[20]

Fearing that the Allied landings north of Sebastopol might be
a feint and that in any case it would be foolhardy to risk battle
in an area where the Allied armies could be covered by the
heavy guns of their fleets, Menshikov did not make a stand above

the beaches of Calamita Bay. Nor did he await the Allied advance in Sebastopol, whose defenses were in a bad state of repair and inadequate to withstand a vigorous attack by land. Instead he moved the bulk of his army to a strategically advantageous position on the heights above the river Alma, where he could intercept the Allies on their march to the city.[21]

On 20 September, six days after their initial landing in the Crimea, the Allied armies attacked the Russians on the Alma River, and despite the superior Russian strategic position, they scored an impressive victory. The Russian generals, overconfident and careless, were guilty of numerous lapses of judgment and failed to take the most elementary military precautions, such as posting troops to guard the routes to the heights the Russians occupied above the river. But the decisive factor in the battle, as in all major engagements of the war, appears to have been the superiority of Allied weaponry, above all the Minié rifle. Allied riflemen taking refuge behind stone walls systematically shot down the crews manning the Russian artillery, while the main Allied forces, relatively unscathed by the ineffective fire of Russian musketry, shattered the morale of Russian infantrymen with their own fire before closing in with small arms and bayonets.[22]

The victory of the Allies might have been even more complete if their leaders had ordered a vigorous pursuit of the retreating Russians. They failed to take advantage of this opportunity, however, nor did they take advantage of temporary Russian demoralization to advance against Sebastopol and attack the northern sector of the city, where the Russin defenses were weakest. Instead the Allied leaders, whose inadequate intelligence services had not provided them with accurate information about Sebastopol's defenses, marched their armies around to the south of the city where they could be more easily supplied by sea, the British taking over the harbor of Balaclava, the French the better harbor of Kamiesh farther to the northwest. Here they made preparations for a siege of Sebastopol, and in doing so gave the Russians the time and opportunity to shore up the city's defenses, with the result that the Allied capture of Sebastopol, which they might have accomplished within the first fortnight of the Crimean campaign, did not take place until after almost an entire year of grim and costly military operations.[23]

Menshikov did not remain in Sebastopol to lead the defense of the city but left the task to the admirals and crews of the Russian Black Sea fleet. Menshikov himself withdrew from the city with a large part of his army to save it from probable capture and to await reinforcements. Once these had arrived and he had had time to reorganize his demoralized forces, he expected that he would again be in a position to achieve the decisive victory over the Allies that had eluded him at the Alma.[24]

It was now the turn of the Allies to fail to take elementary military precautions. Instead of carefully reinforcing their own positions, they devoted their energies to preparations for the bombardment of Sebastopol and left Balaclava weakly defended by Turkish troops and a small contingent of British. It took the Allies almost a month to bring up their guns to the heights above Sebastopol, and not until 17 October did they begin their bombardment of the city, whose defenses had meanwhile been enormously strengthened. Not so the Allied defenses around Balaclava, where on 25 October Menshikov's army launched its first counterattack against the Allied positions. This was the battle that has become famous in British military lore for the stand of the Ninety-third Highlanders ("the thin red line") and for the charge of the Light Brigade, an action of errant folly resulting from confused orders transmitted by a confused orderly to an officer foolish enough to carry them out. Except for the losses in men and horses involved, the charge was of no military significance whatever but only the most celebrated among dozens of similar unnecessary and inexcusable military disasters.[25]

With great difficulty and only after suffering heavy losses, the Allies succeeded in turning back the Russians at Balaclava, but just eleven days later, on 5 November, the Russians, now heavily reinforced, launched a second and far greater attack, this time against the Allied positions around Inkerman to the east of Sebastopol. Again the Russians were turned back, but again only at the cost of heavy Allied losses.[26]

On 14 November the Allies were dealt another severe blow when a hurricane destroyed a large number of their naval and supply vessels at sea and in the narrow harbor of Balaclava, and did immense destruction to their installations on land. As a result of this disaster and the losses in manpower and equipment suffered in their battles with the Russians, the Allies temporarily abandoned their assault on Sebastopol and were obliged to winter in the Crimea.[27]

It was a grim winter, indeed it was a grim year for the Allied armies, but conditions were even worse among the Russian defenders, whose miseries have been movingly described by Tolstoy, himself a member of the Russian garrison, in his *Tales of Sebastopol*.[28]

And so the siege dragged on through the winter and into the spring and summer of 1855. In May the Allies made their most enterprising attempt to break the deadlock at Sebastopol by attacking the Russian city of Kerch, which controlled the narrow waterway between the Black Sea and the Sea of Azov, their object being to open up the Sea of Azov to the Allied fleets and thereby enable them to cut off one of Russia's major line of communication to the Crimean Peninsula. The attack was completely successful, but the victory was never fully exploited, owing largely to the objections of Simpson, Raglan's successor as British commander-in-chief, who opposed any diversion from the siege of Sebastopol.[29]

Major Allied assaults on Sebastopol in April and June were turned back with heavy losses, as was what proved to be the Russians' last major counterattack along the Chernaya River. With that attack the Russians lost their last chance of saving Sebastopol, for by this time the siege and constant bombardment had seriously weakened the city's defenses and sapped the resources of its garrison. Early in September the Allies once again mounted major assaults on the city, and on the eighth of that month the French stormed the Malakov fortress, the key to the

Russian defenses. With the fall of the Malakov, Sebastopol was doomed, and on 11 September the Russian commander withdrew his army from the city.[30]

The siege of Sebastopol is a curious episode in military history. A noteworthy feature about the siege itself, and a major reason why the Russians were able to hold out so long, was that the city was never totally surrounded. Owing to a lack of manpower, or as some critics have suggested, to a lack of imagination on the part of the Allied military leaders, the Allies never succeeded in cutting off all overland routes to the city, so that throughout the siege the Russians were able to send in a steady stream of supplies and reinforcements.

Although the Allied leaders certainly did not plan it that way, their failure to capture Sebastopol in the first weeks of the Crimean campaign, and their subsequent failure to cut off supplies to the city, was the most effective strategy they could have devised to wage war against Russia. While fighting in the Crimea, the Allies could be supplied and reinforced by sea, whereas the Russians, even though fighting on their own territory, were forced to deal with the problems that had so often in the past brought disaster to their invaders: long supply lines, bad roads, and the Russian weather. Men and materiel were sent overland to the Crimea at fearful cost. So severe were the rigors of the long journey, especially in winter, that only one Russian soldier in ten actually reached the front after a three-month march. The Russian medical department estimated the country's losses at half a million men; in comparison, the British and French lost about sixty thousand, two-thirds of whom died of disease. The drain on the Russian economy was on a comparable scale. The defense of Sebastopol bled the country white.[31]

The Baltic and the Caucasus Front

Apart from the Crimea, there were three other areas where military operations might have been expected to take place that would have critically affected the outcome of the war. Two of these have already been mentioned: the Balkans and the Baltic. The Balkans were neutralized when neutral Austria occupied the Danubian Principalities, and because Austria remained neutral the Balkans did not again become a combat zone.

In the Baltic, the Allies soon discovered that naval bombardment alone was not enough to subdue Russia's coastal fortresses (here the inadequacy of wooden ships in facing the rifled shell-firing guns of coastal batteries was again strikingly demonstrated), and as long as those fortresses remained operational they could not afford to risk the landing of a large expeditionary force that alone would have enabled them to score significant victories. Even such victories would not necessarily have been decisive, however, as so many other invaders of Russia, before and since, have discovered.

The Allies did score one success in the Baltic: the aforementioned capture of the fortress-city of Bomarsund on the Aaland Islands in August 1854, but it was hardly a famous victory. At the time of the Allied attack, the fortifications of Bomarsund had not yet been completed and the fortress was scarcely defended by the Russians. The capture of Bomarsund was nevertheless hailed by the Allies, who as yet had no other victories to celebrate, as a major achievement. But Bomarsund proved too difficult and too costly for the Allies to hold in their own right. They offered it to Sweden, which prudently declined to be lured into such a compromising position vis-à-vis Russia. So only one month after their capture of Bomarsund, the Allies withdrew their occupation forces after destroying the remaining Russian fortifications. Shortly afterwards the Russian double eagle once again floated over the city.[32]

So far as the overall conduct of the war was concerned, the Allied Baltic expeditions did accomplish one important objective: they tied down powerful Russian land forces in Finland and along the southern coast of the Baltic and thus prevented them from being used in other theaters of the war.[33]

The other potentially critical area of military operations was the Caucasus region east of the Black Sea to which, most sur-

prisingly, the Allies paid far more political than military attention. There had been intense fighting between the Turks and the
Russians in the Caucasus area since the beginning of the war.
For almost a year the Turks held their own, but in August 1854
the Russians scored a major victory that compelled the Turks to
fall back in confusion to the fortress city of Kars, south of the
Caucasus Mountains. Kars and its surrounding territory was a
region of prime strategic importance, as Allied leaders repeatedly
stressed in their evaluations of the Near Eastern situation, for if
the Russians succeeded in establishing themselves south of the
Caucasus, they would be in a far more favorable position for a
thrust into Anatolia along the south coast of the Black Sea and
thence to Constantinople.

Despite their awareness of the strategic importance of Kars,
the British and French never sent an army of their own there but
restricted themselves to sending advisers to the Turkish army.
Among these advisers, the outstanding figure was the British colonel (later general) Fenwick Williams, who arrived in Kars in
September 1854 and who, together with his small staff, succeeded
in reorganizing the demoralized Turkish armies and the defenses
of the city. These tasks were accomplished so effectively that
Kars managed to hold out for over a year against repeated Russian attacks.

In vain Williams appealed to his superior officers and to his
government to send out a relief expedition, pointing out that if
Kars fell there was nothing to stand between the Russians and
Constantinople. In fact the immediate overall situation was not
so dire as Williams pictured it, except of course for Williams and
the beleaguered Kars garrison. The distances between Russian
supply bases and Kars, and then between Kars and Constantinople, were enormous, and even if the Russians had undertaken a
campaign along the Black Sea coast, the Allies could always have
landed an army almost anywhere along that coast to intercept it.
As the Russians were well aware of their vulnerability in this
regard, it is most unlikely that they would have pressed on much
farther into Turkey even if they had captured Kars in their initial

attacks on the city. The importance of Kars lay far more in its potential than in its immediate strategic significance, for the Russians would require time to develop the city into a major Russian military base in its own right. But once in possession of Kars, and given time, the Russians would pose a far more formidable threat to the Ottoman Empire (and to Allied interests) on the eastern shores of the Black Sea.

For an entire year after the arrival of Williams in Kars, the Allied leadership persisted in its refusal to send out a relief force, but in September 1855 they finally agreed to dispatch a Turkish army to the Caucasus region. By that time it was too late. In November of 1855 the garrison at Kars, decimated by famine and disease, its supplies of ammunition exhausted, surrendered. At the peace conference ending the war, the Russians were compelled to restore Kars and its surrounding territory to the Turks, but they were able to make good use of their capture of the city as a bargaining counter.[34]

Chapter 9

Wartime Diplomacy

Austria's Position

While the siege of Sebastopol wore on and the armies of the belligerents conducted their various military campaigns, the statesmen of Europe were engaged in intense and in the long run far more significant campaigns on the diplomatic front. As in all wars, the primary aim of the diplomats of the belligerent powers was to draw the neutrals into the war on their side, or if this seemed impossible, at least to keep the neutrals neutral.

The prime diplomatic target of the Allies among the neutral powers was Austria, whose entry into the war would have opened up the possibility of major new offensives against Russia. Austria, it was hoped, would draw Prussia and the German Confederation into the war in its wake; Sweden might be tempted to follow the example of the German powers with the promise of annexing Finland; and with that the grand European coalition would have been formed that would have enabled the Allies to roll back the frontiers of Russia as envisaged by Palmerston and the more extreme Western leaders.

Buol, however, after his brief flirtation with the idea of intervention, had become more cautious. With the Russian evacuation of the principalities and their occupation by Austria, one of his own major diplomatic objectives had been achieved. He still continued to pursue his other and far more significant objective, an alliance with Britain and France that would ensure their support for the containment of Russia, but he was now to do everything in his power to secure that alliance without committing Austria to military intervention. As his ministerial colleagues had recognized all along, and as Buol himself once again clearly perceived, if Austria entered the war on the side of the Allies, Austria, because of its geographical position, would be forced to bear the brunt of the conflict, and so long as the war continued Austria would be exposed to the danger of being drawn into it. Thus Buol had come around completely to Hess's point of view, namely, that the foremost task of Austrian statecraft must be to initiate and promote peace negotiations, and to extricate Austria from its perilous position by bringing the war to an end.

The Formulation of the Four Points

In dealing with Britain and France, the Austrians used a stalling tactic, claiming that they could not consider entering the war themselves unless they were given a precise definition of Anglo-French war aims and assurances that the war with Russia was not being fought to promote revolutionary principles. This tactic served several purposes. The first and most important of these was to secure Allied guarantees to respect Austria's possessions in Italy and to repudiate Napoleon's cherished scheme to set up an independent state of Poland and other imperial projects to reorganize the map of Europe along lines of nationality. A second purpose in securing a statement of Allied war aims was that Austria would then be in a position to demand their reformulation if they did not correspond with Austrian interests as the price for Austria's participation in the war. Finally, with a statement of Allied war aims in hand, suitably redefined by themselves, they could present these aims to Russia as a basis for peace negotiations and pressure Russia into agreeing to such negotiations as the price for keeping Austria out of the war.[1]

The Austrians were fortunate that the conservative French foreign minister, Drouyn de Lhuys, shared their anxiety about

Napoleon's revolutionary projects and doubted the willingness of
the French people to participate in the major European wars that
the realization of these projects would entail. He informed the
Austrians that he wished "to master the revolution without the
help of Russia and to check Russia without the help of revolution."[2] The British, on the other hand—or at any rate Palmerston
and his more bellicose cohorts—still insisted on rolling back the
frontiers of Russia and the destruction of Russian sea power—
conditions that Russia would never accept and that could only
be imposed after a decisive and major military victory.

Realizing that he could never get the kind of statement on war
aims he needed from the British, Buol simply bypassed them and
negotiated directly with Drouyn de Lhuys. Together they prepared a formulation of the Allies' major war aims, four in number, and henceforth known as the Four Points, which they then
imposed on the reluctant British as a condition for Austria's join-
ing the Anglo-French alliance.[3] By an exchange of notes between
the Austrian, British, and French governments of 8 August 1854,
the Four Points were officially recognized as the Allied conditions for the restoration of peace.[4]

The Four Points were a far cry from the extravagant war aims
proposed by Palmerston and other extremists. They required 1)
Russia's renunciation of special rights in Serbia and the Danubian Principalities and their replacement by a collective guarantee of the powers in agreement with the Porte; 2) unrestricted
navigation of the Danube for the vessels of all countries; 3) a
revision of the Straits Convention of 1841 "in the interests of the
Balance of Power in Europe"; and 4) Russia's renunciation of all
claims to an official protectorate over Orthodox Christians in the
Ottoman Empire and the protection of the rights of all Christians in the empire by a collective guarantee.

Buol and Drouyn saw no reason why Russia should not accept
the conditions embodied in the Four Points as a basis for peace
negotiations, for they had already agreed to three of them in
principle: the evacuation of the principalities, freedom of navigation of the Danube, and the renunciation of Russian claims

to an official protectorate over the Orthodox Christian subjects of the sultan. The only condition Russia had not yet accepted was the suspiciously vague third point, but that point, after all, remained open to negotiation.

The Russians, however, saw the entire problem in a different light. For them, submission to the conditions of the Allies, now joined by the despised and faithless Austrians, was not a question of the acceptability of the Four Points but a question of pride and honor. So, to the surprise and dismay of Buol and Drouyn, the Russians announced on 26 August 1854, their refusal to accept the Four Points as a basis for negotiation.[5]

Palmerston, on the other hand, was delighted with the news of the tsar's rejection of the Four Points. "If he had nibbled at them," he wrote to Clarendon on 3 September, "we should have been embarrassed though not actually hampered. If Austria now takes her time with Decision, Prussia must follow her, and if Austria & Prussia take the Field in good earnest against Russia, they must restore a substantive Kingdom of Poland . . . when once they draw the Sword they must for their own Sakes throw away the Scabbard."[6]

The Russian attitude changed with changes in the fortunes of war. In mid-August 1854 an Allied naval force operating in the Baltic Sea captured Bomarsund, the main fortress in the strategic Aaland Islands. And on 20 September the Allied expeditionary force that had landed on the Crimean Peninsula earlier that month scored its impressive initial victory at the Alma River. In October the Austrian army was put on a war footing to exert additional pressure on Russia, and the king of Prussia wrote to the tsar imploring him to accept the Four Points as the only means of avoiding a general war. "The green table of the conference room is the sheet-anchor of the world," he said.[7] On 29 November the tsar yielded to this combination of pressure and persuasion. He agreed to accept the Four Points unconditionally, whereupon the Allies agreed to send delegates to a peace conference that was to convene, yet again, in Vienna.[8] It seemed as though the Austrian strategy to initiate peace negotiations had been completely successful and that no serious obstacles remained to the negotiation of a peace treaty and the termination of the war.

Austria Joins the Anglo-French Alliance, 2 December 1854

While holding out the lure of Austria's active intervention in the war against Russia to extract peace conditions from Britain and France, the Austrians had steadfastly withstood all Anglo-French pressures to secure their intervention. With the tsar's acceptance of the Four Points and the Allies' agreement to participate in a peace conference, the Austrians could plausibly argue that the entire question of their entry into the war should await the result of the forthcoming negotiations with the Russians.

The Austrians nevertheless seemed to think that some gesture was necessary to placate the burgeoning hostility and suspicion of Britain and France, and at the same time gain some measure of support against the intense hostility of Russia. So on 2 December 1854, Austria formally joined the Anglo-French alliance.[9] The alliance treaty authorized Austria to occupy the Danubian Principalities, an authorization the Austrians had already obtained by a treaty with the Turkish government; if Austria became involved in war with Russia, the alliance was to be both offensive and defensive; the Allies agreed not to make a separate peace with Russia and to make peace on the basis of previous agreements, presumably the Four Points. Three weeks later Austria concluded a separate treaty with France whereby Napoleon III guaranteed Austria's position in Italy for the duration of the war—hardly a reassuring time limit from the Austrian point of view.[10]

In France, the alliance with Austria was greeted with jubilation because it was seen as a decisive step in the overthrow of the international system established in 1815 for the containment of France. Benedetti, French chargé d'affaires in Constantinople, wrote to Thouvenel, head of the political section of the French foreign ministry: "Politically and militarily, the treaty of 2 December overturns everything and reveals a new horizon. You have mortally wounded the Holy Alliance and given it a first-class funeral."[11]

This contemporary French view of the significance of the 2 December treaty is shared by the British historian Gavin Henderson, who regards it as a diplomatic revolution of far-reaching importance. "The result was the disappearance of the last relics of the system of 1815. . . . No longer were there three powers in favour of the maintenance of the *status quo;* no longer was there any European Concert, even in embryo." The way was paved for the wars and national revolutions of the next decade.[12]

There can be no question about the importance of Austria's abandonment of its position of official neutrality and its alienation of Russia, but it is difficult to see why such importance is attached to the treaty of 2 December for the diplomatic revolution, if one can call it that, had taken place six months earlier when Austria presented its ultimatum to Russia to evacuate the principalities. It seems more reasonable to interpret the 2 December alliance as Austria's payment to Britain and France for the Four Points and as a token of good faith, but a token which would still allow Austria to evade active participation in the war.

Interpretation of the Four Points

Unlike the French, the British were neither pleased nor placated by the Austrian alliance, and extremists within the war party resented having been maneuvered into an agreement to negotiate with Russia on the basis of the Four Points. All was not lost, however, for the success of these negotiations hinged on the interpretation of the third point, which called for a revision of the Straits Convention, and it was over this point that the British war party now proceeded to sabotage Austria's peace campaign.[13]

At a meeting of the British cabinet on 13 December 1854, the British ministers concocted a plan to make a separate agreement with France about the interpretation of the third point that would satisfy British interests but that the Russians would be cerain to reject. To avoid alienating Austria or forfeiting Austrian support in their negotiations with Russia, the British and French would send Austria a weaker and altogether far more vague interpretation of the third point than the one they agreed upon between themselves. According to the interpretation to be submitted to Austria, the object of the revision of the Straits Convention would be to put an end to Russian preponderance in the Black Sea. The proposed Anglo-French interpretation was more specific. It required the demolition of the great Russian naval base of Sebastopol and all other Russian fortresses on the coasts of the Black Sea, and a Russian guarantee never to rebuild them. The Russians were to be allowed to maintain only four warships on the Black Sea, the same number as Turkey. The Anglo-French interpretation thus required not only the elimination of Russian preponderance on the Black Sea, but Russia's relegation to a status of permanent inferiority.

The reaction of the leaders of the French government to the British interpretation proposal was mixed, but throughout this period the guiding principle of Napoleon's policy was to avoid jeopardizing the French alliance with England. Accordingly, the French government accepted the British interpretation in secret notes of 17 and 19 December. On 26 December the British and French governments signed a treaty with Austria agreeing to the "weaker" interpretation of the third point with its vague stipulation to end Russian preponderance in the Black Sea.[14]

On that same day Buol, together with the ambassadors of Britain and France, informed Gorchakov, the Russian ambassador to Vienna, of the weaker interpretation of the third point embodied in the treaty of 28 December.[15] Gorchakov, however, saw nothing weak about the stipulation to end Russian preponderance in the Black Sea: this could only be done through the permanent destruction of Russia's Black Sea fortresses, and to avoid such humiliation Russia would wage war for another six years, if necessary against all of Europe.[16] The British and French were delighted when they learned of Gorchakov's reaction to the "weaker" interpretation. The negotiations at the forthcoming peace conference would fail owing to Russian intransigence, their own intransigent terms would not have to be revealed, and Austria would be obligated to enter the war on their side.[17]

But the consequences of Russia's rejection of Allied terms which so delighted the British and French were also evident to Gorchakov. After his initial indignation had cooled, and upon receiving assurances from the Austrian emperor that he would never agree to Allied conditions that would offend the honor and dignity of the tsar, he recommended to his government that he be allowed to negotiate on the basis of the Allied conditions of 28 December, that is, the "weaker" interpretation of the third point. The Russian government endorsed this recommendation, enabling Gorchakov to inform the Allies on 6 January 1855, that he had been empowered to negotiate on the basis of the 28 December agreement and to express the hope that the Allied governments would soon send plenipotentiaries to Vienna with similar authority.[18]

The British and French governments were now trapped. All their subsequent efforts to avoid serious negotiations with the Russians or to provoke them into breaking off negotiations were unsuccessful.[19] So it was that they found themselves obliged to participate in a peace conference that convened in Vienna in March 1855.

Sardinia Enters the War; the Fall of the Aberdeen Government and the Death of Tsar Nicholas I

Before the peace conference met in Vienna one important diplomatic development took place, and two critical changes occurred in the governments of the belligerent powers that delayed the opening of the conference.

In the field of diplomacy, the northern Italian state of Piedmont-Sardinia joined the Anglo-French alliance on 10 January 1855 and on 26 January concluded a military convention with Britain and France whereby Sardinia promised to supply 15,000 men for the war in return for a monetary indemnity and a guarantee of Sardinia's territorial integrity for the duration of the war.[20]

The entry of Sardinia into the war, under negotiation for some time, had been delayed to avoid offending the Austrians, who regarded Sardinia as a threat to their position in Italy, but the treaty with Sardinia was finally concluded because of the desperate Allied need for additional troops. The Sardinians for their part hoped that their active participation in the war on the side of Britain and France would win them powerful support for their position in Italy vis-à-vis Austria, which was reaping Anglo-French enmity for its continued refusal to participate actively.[21]

The first of the critical governmental changes during this period took place in Britain, where the Aberdeen goverment fell at the end of January 1855, largely because of public indignation over its inept conduct of the war. The successor of the well-meaning, pacific, but generally ineffectual Aberdeen as British prime minister was Lord Palmerston, the most bellicose and extreme of all British political leaders. The resignation of Aberdeen was followed in mid-February by that of three other members of his cabinet who had stayed on under Palmerston: Gladstone, chancellor of the exchequer; Graham, first lord of the admiralty; and Sidney Herbert, secretary for colonies. Although the immediate reason for their resignation was their opposition to the appointment of a commission to investigate the previous government's conduct of the war, they may have been motivated just as much by their differences with Palmerston over foreign policy. Their resignation removed from the cabinet three influential figures whose views about the war were not so extreme as those of the new prime minister. If they had remained in office, the results of the forthcoming Vienna Conference might well have been different.[22]

The second critical governmental change took place in Russia, where Tsar Nicholas I died on 2 March, physically exhausted by overwork and spiritually drained by what he conceived to be the personal betrayal of his fellow rulers and their abandonment of the political principles he had sought to defend on behalf of them all. His successor was Alexander II, the future tsar liberator, who was no more ready to make peace on humiliating terms than his father. Skeptical about the possibility of negotiating an honorable peace, he made preparations for a long military campaign.[23]

The Vienna Conference, 15 March–4 June 1855

When peace negotiations finally began in Vienna on 15 March 1855, there seemed greater reason to hope that they might be successful than many of the delegates had anticipated.[24] As we have seen, the Russians had already accepted three of the Allied Four Points in principle and had agreed to negotiate over the Allied demand to end Russian preponderance in the Black Sea. Drouyn de Lhuys, the French foreign minister who personally assumed the role of French plenipotentiary at Vienna, had long been in favor of a negotiated peace.[25] Even Lord John Russell, the British plenipotentiary, hitherto almost as bellicose and extreme as Palmerston, proved surprisingly conciliatory because, his enemies alleged, having been outmaneuvered by Palmerston as chief of the war party, he now sought to restore his influence and prestige by winning laurels as a peacemaker.[26] For Buol, the Austrian foreign minister and president of the conference, the whole purpose in convening the conference was the restoration of peace in order to extricate Austria from the manifold dangers created or intensified by the war.

The conference failed and was probably doomed to fail from the start, because both Napoleon and Palmerston believed they could not afford to make peace without having gained substantial military successes, and because Palmerston at least still hoped to impose conditions on Russia that would destroy or cripple that power's ability to threaten British interests in the Near East.[27]

Early in the conference, after the Russians had agreed to Allied conditions respecting the first two of the Four Points, the French and British plenipotentiaries put forward proposals on the third point—ending Russian preponderance in the Black Sea—which corresponded with their governments' "harsh" interpretation of that crucial issue. They called for the complete neutralization of the Black Sea, a program that would have required the destruction of all coastal fortifications and the removal of all naval vessels from the Black Sea. The Russians flatly rejected such extreme demands, which in their view would have meant a loss of Russian sovereignty in the Black Sea area and a severe national humiliation.[28]

The Austrians made a well-conceived effort to rescue the conference by suggesting a compromise proposal, which Buol worked out in private negotiations with the British and French plenipotentiaries (Drouyn and Russell). His objective was to formulate conditions that would satisfy the requirements of the British and French governments to reduce the Russian threat in the Black Sea in such a manner as not to compromise the honor of the tsar, and thus make them acceptable to the Russians. To avoid offending Russian sensibilities, the Allies should make no direct or explicit stipulations to limit Russian sea power in the Black Sea, but they should pose conditions that would oblige the Russians to impose limitations on themselves. This was to be done by informing the Russians that any Russian naval buildup would be met by a corresponding buildup (a graduated counterpoise) on the part of the Allies and that a Russian buildup beyond a certain point (Russia's prewar strength) would be regarded as a Russian act of aggression that would be met by an Allied declaration of war.

The principles for peace finally agreed upon by Buol and the British and French plenipotentiaries provided that all the powers, including Russia, should guarantee the sovereignty and independence of the Ottoman Empire; that the Straits be closed to the warships of all states while the Porte was at peace, in accordance with the Straits Convention of 1841, but with the reservation that the Western powers be allowed to send their warships through the Straits in the event of a threat to the Ottoman Empire; that Austria, Britain, and France conclude a military alliance to come to the aid of the Ottoman Empire either in the event of a Russian attack or if Russia built up its navy beyond its prewar strength. (The latter condition was later changed at Drouyn's insistence to *up to* its prewar strength.) If the British and French governments agreed to these proposals, Austria would engage to present them to Russia in the form of an ultimatum and to join in the war against Russia if they were not accepted. In view of the Russian enmity toward Austria that this Austrian ultimatum would engender, Austria required a treaty of alliance with Britain and France which would remain in effect after the resolution of the present crisis. This entire package of Austrian proposals, worked out with the British and French plenipotentiaries, was known as the Austrian Ultimatum[29] (not to be confused with the previous ultimatum or "summons" to Russia of 3 June 1854; see pp. 111–23).

So fully did these Vienna proposals safeguard the fundamental interests of Britain and France and so advantageous was the prospect of Austria's entry into the war on their side, that it is no wonder that Drouyn and Russell, who had of course been closely involved in drawing them up, accepted them. But as in the case of the 3 June ultimatum, the far more difficult question once again arises as to why Austria offered to inflict this fresh humiliation on Russia and thereby absolutely guaranteed Russia's future enmity toward itself. The only explanation for Austria's willingness to submit this new and even more humiliating ultimatum to Russia at this time—and to renew the offer six months later—was a sense of desperation in Vienna, a belief in the need to end the war no matter how great the gamble or high the political cost, to avoid the even greater danger of a continuation of the war and the possibility that the Allies, in a last desperate gamble of their own, might fulfill their oft-repeated threat to unleash the forces of national revolution in the Balkans, Poland, and Italy. By cooperating with the government of Napoleon III, the most fervent advocate of national revolution among the leaders of the great powers, the Austrians may have seen their best and last opportunity to ward off these mortal dangers to the Habsburg Empire and a means of separating France from the more extreme and bellicose policies of Palmerston.

For a time it seemed as though Austrian policy would be suc-

cessful. After listening to the arguments of Drouyn, Napoleon
seemed inclined to accept the Austrian proposals.[30] Not so the
British government. Palmerston called the Austrian plan a contemptible fraud, Clarendon labeled it shameful and treacherous,
and both were certain that British public opinion would be
equally appalled. If Buol's plan were adopted, Clarendon wrote
to Westmorland in Vienna, the British ministers would not be
safe in the streets "and *serve us right.*"[31]

The Austrian Ultimatum was discussed in a British cabinet
meeting on 2 May, where Palmerston argued vigorously against
it. Acceptance, he declared, would be the equivalent of capitula-
tion. No one, in fact, appears to have argued in favor of acceptance. Even Lord John Russell, upon his return from Vienna,
failed to defend the conditions he himself had accepted and
helped to formulate, and declared weakly that he did not profess
to think the Austrian proposals could be the basis for a satisfactory peace.[32] In describing the meeting of 2 May, Lord Lansdowne, minister without portfolio, wrote that "the deliberations
of the Cabinet with respect to the Austrian Propositions were
not deliberations as to the desirableness of their being accepted
or rejected, but as to the conduct we ought to pursue in the event
of their being accepted by Louis Napoleon."[33]

As noted above, for a time it seemed as though Napoleon, on
the advice of Drouyn, might indeed accept the Austrian proposals, but the British government was saved from this embarrassment by the activity of Cowley, the British ambassador to
Paris, who invited himself to Drouyn's meeting with the emperor on the afternoon of 4 May, and together with Marshal
Vaillant, the French minister of war, succeeded in persuading
Napoleon to reject the Austrian terms. "We have beat Drouyn to
pieces," Cowley exulted.[34] "Drouyn de Lhuys has been playing
old Gooseberry at Vienna," he wrote to Stratford, "and agrees
with Buol to support terms that it would be disgraceful for us to
accept, and I have taken the liberty of exposing him to his Imperial Master to his great discomfiture. . . . The Emperor has
come well out of the ordeal."[35]

Although Napoleon had seemed to vacillate over the Vienna

proposals, there is reason to doubt whether he had ever seriously considered making peace at this time. Both he and Drouyn appear to have been primarily concerned with securing Austria as an ally, but unlike Drouyn, who was willing to settle for a negotiated peace, Napoleon had other objectives in view. Once Austria had been ensnared, he told Prince Albert at a dinner party on 26 May, the Allies should refuse to make peace even after their *avowed* objectives had been attained. According to the Duke of Argyll's account of this conversation, Prince Albert had argued that this scheme would not be consistent with their honor, but the emperor had seemed amused that so much stress was placed on such considerations.[36] On the day following Napoleon's conversation with Prince Albert, Persigny, the successor to Walewski as French ambassador to London and as close a confidant as the enigmatic Louis Napoleon ever possessed, assured Palmerston that he should "not for a moment suppose that the Emperor wants peace, or would make it on any terms till he has obtained a military success. All he wants is to prolong negotiation in order to satisfy people's minds in France and to keep Austria from breaking with us."[37]

Palmerston too was anxious to secure Austria's entry into the war, but he was convinced that this objective could not be achieved through diplomacy but only through military victories. On 28 May he urged Napoleon to remain staunch against the subtleties of diplomacy and warned of the grave dangers the Allies would incur if they allowed themselves to be plunged again into the Viennese labyrinth simply to serve Austrian purposes. "Victories in the Crimea will command for us the friendship, perhaps even the sword of Austria; without success in the Crimea, we shall not even have her pen."[38] To Persigny in London he said: "The best and only way of having Austria on our side is to take Sebastopol or win a battle. She will join us if we are strong, and hold aloof from us if we are weak."[39]

Confident in the belief that the French emperor shared his point of view and that the British Parliament, too, would support his policies, Palmerston wrote Clarendon that "we cannot give way to a small knot of gamblers and intriguers at Paris, who want for their own dirty objects to sacrifice the honour of two great countries and the future interests of Europe. We must decline [the Austrian proposals] firmly, but as civilly as possible."[40] Already a week earlier, he had suggested to Clarendon how Britain's rejection of the Austrian proposals might best be conveyed to the Austrian government. "We should thank Austria for her offer, but her proposals to Russia are too harsh if we decide we want peace at any price, and not harsh enough if we think we can win the war. Austria does not hold out the inducement that she will enter the war on our side if Russia refuses, so what motive have we for accepting her intervention?"[41] As the Austrians *had* promised to enter the war on the side of the Allies in the event of Russian rejection, Palmerston's statement suggests that he had never bothered to study the Austrian proposals carefully or that he was deliberately misrepresenting them to justify, if only to himself, the British rejection.

The Vienna Conference continued until 4 June, but all Buol's efforts to revive meaningful negotiations failed—as did all Anglo-French efforts to persuade Buol to blame the failure of the negotiations on the Russians. In his public statements Buol observed great restraint in refusing to apportion blame, but to his ambassadors in London and Paris he wrote that the failure of the conference had been due to the uncompromising attitude of the Western powers, which obviously wanted to force a decision on the battlefield.[42]

Buol had struck the heart of the problem. The French emperor was evidently convinced that his regime could not afford to make peace before achieving substantial military victories, and Palmerston continued to advocate war aims that still required such victories. As the Vienna Conference wound down in the latter part of May, he reiterated his grandiose plans calling for Russia to cede the Crimea to Turkey, restore the independence of Circassia, and evacuate all territory in the Caucasus region conquered or annexed in the preceding twenty-five years. Russia was to cede Bessarabia to Moldavia, which together with Wallachia should be granted self-government within the Ottoman

Empire under the protection of the Allied powers.[43] Because Palmerston knew that Russia would not yet accept such terms, he had never desired the success of the Vienna negotiations and could only welcome their collapse. Throughout this period he had continued to advocate a vigorous prosecution of the war, and he now urged the French government to join Britain in putting renewed pressure on Austria to enter the war on their side.

In defending his policy before the House of Commons, Palmerston once again summed up his conception of the Russian threat. It was as clear as the sun at noon, he said, that Russia intended to partition the Ottoman Empire, "and it is to prevent that [that] we are carrying on the war." But the purpose of the war was not only to protect Turkey, "to protect the weak against the strong, and right against wrong," but to protect the interests of England. If Russia were to gain possession of Turkey, "if that gigantic Power, like a Colossus, has one foot upon the Baltic and another upon the Mediterranean," British trade and commerce would not only be severely injured but would be totally swept away. The alternative to carrying on the war to a victorious conclusion was a Russia dominating both the Baltic and the Mediterranean and exercising dominant control over Germany. Here was a prospect, he warned, that advocates of peace at any price should consider.[44]

Palmerston's policies triumphed all along the line. On 4 June the negotiations in Vienna finally came to an end; two days later Palmerston won a resounding vote of confidence in the House of Commons. At the same time two influential political opponents were removed from the scene. Drouyn, the French plenipotentiary in Vienna who had accepted the Austrian proposals, found himself repudiated by his own government and promptly resigned.[45] He was succeeded as French foreign minister by the more pliant Count Alexandre Walewski, a natural son of Napoleon I and at this time French ambassador to London, who was considered more bellicose and also more pro-British. The perennial political rival of Palmerston, Lord John Russell, the British plenipotentiary who had also accepted the Austrian proposals, was more resilient. Although similarly repudiated, he remained in the cabinet as secretary for the colonies, but he too was subsequently obliged to resign when the Austrians, indignant about Russell's misrepresentation of his position, made public his original acceptance.[46] But on one front, Palmerston was not successful. The Austrians, feeling duped by the Anglo-French scuttling of the Vienna Conference, persisted in their refusal to enter the war on the side of the Allies. On 8 May Buol wrote to Hübner, the Austrian minister to Paris, that Austria could not impose peace on the belligerent powers, but neither could the belligerents force Austria into a war on terms that did not correspond with Austria's interests.[47]

The Fall of Sebastopol, September 1855

As we have seen, since the landing of the Allied armies on the Crimean Peninsula in September 1854 and the beginning of the siege of Sebastopol, the Allies and Russians had been engaged for almost a year in a succession of costly but inconclusive battles outside the city—the Allies to break through the Russian defensive positions, the Russians to break through the encircling Allied armies and drive them into the sea. An Allied breakthrough was finally achieved early in September 1855, and on September 11 the Russian forces withdrew from the city.

With the fall of the great Russian naval base at Sebastopol, the major objective of the Allies in the Crimea had been achieved. Now, however, they faced the perplexing problem of what their next objective should be. How and where could they strike decisive blows against Russia that would compel the Russians to yield to their more extreme demands or even to terms that would allow the Allied governments to justify the war before the tribunal of domestic public opinion? Differences of opinion between the Allied governments and their military commanders about this question led to increasingly strained relations and to a rapid deterioration of Allied solidarity.

Chapter 10

Post-Sebastopol:
The Rocky Road to Peace

Plans for the Continuation and Extension of the War

The fall of Sebastopol did not lead immediately to new peace initiatives, as some writers have suggested. On the contrary, the leaders of the belligerent powers spoke in terms of large-scale new military campaigns. In Russia, Tsar Alexander II hurled defiance at his enemies and announced his determination to fight on. "Sebastopol is not Moscow, the Crimea is not Russia," he declared. "Two years after the burning of Moscow, our victorious armies were in Paris. We are still the same Russia, and God is on our side."[1] In France, Napoleon proposed that the Allies hold on to and fortify Sebastopol, and from there launch "decisive blows" against strategic Russian positions in Bessarabia and Asia,[2] and he gave Vienna to understand that he did not want the Austrians to resume peace negotiations.[3] While in England, Palmerston informed his ambassador to Paris that it was folly even to think of peace and that he anticipated two to three more years of war.[4]

Palmerston, in fact, positively dreaded the prospect of peace. The British army had won no brilliant victories. There was as yet no possibility whatever of imposing the crippling peace terms on Russia that Palmerston thought necessary for the security of Europe. Palmerston therefore continued to press not only for a vigorous prosecution of the war but its extension on a massive scale. Writing to his brother in anticipation of the fall of Sebastopol, he lamented that the real danger would then begin—the danger of peace. "Austria will try to draw us again into negotiations for an insufficient peace, and we shall not yet have obtained those decisive successes which would entitle us to insist on such terms as will effectually curb the ambition of Russia for the future."[5]

Palmerston's bellicosity was still enthusiastically supported by British public opinion, although British popular enthusiasm for the war itself was considerably greater than the average Englishman's desire to enlist and fight in it. A shortage of troops had been an embarrassing difficulty for the British from the beginning, and they had been obliged to scour the world for mercenaries.[6] It was largely to secure more troops that the Allies had promised the Italian kingdom of Sardinia a generous subsidy and secured that country's entry into the war in the previous January.[7] After the fall of Sebastopol, however, Palmerston's principal reason for securing new allies was to enable him to carry on the war with Russia on a broad front and strike at strategic Russian positions. In November 1855 he succeeded in concluding an alliance with Sweden, only a defensive alliance to be sure, but the prospects seemed good that Sweden could be lured into taking the offensive with promises of Finland and other territorial gains.[8] In justifying the defensive nature of the Swedish alliance to Clarendon, Palmerston confessed that Britain had gone to war not so much to keep the sultan and his Moslems in Turkey as to keep the Russians out, and that Britain had a strong interest in keeping them out of Norway and Sweden as well. "The treaty we propose would be *part of a long line of circumvallation* to confine the future extension of Russia even if the events of war should not enable us to drive her outposts in at any part of her present circumference."[9]

In addition to negotiating the Swedish alliance, Palmerston stepped up the pressure to secure the active participation of Austria, Prussia, and the German Confederation; and he proposed to secure the active allegiance of the Poles and the peoples of the Caucasus by promising them their independence. With such a coalition and with the geographical bases these countries would provide, the Allies could extend the war in the Baltic and the entire Black Sea area, attack Russia's naval bases in the Baltic, dislodge Russia altogether from the Danube basin, advance against the Russian Black Sea ports and the naval base of Odessa, gain control of the mouth of the Dniester, and thrust back the Russian frontier in the Caucasus region. In response to news of renewed peace initiatives on the part of France and Austria, which he ascribed to the influence of Russian agents, Palmerston wrote to Clarendon on 9 October that they would find all their "steadiness and skill required to avoid being drawn into a peace which would disappoint the just expectations of the country, and leave unaccomplished the real objects of the war. . . . The fact is, as you said the other day, Russia has not yet been beat enough to make peace possible at the present moment." He still thought it necessary to wrest from Russia permanently "sallying points for attacks upon her neighbours" which would "lastingly diminish her means and power of aggression," and for this purpose still spoke of depriving Russia of its frontier provinces—the Crimea, Georgia, and Circassia.[10]

Stratford in Constantinople was thinking along the same lines. His German colleagues would urge him to make peace now that Sebastopol had fallen, he wrote to Clarendon on 13 September, but Stratford thought that for the sake of its own honor and the interests of Europe, Britain still had exertions to make before the sword could be returned to the scabbard. "Having reduced the Russia of *accumulated power,* we have to guard against the Russia of *prospective growth,*" and for this purpose he advocated the creation of a barrier of independent neutral states along Russia's entire frontier.[11]

If successful, Palmerston's plans for a Continental war might have allowed him to impose those terms he and Stratford thought necessary to deprive Russia of its bases for aggression, at least temporarily. But, although he was a long time in realizing it, there was never any chance that his plans would be successful. The alliance finally concluded with Sweden remained defensive only, despite Palmerston's efforts to persuade the Swedes that

their interests too required pushing back the Russian frontiers.
The Austrians continued to resist Allied pressure for active participation. And Napoleon, for all his loyalty to Britain, no longer
seemed primarily concerned with throttling Russia but with the
realization of his cherished objective of reorganizing Europe
along the lines of nationality: reestablishing an independent
Poland, creating a Rumanian national state through the union of
the Danubian Principalities (Moldavia and Wallachia), and securing the independence of Italy and Hungary, while at the same
time extending the boundaries of France to its "natural" frontiers
by acquiring the left bank of the Rhine.[12] Such a program of national revolution differed fundamentally from the goals of Palmerston, and any move on the part of Britain to rekindle Napoleon's enthusiasm for the war by supporting any part of it was
certain to put an end to any prospect of Austrian intervention.

The French Desire for Peace

While Palmerston was still working to extend the war in order to
wage it more effectively and on a broader scale, Napoleon decided he could no longer afford to ignore the war weariness in
his own country and the pressures of public opinion for peace.
The French had contributed far more to the Allied war effort
than the British and had maintained a far larger army in the
Crimea (the French army was raised through conscription, the
British through volunteers).[13] "France wishes for peace more
than anything else on earth," the Duke of Cambridge wrote to
Queen Victoria, "and this feeling does not confine itself to Walewski or the Ministers—it extends to all classes. . . . No doubt
the Emperor can do much that he wishes, but still he cannot go
altogether against a feeling which so loudly expresses itself on
all occasions, without thereby injuring his own position most
seriously."[14] For Napoleon there was the further consideration
that, unless the British endorsed his idealistic program for re-
structuring the European state system along the lines of nationality, he had little incentive to cooperate in grandiose new military

campaigns. His major political-diplomatic goal, the breakup of the Concert of Europe, had long since been realized. In the final stages of the siege of Sebastopol, the French army had won the major victories and thereby acquired those fresh military laurels for France that Napoleon had considered necessary to live up to the expectations associated with his name. Despite his concern to preserve good relations with Britain, Napoleon was becoming increasingly conscious that the material and moral costs of continuing the war might exceed any advantages that might be gained by doing so.

Napoleon was also under heavy pressure from his advisers. His foreign minister, Count Walewski, had urged him to make peace directly after the fall of Sebastopol. "Who can deny that France comes out of all this enlarged and Russia diminished?" he wrote to the emperor on 11 September. "France *alone* will have profited in this struggle. Today she holds first place in Europe. Unless we want to remake the map of Europe, and I don't believe that is the thought of Your Majesty, we have nothing to gain from a prolongation of the war."[15] As Walewski knew very well, Napoleon was indeed thinking of remaking the map of Europe, and the emperor's first response to his foreign minister's appeal for peace was his proposal for striking "decisive blows" at Russian strategic positions from Sebastopol.[16]

Napoleon's negative response, however, did not deter Walewski from going behind his emperor's back and sounding the Austrian government about renewing its mediation efforts. Nor did it deter the Austrians from entering into negotiations with Walewski, although Napoleon had given them to understand that he did not desire their mediation.[17]

Buol's Peace Initiative, Late September 1855: The Buol-Bourqueney Negotiations

The origin of Buol's post-Sebastopol peace initiative is obscure, which is understandable because in its first phase it had to be conducted in great secrecy—contrary to the wishes of Napoleon

and without the knowledge of the British. What is certain is that
Buol drew up a new mediation proposal based on the old Four
Points, modified to accord with Austrian interests, and that some
time toward the end of September he discussed it with Bourqueney, the French ambassador to Vienna. There is no reliable
evidence about the exact nature of Buol's initial proposal, or how
much Bourqueney or for that matter Walewski were involved in
its formulation. It was to Buol, however, that Bourqueney subsequently ascribed "the honor of first formulating" the proposal
that eventually led to peace.[18]

Buol was undoubtedly encouraged to take this initiative by reports of the attitude of the Russian government, which was having grave difficulties finding the resources to carry on the war
and which, like the French government, was confronted with a
terrible war weariness on the part of its population that found
expression in revolutionary disturbances throughout the tsarist
empire. The Russian government could not initiate peace negotiations itself for fear that such a move would be interpreted as a
sign of weakness and because Russian ministers were anxious
above all to safeguard their new emperor from humiliation. The
Russians, however, let it be known that they would be receptive
to peace proposals, an attitude succinctly summed up by Gorchakov, the Russian ambassador to Vienna: "We will be mute, but
not deaf." Nesselrode in St. Petersburg was more specific. It was
not possible for the Russians to make proposals at this time, he
told the Austrian emissary to St. Petersburg, but they were prepared to receive favorably any proposals made to them that were
compatible with their honor.[19]

To judge from the subsequent course of events, the strategy
worked out between Buol and Bourqueney was almost identical
with that of the Austrian ultimatum stemming from the Vienna
Conference of the previous spring, except that it was supported
from the beginning by leaders of the French government, even if
initially behind Napoleon's back. As the first step in the Buol-
Bourqueney campaign, Bourqueney was to take the Austrian
proposal to Paris, where Walewski would arrange its acceptance
by the French government and make whatever modifications

might be desired by France. Walewski would then send it along to London to secure its acceptance by Britain. The bait Buol dangled before the French and British governments to win their adherence to his peace proposal (which in its final form would embody peace terms agreed upon by all three governments) was that the Austrian government was prepared to submit this proposal to the Russian government in the form of an ultimatum, and that Austria would break off diplomatic relations with Russia if the ultimatum were rejected. With this strategy, Austria could exert pressure on both Britain and France to exercise moderation in naming their conditions for peace as the price for the Austrian government's willingness not only to participate in the Allied ultimatum but to undertake the onerous task of submitting it to Russia. The advantage in all this for Austria was that if the Allied terms were sufficiently moderate, there was a good chance that Russia would accept them and with that the war which held so many dangers for Austria would be brought to an end.

If Russia did not accept, on the other hand, the dangers for Austria would be infinitely greater. Although Buol specifically stated that a break in diplomatic relations would not obligate Austria to participate actively in the war, the British and French assumed that Austria could hardly avoid such participation and were certain to bring renewed pressure to bear on Austria to do so. Whether Russia accepted or rejected, however, the mere act of presenting such an ultimatum was certain to add substantially to Russia's hatred for Austria and correspondingly increase the danger of Russian enmity toward Austria for the future.

Once again, the only explanation for Austria's willingness to inflict on Russia the humiliation of an ultimatum was a sense of desperation in Vienna about the need to end the war regardless of the political cost.

Concurrent Peace Negotiations

The story of the Buol-Bourqueney negotiations in the autumn and winter of 1855 that finally led to peace in the following years is difficult to reconstruct, for it is badly blurred by the deliberate misrepresentations and dishonest stratagems employed by the various governments involved. It is complicated still further by the profusion of other negotiations conducted during this period by a variety of intermediaries acting on behalf of (or purporting to be acting on behalf of) one or another of the belligerent or neutral powers. Thus Counts Pfordten and Beust, the minister-presidents of Bavaria and Saxony, acted as intermediaries between France and Russia, as did Baron Seebach, the Saxon minister to Paris, who as Nesselrode's son-in-law maintained especially close contacts with the Russian government. Another set of negotiations was conducted between the Duke of Morny, the architect of Napoleon's coup d'état and at this time president of the French legislative assembly, and Count Gorchakov, the Russian ambassador to Vienna, who aspired to and eventually succeeded to Nesselrode's position as Russian chancellor and minister of foreign affairs.[20]

All these supplementary negotiations took place after the Buol-Bourqueney peace iniative was well under way, and they might have assumed critical importance if the Buol-Bourqueney negotiations had broken down. As it was, their chief significance lay in keeping separate channels of communication open between the belligerent and neutral governments, allowing one government to reassure another secretly about its true intentions, or enabling one government to put pressure on another in the form of secret threats or promises.

Even by eliminating consideration of these supplementary negotiations, however, the story of the Buol-Bourqueney negotiations remains complicated and often unclear.

The Reception of the Buol-Bourqueney Proposals in Paris and London, October 1855

Early in October 1855 Bourqueney conveyed Buol's peace proposal to Paris, where it was well received by Walewski, who may have inspired it in the first place.[21] There is no record of how Walewski secured Napoleon's approval of the Austrian peace plan, but it is safe to assume that he reminded the emperor of his nation's desire for peace and that he pointed out the thoroughly satisfactory nature of the Austrian proposals from the point of view of France's national interests—the advantage to France of Austria's probable participation in the war in case Russia rejected the Austrian ultimatum, and the fact that Britain would be consulted about the Austrian proposals and thus be associated with the entire peace initiative. Whatever arguments Walewski and other partisans of peace brought forward, they were obviously convincing, for on 17 October Napoleon and his council decided to accept Buol's proposals, as modified by France and Britain, as conditions for peace, and to encourage him to submit the Allied terms to St. Petersburg.[22]

Walewski had greater difficulty dealing with London. Clarendon expressed dismay about Napoleon's new pacific attitude, which Clarendon was convinced was the product of the emperor's fear of higher prices and a financial crisis, and about the difficulty the British government would now have to avoid being hustled into a shameful peace.[23] The French must put pressure on Austria, he wrote to Cowley, the British ambassador in Paris, to submit conditions Russia could not possibly accept, including the cession of the Crimea, Georgia, and Circassia. "The more [conditions] we are able to impose the longer Russia will be in shaking them off and the more time Europe will have to prevent her."[24]

Cowley undoubtedly informed Walewski of the extreme nature of the British conditions, which were not mere modifications of the Austrian proposals but an entirely new set of peace terms. The British, however, had not rejected the Austrian peace initiative outright and that was evidently good enough for Walewski. On the evening of 22 October he informed Hübner, the Austrian ambassador to Paris, that he had just received the agreement of the English cabinet to negotiate with Vienna (he told Hübner nothing about the British conditions for peace) and that Bourqueney would shortly be returning to Vienna for that purpose. Before his departure Bourqueney told Hübner that he would discuss with Buol "the conditions for peace agreed upon [*concertées*] between Paris and London." If Austria accepted the "very moderate" proposals he was bringing to Vienna, the result would be a union of Austria with France and England for peace or war. If Austria did not accept, the result would be a "moral rupture" with France, and France would regard its treaty of alliance with Austria of the previous December as null and void.[25] Thus Walewski and Bourqueney brought pressure to bear on Austria, not in Clarendon's sense of forcing Austria to submit impossible conditions to Russia but, rather, to carry on with its peace initiative, and they deliberately and dishonestly misrepresented the attitude of the British government. The British had not agreed to anything at all, certainly not to the "very moderate" proposals Bourqueney was bringing to Vienna. What Bourqueney actually brought to Vienna were the counterproposals of France, which were indeed moderate.

The French asked for revisions of only two of the Four Points: the union of the Danubian Principalities of Moldavia and Wallachia into a single state under a foreign prince, but still under the nominal suzerainty of the Porte; and the retrocession by Russia to the principalities of Bessarabian territory at the mouth of the Danube acquired by Russia through the Treaty of Adrianople of 1829. France's reason for desiring the union of the principalities was to create a more viable state along this critical frontier between the Russian and the Ottoman empires, but it was also well known that Napoleon believed the inhabitants of these principalities to be members of the same Rumanian nationality, so that their union would represent a stage in the realization of his nationalities program. The reason for France's other revision, the cession of Bessarabian territory at the mouth of the Danube, was to remove this strategic area from Russian control and thus free the Danube to international shipping.[26]

Final Negotiations with Austria, Late October–Early November 1855

The Austrians objected to both French revisions: to the first precisely because it would be a stage in the reorganization of Europe along the lines of nationality, which if carried further would result in the dissolution of the Habsburg Empire; to the second because Austria, or at any rate Austria's military leaders, wanted the cession of a far larger portion of Bessarabia than France demanded in order to establish an even better strategic frontier against Russia.

In response to Austria's objections, Bourqueney agreed to drop the French demand for the union of the principalities and to support the Austrian position on the Bessarabian question, but he asked for a great deal in return: the inclusion of a fifth point stating that "the belligerent powers reserve the right vested in them to bring forward in the European interest special conditions in addition to the Four Points."[27]

Once again the French (or more accurately, the Walewski-Bourqueney) stratagem was far from honest. They would conclude an agreement about peace terms with Austria, including the fifth point, which Austria would submit to Russia; but, to have any chance of securing Britain's adherence to that agreement, they would have to assure the British secretly that they would support any demands Britain might make on the basis of the fifth point at a future peace conference; and to have any chance of securing Russia's acceptance of the ultimatum, they would have to assure Russia, also in secret, that the fifth point had been inserted into the peace terms pro forma and was otherwise meaningless—as they must have assured Buol to secure his agreement to this dangerously ambiguous condition. If the Russians did accept (and there can be no doubt that Walewski at least sincerely hoped they would), then the combined pressure of France and Austria, plus Russia, at a future peace conference could compel the British to relinquish any extreme demands they might make under the fifth point (this is in fact what happened), and the restoration of peace would be assured. If the Russians did not accept, the war could be resumed under more favorable circumstances for the Allies with the likely participation of Austria and perhaps other German states on their side.

It should be noted here at once that the British saw through

the French stratagem, or at least suspected Walewski of playing
them false, for in subsequent negotiations they were to demand
that their special conditions be incorporated into the Austrian
Ultimatum so as to make quite certain that the Russians would
not accept it. Precisely for this reason, of course, the Austrians
refused to do so.[28]

Even as it stood, the ultimatum seemed likely to be rejected.
Austria's inclusion of the demand for Russia's cession of a substantial part of Bessarabia has been called yet another great mistake on the part of the Austrians, for by requiring that Russia
submit to the humiliation of a cession of territory they further
reinforced Russian hostility to the Habsburg Empire. Both Britain
and France, however, were also demanding the cession of Bessarabian territory, even if France was not demanding so much as
Austria, and the Austrians believed, probably correctly, that the
hostility aroused by their presentation of an ultimatum could
hardly be intensified and that the acquisition of a more defensible
strategic frontier was therefore both desirable and necessary.
Moreover, the territory in question was not merely a matter of a
few marshes at the mouths of the Danube, as Napoleon was later
to describe it, but one of the most important commercial arteries
of central and southeastern Europe: the Russians had allowed
the navigable channels of the Danube delta to silt up so that they
were impassable for larger vessels, and they had imposed restrictions on the transport of goods between the Danube and the
Black Sea so as to divert commerce to their own Black Sea port
of Odessa.[29]

The importance of the Danube question for Austria was clearly
expressed when Buol presented the tentative agreement arranged
between himself and Bourqueney to Emperor Francis Joseph on
9 November. Buol was only too conscious of the onerous nature
of the conditions he was proposing and fearful that Francis
Joseph would not consent to having them presented to Russia in
his name. Buol therefore stressed that France and Britain would
never give up their demand for the neutralization of the Black
Sea and the conditions associated with it. If the Russians were

prepared to make this sacrifice, however, Buol was convinced
that they would also yield to the demand for the territorial cession in Bessarabia, which promised such incalculable advantages
to Austria. The removal of all Russian influence from the Danube
would send shock waves throughout Germany and contribute
more to Austria's ability to assert its authority over the other
states of Germany than any policy Austria could adopt. "The
Danube all the way to its mouth would become a German river
for all practical purposes, and Germany would give us thanks for
this achievement which it now expresses so reluctantly." To gain
such advantages, Buol believed Austria should risk going to the
brink of war "so long as we can avoid the ordeal of actual participation in war."[30]

The Buol-Bourqueney Agreement, 14 November 1855

The Austrian emperor agreed to the recommendations of his foreign minister, and on 14 November Buol and Bourqueney ini-
tialed a memorandum embodying the results of their negotiations, the *"Projet de préliminaires de paix."*[31] In this memorandum the original Four Points were restated but with significant
revisions and clarifications. To the first point, the abolition of
Russia's "special and exclusive right of protection" over the Danubian Principalities and Serbia, was added the demand for a
rectification of the Russo-Turkish frontier in Bessarabia that required Russia to cede to the Danubian Principality of Moldavia
a strip of territory east of a line running from Chotin in the north
in a southeasterly direction along the line of the mountains to
Lake Salsyk in the south, thus removing Russian control over the
mouths of the Danube as well as over the lower course of the
Pruth River, heretofore the boundary of Bessarabia. The new
second point provided for freedom of navigation on the Danube
"and its mouths," which was "to be effectively assured through
European institutions." In the third point, the provision for the
neutralization of the Black Sea was clarified: the sea was to be
thrown open to the commerce of all nations, all military and

naval arsenals along its shores were to be abolished, and the
number of light naval vessels that were to be permitted to the
Black Sea countries for police or coast guard purposes was to be
regulated in a separate treaty between Russia and Turkey. The
fourth point on the protection of the rights of Christians in the
Ottoman Empire remained substantially unchanged. Added was
the fifth point giving the belligerent powers the right to add special conditions (*conditions particulières*) that were in the European interest (*dans un intérêt Européen*).

In addition to these peace preliminaries, Buol and Bourqueney
drew up another agreement on Austria's future procedures in
dealing with Russia: Austria was to present the Allied peace conditions to the Russian government with the demand that they be
accepted unconditionally; if Russia refused, Austria was to break
off diplomatic relations with Russia and consult with its allies
about further measures. To avoid any misunderstanding or am-
biguity on this last point, Buol stated specifically "that the means
of pressure to be used against Russia did not include an [Aus-
trian] commitment to fight . . . this could only occur after all
other expedients had been exhausted."[32]

British Reaction to the Buol-Bourqueney Proposals

Following the conclusion of his negotiations with Buol, Bourqueney brought the draft of the Buol-Bourqueney agreement to
Paris, where there was no question of its approval by the French
government since it was the product of a French negotiating
effort. On 18 November Walewski sent it on to London with the
request that the British government agree to it without further
deliberation.[33] Here the prospects of its acceptance, much less
acceptance without further deliberation, seemed very doubtful
indeed.

Palmerston's demands remained as extravagant as ever. He insisted on Russia's granting independence to Georgia and Circassia; the cession of the strategically important Aaland Islands in
the Baltic Sea to Sweden or their permanent demilitarization; the

neutralization not only of the Black Sea but of the adjoining Sea of Azov and the Bug and Dniester rivers on the grounds that if Russia were allowed to maintain naval vessels and arsenals on these waterways, the neutralization of the Black Sea itself would always be in jeopardy.[34] In a letter to Persigny, he charged that France and Austria had negotiated behind Britain's back, that Britain would be delighted with a good peace "which would assure the objects of the war," but rather than be dragged into a peace on inadequate terms, Britain would prefer to go on fighting with no other allies than the Turks.[35]

Clarendon, on the other hand, found the Buol-Bourqueney peace terms surprisingly good, by which he meant that they were so onerous that Russia could not possibly accept them. "If Louis Napoleon for his own interest really wants to slip out of the war, then these propositions may be a godsend." Clarendon thought it absurd, however, and very *Austrian,* that Austria did not intend to back up its proposed ultimatum to Russia with anything more than a mere threat to break off diplomatic relations—*la guerre sans bataille,* as Buol had called it.[36]

Queen Victoria also found the Buol-Bourqueney proposals good, and she wrote Clarendon urging that they be accepted. She thought it would be the height of impolicy if Britain did not enter fairly and unreservedly into the French proposals, and she asked him to express her opinion to the cabinet. "The terms of the Austrian Ultimatum are clear and complete and very favourable to us, if accepted by Russia. If refused, which they almost must be, rupture of diplomatic relations between Austria and Russia is a decided step gained by us, and will produce a state of things which can scarcely fail to lead them to war. A refusal to entertain the proposal may induce and perhaps justify the Emperor of the French in backing out of the War, which would leave us in a miserable position."[37]

On 20 November the Buol-Bourqueney proposals were the subject of a six-hour debate in the British cabinet, which finally overrode the objections of Palmerston and voted to accept the preliminary peace conditions subject to British modifications. This vote in the cabinet has been interpreted as a defeat for Palmerston and a turning point in British policy, but as Palmerston and Clarendon were left to formulate the British modifications, they were still in a position to put forward conditions that would be unacceptable to the Russians and thereby wreck any peace negotiations.[38]

Queen Victoria urged moderation. Her greatest concern at this time was that the Austrians would get cold feet and use any unreasonable British demand for modifications to back out of their peace initiative altogether. She therefore thought it would be a grievous mistake to risk the inestimable advantages of Austria's presentation of an Allied ultimatum by quibbling with Austria over points of detail.[39]

The modifications formulated by Palmerston and Clarendon seemed moderate enough. They wanted the neutralization of the Black Sea to include the adjoining Sea of Azov; they wanted the provisions concerning the number of naval vessels to be maintained in the Black Sea to be included in the peace treaty signed by all the great powers and not left as a separate agreement signed only by Russia and Turkey. They also wanted their special conditions provided for under the fifth point to be made part of the Austrian Ultimatum. Under this point they demanded the permanent demilitarization of the Aaland Islands, a condition that seemed to pose no serious obstacle to Russian acceptance since the Russians had already agreed to it unofficially. More serious was their demand for diplomatic consulates in Russia's Black Sea ports, presumably to supervise Russia's adherence to any future treaty agreements. A potentially insuperable obstacle, however, was the superficially innocuous Palmerston-Clarendon demand for a discussion at a final peace conference of the status of the populations inhabiting Russia's provinces on the east coast of the Black Sea, a provision that would allow them to bring up Palmerston's cherished war aims of securing the independence of Georgia, Circassia, and other territories in the Caucasus region.[40]

So vague a formulation involving areas of critical strategic importance was certain to be rejected by Russia, and this is clearly what Palmerston and Clarendon intended. They had only agreed to negotiate over the Franco-Austrian proposals to avoid giving France an excuse to withdraw from the war and to secure the participation of Austria if the Russians rejected them, and they were determined to make sure that Russia *would* reject them. Both Palmerston and Clarendon thought a continuation of the war essential in order to bring about a peace that would justify having fought it in the first place. While they negotiated over the Franco-Austrian peace proposals, they were discussing plans for opening up a major new front in the Baltic in 1856 and sending a British expeditionary force into Georgia, a campaign Clarendon was confident would not be "interfered with by negotiations."[41]

The modifications formulated by Palmerston and Clarendon now became the subject of negotiations between London and Paris. Upon the objection of Walewski, the British agreed to drop their demand for the neutralization of the Sea of Azov;[42] they agreed not to insist on their demand to maintain consuls in Russia's Black Sea ports, provided that France guaranteed to secure the inclusion of this condition in a final peace treaty; and they agreed that the provisions about naval vessels to be maintained in the Black Sea might be left to a special bilateral treaty between Russia and Turkey provided that the terms of that treaty could not be changed in any way without the consent of all the signatories of a general final peace treaty. Walewski for his part agreed to inform Vienna of Britain's special conditions provided through the fifth point, including the demilitarization of the Aaland Islands, commercial concessions that would be the equivalent of a war indemnity, and, most important of all, the right to make stipulations regarding Russian territories on the east coast of the Black Sea if the military situation were favorable.[43]

In fact, the military situation for the Allies turned distinctly unfavorable at this time, for on 26 November the Russians captured the strategic Turkish fortress-city of Kars south of the Caucasus Mountains, a military success that may have predisposed the Russians to peace. Their army had saved face through the capture of Kars, and Kars itself might be used as a bargaining counter to offset the demands of the Allies at a future peace conference. In Britain, on the other hand, news of the fall of Kars only strengthened the belief of Palmerston and Clarendon that the war must be continued to achieve a satisfactory peace.[44]

While allowing the British to assume that he had accepted all their demands, Walewski neglected to inform them that he had no intention of allowing their special conditions to be incorporated in the Austrian Ultimatum, because doing so would ensure its rejection by Russia. At the same time he allowed the Austrians to assume that the British government was now committed to supporting the Franco-Austrian peace terms. On sending the final version of the British amendments to Vienna (minus Britain's special conditions or reservations), he described them as "disguised adherence" (*"adhésion dissimulée"*) to the Franco-Austrian proposals, thereby disguising the true state of affairs from the Austrians as well as the British.[45]

The British, however, suspected that Walewski would try a trick of this kind and instructed Seymour, their ambassador to Vienna, to approach Austria directly with the demand that their special conditions be included in the Austrian Ultimatum to Russia. Buol refused on the grounds that Austria had merely agreed to submit preliminary peace conditions to Russia, not negotiate a final peace treaty. If Russia accepted, Britain could present its special conditions at a peace conference as provided under the fifth point, but Austria was under no obligation to do so.[46]

Palmerston and Clarendon were infuriated, convinced that Buol and Walewski had betrayed them, as Walewski indeed had done. Clarendon wrote to his wife that Palmerston was positively rabid, "his feelings about Austria are so savage that he almost compels me to take her part."[47] Walewski for his part was infuriated with Britain. He considered the attitude of the British cabinet incredible and Palmerston himself mentally deranged (*une abérration*).[48] In Vienna, Buol continued to persevere. Together with Seymour and Bourqueney, he worked out yet another compromise proposal that Seymour sent to London by telegraph.[49]

It was now the turn of the British to cheat. They did not want to forego the benefits of an Austrian Ultimatum, which they believed would be rejected by Russia even in its current form, and thereby oblige Austria to break off diplomatic relations. At the same time the British ministers shared the queen's fears that if they insisted on conditions that would be clearly unacceptable to Russia, the Austrians would get cold feet and withdraw from the peace project altogether.[50] They therefore informed Buol, through Seymour, of the British cabinet's approval of the latest version of the Austrian peace terms.[51]

What the British did not tell Buol was that their acceptance of the Austrian Ultimatum had been hedged with secret reservations. Palmerston and Clarendon were to maintain later that they had only approved the Austrian Ultimatum as a statement of *Austrian* conditions; and because the Austrians had refused to include Britain's conditions in their ultimatum, the British government reserved the right to secure Russia's acceptance of *British* conditions before Britain would agree to an armistice.[52] Palmerston and Clarendon had a case. The only trouble with it was that they did not inform Austria or France of their reservations at this time. On the contrary, in response to Buol's enquiry Seymour specifically assured him that the British government had agreed to the terms of the Austrian Ultimatum as the basis for future peace negotiations.[53]

The Austrian Ultimatum Presented to Russia, 28 December 1855

The final text of the Austrian Ultimatum embodying preliminary conditions for peace ostensibly agreed upon by the Austrian, British, and French governments was drawn up on 16 December.[54] On that same day Count Valentin Esterházy, the Austrian ambassador to Russia, left Vienna to convey the ultimatum to St. Petersburg, where he officially submitted it to the Russian government on 28 December.[55]

In accordance with his instructions, Esterházy demanded Russia's unconditional acceptance of the terms agreed upon by the Allies within eight days. If he did not receive a satisfactory reply by that time, he was to inform the Russian government that Austria would break off diplomatic relations on 18 January. Russian acceptance, on the other hand, would be followed by an immediate armistice and peace negotiations. In strictest confidence, Esterházy was to explain to the Russians that the special conditions mentioned in the fifth point had never been the subject of a treaty between Austria and the Western powers, and that Austria could assure the Russians that these conditions did not involve either a cession of territory or an indemnity and would therefore present "no serious obstacle to the conclusion of peace."[56] As the French were giving the Russians similar assurances with respect to the same point at this time, Palmerston and Clarendon were absolutely correct in believing that Buol and Walewski would fail to back up Britain's special conditions at a peace conference and that the British would therefore have to secure Russia's acceptance of these conditions before they could agree to an armistic. The motivation of Palmerston and Clarendon throughout, however, was not to secure acceptance of their conditions but, rather, to retain the opportunity of presenting conditions that Russia was certain to reject and thereby ensure the continuation of the war.

Russia's Unconditional Acceptance of the Austrian Ultimatum, 16 January 1856

Contrary to the expectations of most Allied observers, the Russians agreed to the terms of the Austrian Ultimatum, though in the first instance with two major reservations: they rejected the fifth point altogether, and they rejected the cession of territory in Bessarabia required in the first point.[57] Buol refused to make concessions of any kind, but in reiterating Austria's demand for unconditional acceptance he reminded Esterházy of his secret instructions enabling him to reassure the Russians about these controversial points. Russia's acceptance of the fifth point would not commit the Russians to anything but would give them the same latitude with respect to special conditions as all other belligerents; and the final delimitation of territory to be ceded in Bessarabia remained open to negotiation.[58]

The Russians yielded unconditionally on 16 January. At a meeting of the Imperial Crown Council on the previous day Russian leaders had set forth their principal reasons for doing so, their arguments supported by detailed memoranda from various government departments describing the condition of the Russian economy and armed forces. The gist of these arguments was that the Russians could not afford to continue to fight and that if they nevertheless attempted to do so their situation could only grow worse. If they rejected the Austrian Ultimatum, they had every reason to expect that Austria would enter the war against them and that Allied pressure on Prussia and the other German states might bring the entire German Confederation into the war as well. On 17 December the Russian government had been informed of the Swedish alliance with Britain and France, which increased the danger of an Allied offensive in the Baltic. If the war were extended through the entry of these other states into the conflict, the military situation for Russia would become desperate, and future Allied peace terms were certain to be far harsher. Sweden was known to have designs on Finland, the British made no secret of their desire to set up independent states in the Crimea and the Caucasus region, Napoleon spoke of establishing an independent state of Poland.

Within Russia itself there were grave dangers and difficulties that would only grow more serious if the war were continued. The Russian people were clearly tired of the war and the burdens it entailed. There were stirrings of revolt in every part of the empire that might get out of control if the bulk of the Russian army remained deployed against a foreign foe. National revolts in Poland, Finland, or the Caucasus might well result in the loss of all of Russia's border provinces. Recruitment for the army had drained Russia's labor force terribly, and human reserves were exhausted, as were Russia's supplies of arms and ammunition. The minister of finance warned that a continuation of the war would inevitably lead to national bankruptcy. In sum, a Russian effort to hold out might lead to disasters far greater than any losses of territory or prestige Russia might incur by accepting the relatively mild Allied peace terms.

There was also the present attitude of the French government to be considered. The Russians were well informed about the war weariness in France and had received secret assurances from members of the French government about their willingness to cooperate with Russia to block extravagant demands on the part of the British. If the Russians rejected the present Allied terms, they would throw France back into the arms of England, whereas through acceptance the chances seemed good of driving a wedge between the Allied powers.

In overcoming the resistance of Russian patriots to the humiliation of surrender, the most persuasive argument brought forward by advocates of peace may have been that the present Allied terms would in no way hamper Russia's capacity to develop its resources or otherwise prejudice the country's future. In a few years Russia would again be as strong as before the war and could then pursue policies that were rendered impossible by present circumstances. A peace made today would be no more than a truce, but if it were postponed for a year or more the country might be reduced to such a state of weakness and exhaustion that it might require at least fifty years to recover. A peace made under such conditions would leave future Russian governments no alternative but to adhere strictly to the terms of peace imposed upon them during that half-century of weakness because they could not afford the risk of war to recoup their losses.[59]

Palmerston himself could not have summed up more effectively his own arguments for continuing the war against Russia. And Palmerston did his best to see that it was continued.

Final British Efforts to Prevent an Armistice, January 1856

Even before Russia's final acceptance of the Austrian Ultimatum, news of the possibility of Russian acceptance was not happily received in Britain. "We must not let Walewski and Buol drag us into the mire," Palmerston told Clarendon after hearing of Russia's conditional acceptance. "If we hold out the French government must stand by us."[60] On 1 January Palmerston gave the Austrians the first hint that Britain did not feel bound by the Austrian Ultimatum. Even if Russia should accept unconditionally, he told the Austrian ambassador, he personally felt that Britain could not agree to an armistice until Russia had also accepted Britain's special conditions, which the Austrians had refused to include in their ultimatum or otherwise communicate to Russia.[61]

Palmerston's personal opinion quickly became Britain's official policy. On 8 January Clarendon instructed Seymour to demand that the Austrians communicate Britain's special conditions to Russia and that Russia accept them before Britain would consent to an armistice. The conditions remained the same: demilitarization of the Aaland Islands; admission of foreign consuls to Russia's Black Sea ports; discussion of the status of the Caucasus region at the peace conference.[62]

It was now Buol's turn to become indignant. He did not reply to Britain directly but appealed to Walewski to bring the British government to reason. As in the previous December, he argued that the whole object of the fifth point was to allow all belligerents to pose special conditions in the European interest at a peace conference and that Britain had no right to demand the acceptance of its special conditions in advance.[63]

Unable to get anywhere with Austria, the British turned to France, or rather to Napoleon, for they no longer had any confidence whatever in Walewski.[64] Napoleon was torn between his fear that his position in his own country would be compromised if he failed to respond to the French nation's desire for peace and his desire to avoid a breach with England. In vain the emperor appealed to Queen Victoria that all the goals they could possibly desire from the war had been achieved; in vain Persigny argued that the emperor could not afford to ignore the pressures of French public opinion for peace or the financial difficulties that a continuation of the war would entail.[65]

Palmerston brushed aside these considerations. He assured the queen that these representations of the emperor's domestic difficulties were greatly exaggerated, that he was in complete control in France, "and that he can as to peace or war take the course which he may determine to adopt. The cabal of stock-jobbing politicians, by whom he is surrounded, *must* give way to him if he is firm." In congratulating the queen on Russia's acceptance of the Austrian Ultimatum, he pointed out that this success was a tolerably sure indication that perseverance along a similar course would bring the Russian government to accept the British conditions that Austria had not yet communicated to St. Petersburg.[66] Palmerston wrote to Seymour in Vienna urging him to put more starch in his neckcloth.[67] And to the Austrians he said: "England cannot consent to be told by any foreign government that England must sign without hesitations or conditions a national engagement. . . . England cannot recede from her position."[68] Finally on January 24 he formally requested the French government to join with Britain in demanding Russia's acceptance of Britain's special conditions before agreeing to an armistice.[69]

For Walewski the success of the peace campaign now hinged on whether Napoleon would stand up to the pressures of the British government. It was almost certainly because of his lack of confidence in the steadfastness of the emperor that he worked out a compromise with him in typical Walewski fashion. To satisfy the demands of the British, the French would communicate Britain's special conditions to Russia; but to avoid committing themselves against Russia, they would only do so unofficially; at the same time they would secretly assure the British that France would support Britain to secure the unconditional acceptance of their special conditions at the peace conference.[70]

With this assurance Palmerston had to be satisfied. It still left the door open for Britain to raise the question of the future of the Caucasus provinces at the peace conference, and even if he received no support for his program of detaching these provinces from Russia, he might yet use the issue to scuttle the peace conference as he had scuttled previous conferences in Vienna.

On 1 February 1856, the protocol on the preliminaries for peace was signed in Vienna by representatives of all the belligerent powers and Austria, and on 25 February the peace conference that was to end the Crimean War opened in Paris.[71]

Chapter 11

Peacemaking, 1856

The Position of the British Negotiators

Palmerston did not succeed in breaking up the Congress of Paris. He was never given an opportunity to do so, for all the other European powers at the congress, with the possible exception of Sardinia, were desperately anxious for peace, and this general desire for peace proved the determining factor in the negotiations.

Britain was represented at the congress by Clarendon, the foreign secretary, and Cowley, the British ambassador to Paris, both advocates of continuing the war until harsher peace terms could be imposed on Russia.[1] Even before the congress convened, however, Clarendon had begun to have doubts about Britain's military prospects if the war went on. "I should have liked another campaign . . . ," he wrote to Stratford after Russia's acceptance of the Austrian Ultimatum. "Then again, we cannot feel sure that another campaign *would* have restored our military prestige—on the contrary. . . . There is still so much that is radically defective in our military administration that the chance of failure would be quite as great as that of success."[2] Thus from the outset Clarendon was not at all sure whether it would be wise to resort to tactics designed to bring about the failure of the negotiations.

Clarendon also came to realize early that Britain could expect no support from France for a continuation of the war. Before going to Paris, he learned of France's enthusiastic reaction to Russia's acceptance of the Austrian Ultimatum, and in some contempt he wrote to Stratford that all of France—government, people, army, were now "bent on peace *at any price. . . .* The French people have gone mad, kissing each other upon the *restoration of peace.*"[3] After his arrival in Paris, Clarendon took a more sympathetic view of the French desire for peace and perceived that the difficulties confronting the French government were not merely fictitious representations on the part of unscrupulous speculators in the imperial entourage. He also saw that those difficulties had mounted sharply shortly before the congress convened. "Unluckily, too," he explained to Stratford some time later, "just as the negotiations began, the French army fell ill, and the Emperor himself admitted to me that with 22,000 men in hospital, and likely to be more, peace had almost become a military as well as a financial and political necessity for him."[4]

From London Palmerston bombarded Clarendon with instructions to stand firm and insist on stringent conditions. Clarendon was to impress upon Napoleon that, rather than sign an unsatisfactory peace, Britain and France must be prepared to allow the negotiations to break down and to resume the war.[5] By the time negotiations began, however, Clarendon had a very different view of the situation. He told Palmerston bluntly that he did not make sufficient allowance for the change in the attitude of France. "When you talk of 'we' and of 'our' going on with the war if the Russians are intractable, you are probably thinking of the France of two years ago, whereas it is no such thing. Except the Emperor and Walewski, who does not dare to act contrary to the Emperor's orders, we have nobody here who is not prepared to make *any* peace." The entire alliance with France was now in jeopardy "quite as much as the conditions of peace for which we are contending." He, Clarendon, was regarded as a slave of the English newspapers and the representative of Palmerston's anti-Russian feelings; the general opinion seemed to be that peace would be fatal to Palmerston's government and that "I am here for the purpose of making it impossible."[6] To his friends Clarendon admitted that he would indeed have preferred a continuation of the war so as to be able to impose very different conditions on

Russia, but, as he explained to the Liberal leader Lord Granville, Britain would find itself isolated if it attempted to do so. For "France was determined on peace; and whatever Palmerston in his jaunty mood may say, we could not have made war alone, for we would have had all of Europe against us at once, and the United States would soon have followed in the train."[7]

The Congress of Paris

The Congress of Paris convened on 25 February 1856 and officially ended with the signature of the Treaty of Paris on March 30, although the delegates were to remain in Paris for almost a month longer to negotiate over related problems. Represented at the congress were all the belligerent powers (Britain, France, the Ottoman Empire, Russia, and Sardinia) and Austria. Prussia, which had steadfastly refused to join in the war against Russia or to be associated with the Austrian Ultimatum, was not invited to participate in the congress until it discussed a revision of the Straits Convention of 1841, to which Prussia was a signatory, and even then the Prussian delegates were received with bad grace. When the chief Prussian plenipotentiary joined the congress for the first time on 18 March, Buol described his entrance into the conference room as that of a poor miserable sinner.[8]

Representing France at the congress was Walewski, the foreign minister, who as chief of the host delegation was elected president of the congress. The second French plenipotentiary was Bourqueney, the ambassador to Vienna. The British delegates, as mentioned, were Clarendon and Cowley. Austria was represented by Buol and Hübner, the ambassador to Paris; the Ottoman Empire by Aali Pasha, the grand vizier, and Mohammed Djemil Bey, ambassador to Paris and Turin; Sardinia by its minister-president, Cavour, who had not yet established his reputation as one of the great diplomats of the nineteenth century, and by Villa-Marina, the minister to Paris; Prussia by Manteuffel, the minister-president and foreign minister, and Hatzfeldt, the minister to Paris. Representing Russia were Orlov, chief of the abortive mission to Vienna in January of 1854, and Brunnow, the ambassador to London.

An important role at the congress was played by Napoleon III, who frequently received the delegates in private audience and mediated between them on several critical occasions. Though still primarily concerned with preserving good relations with Britain, the French ruler had come to realize he could not afford to ignore his own country's desire and need for peace. Napoleon also recognized that there were positive advantages to be gained from promoting the chance for peace, for by scaling down Allied demands he was able to go a long way toward reestablishing good relations with Russia that might be put to good use in promoting imperial projects in the future. In the course of the congress the French were to side with Russia on numerous controversial issues, with the result that the British found themselves without support for their more extreme demands. On certain issues, for example the Allied demand for Russia's cession of territory at the mouths of the Danube, the British formed an uneasy partnership with Austria. But the British, like all other governments represented at the congress, were fundamentally hostile to the Austrians, who received no thanks for their persistent efforts to restore peace but were on the contrary vilified for their pusillanimity during the war and suspected of seeking to make cheap territorial gains from the sacrifices of the belligerents.

The final Treaty of Paris confirmed and clarified but did not substantially alter the preliminary agreements concluded among the powers as the basis for peace. Although the controversies over certain points were often bitter, the general desire for peace among the major powers, apart from Britain, was sufficiently great to overcome these obstacles and permit the resolution of all problems through compromise. As usual in all international conferences, much of the work was done in small committees dealing with specific problems, and the most significant agreements and compromises were arranged in confidential meetings among the principal negotiators—the plenipotentiaries of Austria, Britain,

and France, who were in fact to settle all major questions between them.[9]

The Issue of Russia's Caucasus Provinces

The first of the confidential meetings of the plenipotentiaries of
Austria, Britain, and France took place on 21 February, four days
before the congress officially convened. At this initial meeting,
Buol appears to have deliberately brought up the one major issue
over which the Allies had not reached agreement in their preliminary negotiations and that Buol must have feared Britain
would attempt to use to break up the congress, namely, Britain's
demand for a discussion at the peace conference of the future
status of Russia's territories on the east coast of the Black Sea.
Would the British clarify what they hoped to achieve through
such a discussion? Buol's initiative on this question was a bold
move, and it evidently took the chief British plenipotentiary by
surprise. Without adequate opportunity to bring pressure to bear
on other plenipotentiaries or otherwise prepare his case, and deprived of any chance to select his own time for presenting Britain's demands on this crucial issue to the congress, Clarendon
was obliged to reveal the most extreme of Britain's war aims.
Evidently in some embarrassment, Clarendon said that it was
difficult to be precise about this matter, but he believed the congress should call upon Russia to rectify its frontiers with Turkey,
and that the Kuban River might be considered in advance as the
boundary between these two empires. Although Clarendon's language was certainly imprecise, his description of Britain's special
conditions was clear enough: what he was proposing was the
amputation of all Russian territory south of the Kuban River,
and by implication either the establishment of Georgia, Circassia,
and other Russian frontier provinces in this area as independent
states or their restoration to the Ottoman Empire.[10]

As everyone at the conference realized, such a program would
have required a continuation of the war on a major scale. But
quite apart from the determination of the other powers to pre-

vent a resumption of the war, the Allies were hardly in a position to impose demands on Russia in the Caucasus region. As mentioned earlier, the Russians had captured the strategic fortress-city of Kars south of the Caucasus Mountains in the final stages of the war, so that the Russians were now in a position to demand border rectifications in this area in *their* favor or to use Kars as a bargaining counter for Bessarabia, which is what they did. When Buol first raised the Caucasus question, Clarendon spontaneously admitted that the Allied military situation in the Asian theater did not allow for excessively grandiose pretensions. And as the British negotiators received no support for continuing the war or for posing demands of any kind in the Caucasus area, they quietly dropped what might have been the most dangerous issue at the peace conference.[11]

In the final treaty, the prewar territorial status of both the Russian and Ottoman empires in Asia was reestablished, and an international boundary commission to verify the frontiers was set up to prevent all local territorial disputes.[12] "It was quite out of the question contending for Circassia and the adjacent territories," Clarendon explained to a disappointed Stratford in Constantinople, "for the Emperor said he could not conscientiously insist upon them and would not support us—in fact upon the Bessarabian frontier we had to choose between a concession to Russia or something very like a rupture with France."[13]

Bessarabia and the Danubian Principalities

Bessarabia, rather than the Caucasus, developed into the most thorny territorial problem at the congress. As we have seen, the Austrians not only wanted to remove Russian control over the mouths of the Danube but also the cession of a large slice of territory north of that river so as to give the Ottoman Empire and its allies (and thus also Austria) a better strategic frontier against Russia.[14] The Russians, of course, were equally aware of the strategic and economic value of this area, and they were also anxious to avoid the humiliation of having to make a territorial concession of any kind. They therefore proposed that, in return for yielding to the Allied demand for the restoration of Kars to the Ottoman Empire, the Allies give up all claims to Bessarabia.

The problem was finally settled by compromise, with most of the arrangements being made behind the scenes or under the table, as are most compromise settlements in international affairs. In return for the restoration of Kars and all other prewar Ottoman territory in Asia, the Russians were allowed to retain about two-thirds of the Bessarabian territory they had agreed to relinquish in the preliminary peace agreements, but they did give up the crucial area at the mouths of the Danube and thereby lost this strategic frontier as well as control over Danube shipping at the entrance to the Black Sea.[15] Thus the essential objective of the Allies with respect to Bessarabia had been attained, an advantage that the Austrian negotiators hailed in their report to Emperor Francis Joseph as "the liberation of that great artery of Austria, of that essentially German river . . . which will be in the sight of Austria, Germany, and Europe the most striking justification of Your Majesty's diplomacy."[16]

The territory ceded by Russia in Bessarabia was to be attached to the Principality of Moldavia, the final details of the new frontier to be worked out in later negotiations.[17]

The major controversy over the Danubian Principalities themselves (Moldavia and Wallachia) was whether they should be united under a single rule and how they were to be governed in the future. Napoleon continued to advocate their unification as a step in the realization of his nationalities program and to create a more viable state to serve as an obstacle to Russian expansion in this area. The Austrians, British, and Turks all opposed unification, the Austrians because they disliked any recognition of the principle of nationality and feared a weakening of their own influence in the principalities; all three because they feared a union government might be strong enough to attempt to break away from the suzerainty of the Porte and thus violate the integrity of the Ottoman Empire, which the present war had allegedly been fought to preserve. But if a Danubian union might constitute too strong a state vis-à-vis the Porte, it would be too weak to pursue an independent course and would therefore almost certainly gravitate to Russia, to which the peoples of the principalities already had so many close ties through religion, culture, and common antipathy toward the Turks.[18]

The opponents of unification triumphed. In its final arrangements for the principalities, the congress maintained the separate status of Moldavia and Wallachia, which, together with Serbia, were to remain under the suzerainty of the Porte, their privileges and immunities henceforth guaranteed by all the states signing the Treaty of Paris. To prevent a renewal of Russian pretensions in these principailties and forestall the ambitions of anyone else, the treaty stipulated that "no exclusive Protection shall be exercised over them by any of the guaranteeing Powers" and that none should have a "separate right of interference in their Internal Affairs." Turkish control over the principalities was also strictly limited, for the Porte was obliged to preserve "an Independent and National" administration in all three, and the final treaty included detailed provisions as to how they were to be governed.[19]

In the course of the negotiations over the principalities, Emperor Francis Joseph had described the union issue as "a question of life and death for his empire."[20] The prevention of the union and therewith the avoidance of international recognition of the nationality principle was therefore regarded as a major diplomatic victory by the Austrian negotiators.

Freedom of Navigation on the Danube

In dealing with the question of freedom of navigation on the Danube, the major problem raised at the congress was whether the provisions of the final treaty should apply to the entire course of the river, and thus also to those sections flowing through Austria, Bavaria, and Württemberg. The Austrians wanted to restrict all such provisions to the lower Danube to avoid international supervision of their segment of the river. All other states represented at the congress, however, wanted these provisions to apply to its entire course.

Closely connected with this problem was that of membership on international commissions that would have to be set up to regulate navigation on the Danube. The states bordering on the river maintained that they alone should be represented on such commissions, whereas the nonlittoral states argued that the Danube was a pan-European concern and that representatives of all the signatory powers of a final peace treaty should be represented on any future commissions.[21]

The Austrians were soon forced to realize that they would be unable to prevent the application of final treaty provisions concerning the Danube to the entire course of the river, but they did succeed in preventing the establishment of a pan-European Danube commission. A Danubian European Commission consisting of representatives of all the signatory powers was in fact created, but its duties were confined to clearing the mouths of the Danube and the neighboring waters of the Black Sea of sand and other impediments in order to make this part of the river navigable. This European commission was expected to complete its work within two years and would then be dissolved.

To regulate shipping along the entire course of the Danube and take over the functions of the European commission after its dissolution, the congress provided for the creation of a permanent Danube River Commission that was to be composed only of representatives from the states bordering the river—Austria, Bavaria, the Ottoman Empire (in its capacity as suzerain over the Danubian Principalities and Serbia), and Württemberg—to whom were to be added commissioners from Moldavia, Wallachia, and Serbia, whose nomination was to be approved by the Porte.

To enforce treaty provisions for freedom of navigation of the Danube, the final treaty provided that each of the signatory powers was authorized to station light warships at its mouths (never more than two at a time), and the sultan was authorized to grant special permission for the passage of these warships through the Straits.[22]

The Neutralization of the Black Sea

Quite as controversial as Bessarabia, and far more complicated, was the question of the neutralization of the Black Sea. The Russians had accepted the Allied demand that no ships of war be allowed on the waters of the Black Sea and that no naval arsenals be maintained on its shores, but this restriction would lose much of its value to the Allies if the Russians were allowed to have warships and arsenals on the rivers flowing into the Black Sea and on the adjoining Sea of Azov.

This question too was settled by compromise, and far more quickly and easily than the negotiators in Paris had anticipated. The Russians refused to give up the right to maintain shipyards and fortifications in cities on their inland waterways, notably Nikolaev near the mouth of the Bug River and Kherson near the mouth of the Dnieper. They promised, however, not to build warships in their inland shipyards beyond the number of police or coast guard vessels they would be permitted to maintain on the Black Sea. But this was as far as the Russians would go. As we have seen, the British had attempted to secure the neutralization of the Sea of Azov as one of their special conditions. They had failed to do so in preliminary peace negotiations, and they were no more successful in Paris. The Russians refused to make concessions or promises of any kind regarding the Sea of Azov: this subject was and must remain separate from the deliberations of the congress, which should confine itself exclusively to the problems of the Black Sea.[23] The final treaty provided that the Black Sea be neutralized, that its waters and ports be open to the merchant fleets of all nations, and that neither Russia nor Turkey should maintain or establish arsenals along its coasts. No mention was made of the Sea of Azov.[24]

The British had greater success with another of their special conditions, namely, the right to maintain diplomatic representatives in Russian and Turkish Black Sea ports. In an article in the final treaty dealing with commercial regulations for the Black Sea, Russia and Turkey agreed to admit foreign consuls to their

Black Sea ports "in order to afford to the Commercial and Maritime interests of every Nation the security which is desired."[25]

Contrary to the wishes of the British, the final agreement of the powers on the controversial questions of the number and size of police vessels to be permitted on the Black Sea was not made part of the general final peace treaty but was recorded in a special convention between Russia and Turkey annexed to that treaty. This procedure was adopted in order to spare Russia the humiliation of submitting to the dictates of the European powers on a question affecting Russia's sovereign rights. Instead, the naval limitations desired by the powers were made to appear as the product of an agreement freely negotiated between Russia and the Ottoman Empire. To allay the fears of the British and others that Russia might find means to circumvent the terms of a separate convention, an article was inserted in the final general peace treaty that the Russo-Turkish convention should have the same force and validity as though it were an integral part of the final treaty and that it could not be annulled or modified without the consent of all the powers signing that treaty.[26]

The Straits and the Aaland Islands

Also annexed to the general final treaty were two other separate conventions dealing with the Turkish Straits and the Aaland Islands.

The Straits Convention, signed 30 March (the same date as the main treaty and by the same signatory powers), reaffirmed the provision of the Straits Convention of 1841 that the Straits be closed to foreign warships while the Ottoman Empire was at peace. The new convention, however, provided that the sultan might permit the passage of light naval vessels "in the service of the [diplomatic] missions of foreign powers." It also contained the provision, previously mentioned, that the sultan might permit the passage of similar light naval vessels to safeguard international shipping at the mouths of the Danube.[27]

Among the special conditions put forward by Britain in preliminary peace negotiations was a demand for the permanent elimination of all fortifications on Russia's strategic Aaland Islands in the Baltic Sea. The Russians indicated early in the congress that the tsar attached little importance to these fortifications and that the Russian government was willing to conclude a separate convention with Britain and France to regulate this question.

Once again the British demanded that such an agreement be made part of a general final peace treaty, and once again the congress resolved to spare Russia the humiliation of having an issue affecting Russia's sovereign rights submitted to an international tribunal. The Aaland Islands question was settled in a separate convention signed only by the plenipotentiaries of Britain, France, and Russia. It provided that "the Aaland Islands shall not be fortified, and that no Military or Naval Establishment shall be maintained or created there." Like the Russo-Turkish convention over naval vessels, however, both the Straits Convention and Aaland Island Convention were annexed to the general final treaty, which included articles that they too should have the same force and validity as though they formed an integral part of that treaty.[28]

The Protection of the Ottoman Empire and the Rights of Christians

The question of safeguarding the sovereignty and territorial integrity of the Ottoman Empire, the ostensible reason for the Crimean War in the first place, aroused little controversy at the congress and was easily settled by the negotiators. In the final Treaty of Paris, all the signatory powers engaged to respect and guarantee the independence and territorial integrity of the Ottoman Empire, and the Sublime Porte was "admitted to participate in the advantages of the Public Law and System (Concert) of Europe." Any dispute between the Porte and one or more of the signatory powers was to be submitted to the other contracting parties for mediation.[29]

Less easily settled was the question of the rights of Christians in the Ottoman Empire, the original cause of (or pretext for) the entire crisis in the Near East. This question had received relatively little attention from the Christian powers once the war was under way, but the possibility that the protection issue might still be used as a pretext for European intervention in Ottoman affairs remained a major concern of the Ottoman government. As the Turks saw it, the incorporation of articles dealing with the religious question in a final peace treaty would have provided just such a pretext, for it would make the rights of Christians the subject of a general European guarantee and thus give international sanction to foreign interference in the Ottoman Empire. To anticipate any discussion of this question at the peace conference and the introduction of special provisions dealing with it in a general European peace treaty, the sultan issued a decree (*firman*) on 18 February, before the Congress of Paris convened, confirming and guaranteeing all privileges and special immunities granted *ab antiquo* to all Christian and other non-Moslem communities in the Ottoman Empire, promising complete freedom of religion, and providing for a wide variety of political, administrative, legal, economic, taxation, and other reforms.[30]

Roderic Davison, a foremost authority on Turkish reforms in the nineteenth century, calls this reform decree of 1856 the magnum opus of Stratford, who throughout the month of January had met regularly with leaders of the Turkish government and with the Austrian and French ambassadors to Constantinople to discuss the project. Stratford was pushing the Turks to complete work on the reform decree and to issue it before the opening of the Paris conference so as to deprive the Russians of any opportunity to participate in drawing up provisions affecting the rights of Christians in the Ottoman Empire and to present them instead with a fait accompli.[31]

It may have been Stratford who actually conceived the idea that the Turks issue a decree on the rights of Christians to stave off any possibility of Russian influence in this matter, and he certainly played a major role in drafting it. But the Turks had demonstrated throughout the crisis that they were not nearly so politically naïve as their European friends often seemed to assume. They were perfectly aware of the issues at stake and needed no prompting from Stratford or anyone else to endeavor to prevent the European powers from inserting provisions for Ottoman reform in a general peace treaty. They had always resented European interference in their affairs, and during the Crimean War had conceived an intense dislike for their European allies and protectors because of their high-handed behavior. For their most ardent champion, Stratford, whose pressure for reform and assumption of authority in Ottoman affairs had grown steadily over the years, many Turks had come to feel an outright hatred.

The promulgation of the Turkish reform decree did not save the Turks from having the question of the rights of Christians in the Ottoman Empire introduced in the final peace treaty. To spare the sensibilities of the Turks, however, this introduction was no more than a simple reference to the Turks' own decree of 18 February, which, so the final treaty stated, had emanated from the sovereign will of the sultan, and its mention in the final treaty was made in accordance with a resolve on the part of the sultan to communicate this proof of his solicitude for his subjects to the signatory powers. To reassure the Turks still further, the treaty went on to state that the sultan's communication did not give the European powers the right to interfere, collectively or separately, in the relations between the sultan and his subjects or in the internal affairs of the Ottoman Empire. With this statement the treaty seemed to cancel all European claims to any kind of protectorate over Christians or the Christian Holy Places in the Ottoman Empire, but as a guarantee for European noninterference in Turkish affairs it was about as meaningful as Turkish promises of reform.[32]

The Results of the Treaty of Paris for Russia

The tsar chose to hail the 18 February Ottoman decree for the protection of Christians as an act of Providence that had brought to pass the "original and principal aims of the war," and in a proclamation to the Russian people he declared: "From now on, the future destiny and the rights of all Christians in the Orient are assured. The Sultan solemnly recognizes them, and in consequence of this act of justice the Ottoman Empire enters into the community of European states! Russians! Your efforts and your sacrifices were not in vain. The great work is accomplished."[33]

The tsar's proclamation represented a face-saving interpretation of Russian accomplishments on behalf of Christians in the Ottoman Empire, but in a literal sense it was also true, for Russia's principal avowed aim throughout the Crimean crisis had been the promulgation of a formal Ottoman decree guaranteeing the rights of Christians. The crucial difference between the 18 February decree and Russia's original demands, of course, was that all specific Russian claims for the protection of Christians had been eliminated.

Quite apart from the question of Christians in the Ottoman Empire, the Russians had reason to congratulate themselves on the success of their negotiations in Paris, for the terms of the final treaty were remarkably lenient, especially when compared with the extravagant war aims formulated by Palmerston and Stratford. At the conclusion of the congress, Bourqueney complained that anyone reading the treaty would find it impossible to determine who was the victor and who the vanquished.[34]

In the end, the Russians made only one cession of territory they had not been prepared to make before the war began—the strategically and economically important segment of Bessarabia at the mouths of the Danube. The cession of this territory represented a significant gain for Europe as a whole in that it enabled the powers to ensure the freedom of navigation of the Danube at the entrance to the Black Sea. But, except in terms of prestige, it did not represent a correspondingly critical loss to Russia, which had less at stake in Danubian commerce than many other states and which retained its strategic positions in Bessarabia north of the Danube.

The Russians were deprived of their preponderant influence in the Danubian Principalities and Serbia, but they had been prepared to relinquish such influence before the war began. Their troops who had moved into the principalities in July 1853 to exert pressure on Turkey had already been withdrawn in July of the following year. And no treaty could sever the close religious, ethnic, and cultural ties between Russia and the peoples of these principalities, ties that many contemporary observers feared would ensure their ultimate gravitation to Russia.

The Russians were obliged to agree to freedom of navigation and commerce on the Danube and the Black Sea, but these concessions, far from being detrimental to Russia, were a positive advantage, for they provided Russia, too, with fresh economic opportunities and were a potential stimulus to Russian enterprise.

The harshest part of the treaty and the most damaging blow to Russian power, or so it seemed at the time, were the provisions of the supplementary Russo-Turkish convention prohibiting Russia from maintaining a navy or naval bases on the Black Sea. As a blow to Russian prestige these terms were undeniably harsh, but the blow to Russian power was less significant than it appeared or was meant to be. For the Turks were subjected to similar restrictions, and the reaffirmation of the provision that the Straits remain closed to the warships of foreign powers while the Ottoman Empire was at peace meant that Russia was safeguarded from any immediate threat of British or French sea power on their southern flank. The Turks, to be sure, could still retain warships and naval arsenals of their own in the Straits proper, but they too were prohibited from using them to menace Russia's Black Sea coasts.

The Results of the Crimean War for Austria

Shortly after the signing of the Treaty of Paris, that treaty was buttressed by a separate treaty between Austria, Britain, and France, signed in Paris on 15 April 1856, which was in effect a defensive alliance against Russia. In this treaty the Allies promised yet again to guarantee the independence and territorial in-

tegrity of the Ottoman Empire, but its key provision was that
the signatory powers agreed to regard any infraction of the terms
of the Treaty of Paris as a *casus belli*.[35]

Buol was delighted with this treaty, and in describing it to
Emperor Francis Joseph he expressed the belief that it would
"oppose a firm barrier to the adversaries of the new European
system, will put an end to the intrigues of some and the illusions
of others, and preserve Austria from the dangers of isolation."[36]

Alas, poor Buol. It was he who harbored the illusions. An international treaty is only valuable so long as the contracting
parties find it in their own interests to adhere to it in letter and
in spirit, but neither Britain nor France were to see their interests served by bolstering the European position of the Habsburg
Empire in the years to come. Russia, of course, had been irretrievably alienated. It did not take long for the Austrians to discover how isolated they in fact were.

Already during the Congress of Paris, the Austrians found
themselves under pressure from all the powers to evacuate the
Danubian Principalities, which they did in March 1857.[37] During
the next decade, against the vigorous opposition of Austria, the
powers agreed to the union of the principalities. This union was
to become the state of Rumania, and although still under the
nominal suzerainty of the Porte, its establishment set yet another precedent for the creation of national states for all the other
nationalities under foreign rule, including those of the Habsburg
Empire.

Elsewhere in Europe, the Austrians found themselves alone to
deal with the rivalry of Sardinia and France in Italy, which
ended with the loss of Austria's Italian provinces and the establishment of an Italian national state; and with the rivalry of
Prussia in Germany, which resulted in the loss of Austrian influence in Germany and the creation of a German national state.

Austria, not Russia, was eventually the greatest loser in the
Crimean War.

Chapter 12

Conclusion

For all their leniency, the provisions of the Treaty of Paris together with the Allied coalition formed directly afterwards to ensure their observance might have created a permanent obstacle to further Russian aggression at the expense of Europe and the Ottoman Empire had they been permanently enforced. But international settlements are never permanent. The coalition that imposed the Treaty of Paris on Russia had already begun to break apart during the peace negotiations, and Russia was quick to take advantage of the quarrels among its former enemies.

In 1870, while France and Prussia struggled over the fate of Germany, Russia repudiated the Black Sea clauses of the Treaty of Paris; in 1877 Russia was again at war with Turkey; in 1878 Russia regained the greater part of the ceded territory in Bessarabia (to the Pruth River in the west and the northernmost mouth of the Danube in the south), together with Kars and a large section of surrounding territory in the Caucasus area east of the Black Sea. Nor was Russia's behavior unexpected. As Lord John Russell observed to the House of Commons shortly after the signing of the Treaty of Paris: "If a treaty be found to be injurious to the interests of a country, and some means of violating it are obvious, I do not know of what country in Europe we could predicate a strict observance of the treaty."[1] It was ever thus.

The most permanent result of the Crimean War was the disruption of the Concert of Europe. Forty years of peace were now followed by four wars (fought from 1859 to 1871) that revolu-

tionized the power structure of the Continent. Defeated and hu-
miliated, Russia was determined to break the restrictions imposed
by the Treaty of Paris and thus became a revisionist state, although it refrained from active intervention in European affairs
during the next two decades while setting its own house in order.
Britain, disillusioned by an inglorious war and an inconclusive
peace, adopted an attitude similar to that of Russia by concentrating on domestic problems and largely withdrawing from
European affairs. Austria, as we have seen, was isolated. During
the Crimean War both sides had confidently anticipated Austrian
backing: Russia had expected Austria to support the 1815 peace
settlement against France and to repay a debt of gratitude for
recent military and diplomatic aid; Britain and France had been
certain that Austria would recognize the necessity of halting Russian expansion in southeastern Europe, where vital Austrian interests were at stake. Austria's neutrality antagonized all the
belligerents, with the result that until 1879 Austria was without
friends among the great powers. Prussia's policy during the war
was so flaccid and its strength seemed so inconsequential that it
was almost dismissed as a major power.

France was the state that seemed to have gained most from the
war. French armies had won the most impressive victories in the
final attacks on Sebastopol; the international system of 1815 and
its restrictions had been swept away; France had supplanted
Russia as the dominant power in Europe. But France's position
was not as strong as it appeared. Britain was apprehensive about
the revival of French power and the renewed danger of French
hegemony on the Continent. Russia, already antagonized by the
Crimean War, was further alarmed by Napoleon's talk of an independent Polish state, the creation of which would deprive Russia of its Polish provinces. A similar reaction occurred in Austria
and Prussia, both of which contained large Polish minorities of
their own, and these states also resented Napoleon's interference
in German and Italian affairs. France was as isolated among the
great powers as Austria, a situation Napoleon never seemed to
understand. He pursued an ambitious foreign policy and at-

tempted to push forward his program for reestablishing French predominance in Europe by championing the nationalities movement. But his policies were inconsistent and frequently quixotic; he was unable to control the momentum of the nationalities movement he had hoped to lead; and in the end he was to see the establishment of two new national states on France's frontiers, one of which was to destroy his empire and engage in a quest for European predominance of its own.

Meanwhile the Russian threat remained as though the Crimean War had never been fought. Because the results of that war had been so meager, it is easy to conclude that Palmerston and Stratford had been right, that the European powers should have recognized the need to join in a great anti-Russian coalition to roll back Russia's frontiers on every front and impose conditions that would have permanently diminished that country's capacity for aggression. But, given the geographical nature and sheer size of the Russian Empire, it is doubtful whether such conditions could ever have been imposed on Russia, or, if imposed, whether they could have been enforced over a significant period of time. Russia was simply too large, its power base too broad; there was no place in Russia where an enemy could strike a mortal blow or even a blow that would substantially reduce Russian strength.

But even if Russian power could have been destroyed and the danger of Russian aggression permanently eliminated, would this have led to a new era of peace and security for the peoples of Europe and Asia? Historical experience indicates that it would not. The belief that security can be achieved through the destruction of the power of the state that seems the greatest menace to such security is based on the supposition that only this state is a threat to international peace and that with its defeat all the world will breathe easily. But this is not the case. The elimination of one threat has always been accompanied by the rise of new threats as other states move to fill the power vacuum. Even before the end of the Crimean War, Palmerston's chief concern for the interests of England had shifted from the threat of Russia to the threat of France, just as after the Second World War the elimination of the German threat was succeeded almost immediately by a renewed fear of the threat from Russia—or, from the Russian viewpoint, the threat from the United States.

The moral of the story, and there is a moral, is that absolute security cannot be achieved on the international level any more than in one's personal life. Admirers of the famous Pax Romana tend to forget that after the apparent elimination of all foreign threats to the security of the Roman Empire (and even these were never eliminated but simply pushed to more distant frontiers) that empire was plagued by a succession of bloody civil wars which hardly contributed to the security of the persons involved, certainly not that of the losers.

The preservation of peace, then, cannot be achieved through programs for the elimination of threats to international or domestic security, for such threats never can be eliminated. Nor can it depend on international treaties or institutions designed to preserve peace, valuable as these may be as mechanisms for implementing or pursuing pacific policies.

Fundamentally, the preservation of peace requires a recognition on the part of all statesmen, but especially leaders of the great powers, that the preservation of peace itself is the only *certain* way to ensure the security of their respective states and that wars are always and inevitably a threat to such security and to the stability of the governments which they lead.

Such recognition had been fundamental to the political thought of the statesmen of the Concert of Europe, their views conditioned by the horrors of the French Revolution and the Napoleonic Wars. They understood the threat to their countries' and to their governments' security inherent in both international and domestic wars (that is, revolutions), and believed that the preservation of peace was not only the most certain means of preventing such threats but the highest duty of civilized men.

In their reconstruction of Europe after the Napoleonic Wars, the statesmen of the concert designed an international system to control international anarchy and to make it unprofitable as well as extremely dangerous for sovereign states to engage in aggression or otherwise threaten the international order. They concluded treaties and alliances amongst each other to protect and promote the interests of all contracting parties, but they were acutely conscious that treaties are frequently disregarded by statesmen who believe they can afford to do so with impunity and are tempted to score personal triumphs through unilateral action. In drawing up postwar boundaries, therefore, the statesmen of the concert consciously sought to establish an equilibrium among the great powers so that none should feel sufficiently strong to ignore international treaties or threaten the security or national interests of others.

A most important feature of this postwar balance of power was that it included defeated France, which was not divided, stripped of its territories, or saddled with a crippling reparations burden, but was instead restored to its prewar status and not compelled to pay reparations of any kind.[2] This leniency on the part of the victors was not the product of magnanimity but, rather, a realistic awareness that the French nation existed, that the power inherent in that nation could not be eliminated permanently, and that the elimination of French power was not even desirable, for it might be sorely needed in the postwar world to balance the power of other states, notably Russia. Quite apart from these practical considerations, the victors believed that the most effectual way to ensure France's future good behavior was not to punish or humiliate that proud country but to bring it back into the community of nations and convince the French that their own interests were best served by becoming a cooperative and supportive member of the postwar international system.

The policy of bringing all the great powers into the system, of keeping them "grouped," as the technique came to be called, appears in retrospect to have been the most effective method employed by the statesmen of the concert for the preservation of peace. This policy required the maintenance of the closest possible diplomatic relations among the great powers so that none should feel threatened or isolated, and so that the means were always available to deal with the crises that are endemic to any international system through negotiation.[3]

In persuading the leaders of the great powers to allow their

countries to be grouped, and in dealing with recalcitrant statesmen tempted to exploit crisis situations for unilateral advantages,
the only means available to the statesmen of the concert was to
reinforce or awaken in them the aforementioned recognition:
that the preservation of peace was the only certain way to ensure their own security and that war, far from protecting or promoting their interests, was far more likely to benefit the forces of
anarchy and revolution and might very well prove catastrophic
to them all.

The statesmen of the concert have been bitterly criticized for
not making sufficient allowance for change, and because, in the
interest of preserving the existing international and domestic
order (and their own privileged position in it), they were willing to support corrupt and tyrannical regimes and attempted to
suppress revolutions of every kind. The concert system, however,
was far more rigid in theory than in practice. The statesmen of
the concert did not succeed, and could not have succeeded, in
preventing all wars and revolutions in the post-Napoleonic world.
Moreover they were painfully aware of their vulnerability in this
regard, and it was precisely for this reason that they made arrangements which would give them the opportunity to deal with
international crises at the conference table. What they did succeed in doing was to prevent minor wars and revolutions from
developing into a conflict amongst themselves, and through conference diplomacy to register changes in the international order
that they were unable to prevent or found expedient to condone.[4]

Not least among the accomplishments of the statesmen of the
concert was the peaceful containment of Russia, which was not
only successfully grouped but after the 1848 revolutions became
the foremost champion of the concert system. As we have seen,
however, the very fact that Russia, potentially the most powerful
of European states, had emerged as the staunchest supporter of
the concert evoked a fear among other European powers that
Russia would use it as an instrument for the extension of its own
influence. That fear, combined with Napoleon III's determination to break up the concert to regain France's freedom of action,

the growing popular conception of Russia—and the concert—as bulwarks of despotic government, and the diminished awareness among a new generation of European leaders of the hazards of war, all help to explain the abandonment of concert diplomacy in favor of the policy of confrontation that led to the Crimean War.

The advocates of confrontation in the mid-nineteenth century still have their defenders, and the arguments used today on their behalf are almost identical with those employed by their contemporaries. "Russia," says a British historian writing in the 1960s,

had been at her old game of invading countries not her own, had inflicted 'wrong' upon Turkey and the inhabitants of the Principalities and had brought on war with the former. A war to cut [Russian aggression] short and make it highly unlikely in the future was certainly justified, given the amount of trouble that same phenomenon had already occasioned this country in earlier crises. . . . Without a reverse the Tsar would be able to restart his little game with impunity later on. A lunge at his underbelly therefore made very good sense and the results more than justified the effort. . . . The effective nature of the war was proved by events. Two decades is a long time in international relations, yet for that period and more Russian activity in the Near East was severely hampered. That the Crimean victory did not last forever is no real argument either against the war itself, or against the terms of peace imposed.

The Crimean War, this British historian goes on to say, had not only been the best means of injuring Russia's own war capabilities, but "let it not be forgotten—Britain, France, Turkey, and Piedmont [Sardinia] won."[5]

Yes indeed, they won, and seemingly without serious risk to themselves, much less the catastrophic consequences predicted by the Cassandras of the concert. Through his victory in the Crimean War, Napoleon III actually achieved one of his major foreign policy objectives—the breakup of the concert and the recovery of France's freedom of action. What Napoleon failed to consider, however, was that by casting off all restraints on the policy of France, he also destroyed all restraints on the policies of other powers. Within just a decade and a half he was to discover that it was not France but Sardinia and Prussia which were to harvest the fruits of his Crimean victory, and with disastrous consequences for France.

For another of the victors, Britain, the consequences of the destruction of the concert were not so quickly apparent or so obvious. Yet the metamorphosis of Russia from a conservative into a revisionist power, and the withdrawal of Russian support from the concert system that opened the way to the unification of Germany and Italy, were eventually to prove catastrophic for Britain as well.

As for that other victor in the Crimean War, the Ottoman Empire, the war that had ostensibly been fought for its preservation actually hastened its disintegration. In their efforts to safeguard the rights of Orthodox Christians and non-Turkish inhabitants of the Ottoman Empire, the European powers had stimulated the aspirations of these peoples to seek complete emancipation from Ottoman rule, and in the years before 1914 almost all the peoples of European Turkey had succeeded in this endeavor. Champions of the principle of national self-determination hailed the establishment of new national states in the Balkans as the most positive and lasting achievement of the Crimean War. Whether or not one agrees with this view, the establishment of these new national states hardly represented a victory for or a strengthening of the Ottoman Empire, and in the end the major beneficiary of the disintegration of that empire, as European statesmen had so long and so correctly feared, was Russia.

Russia was indeed weakened by its defeat in the Crimean War and its activity in the Near East severely hampered, but only very temporarily—two decades is surely not a long but an extremely short time in international affairs. Moreover, Russia was soon to be actually strengthened as a result of its defeat. Immediately after the war, Russian leaders, dismayed by the weaknesses of their country that the war had revealed, undertook sweeping reforms of Russia's political and social institutions in order to overcome the tsarist empire's military and economic backwardness in relation to the West and mobilize its resources more effectively. Just twenty-one years after the Treaty of Paris, Russia was again at war with the Ottoman Empire, and this time it was Russia that won.

Once again Russia stretched the bow too tight and attempted to establish a protectorate over the greater part of the Balkan region. This time, however, Russian ambitions at the expense of the Ottoman Empire were not curbed through war but through the conference diplomacy of a briefly revivified Concert of Europe. This diplomacy was backed up by a tacit threat of war, to be sure, but such a threat is necessarily implicit in any diplomacy designed to control anarchy among sovereign states. At the Congress of Berlin in 1878 Russia was compelled to give up the greater part of its gains in the recent war against Turkey. Russia had been contained quite as effectively, and in terms of human suffering and sacrifice, infinitely more cheaply, by diplomacy than by war, and Russia was once again successfully, albeit reluctantly, grouped.

In the years before 1914 the policy of grouping broke down as the threat of Germany began to loom even larger than that of Russia, and the great powers once again resorted to the politics of confrontation—with results even more disastrous than the most pessimistic of concert statesmen could have envisaged.

After two world wars, in which a primary objective of the Germans was the elimination of the Russian threat to German security, Russia continues to exist as a great power, as it did after the Crimean War, and remains an inescapable fact of international political life. The bolshevik government, the legatee, if only for reasons of geography, of so many traditions of imperial Russian foreign policy, remains in a position to play a waiting game, to take advantage of the mistakes and imbroglios of others in order to advance its interests (or presumed interests) along any point of its vast frontiers.

Until the recent revolutionary events in Eastern Europe, the bolshevik government seemed to have in communism an ideological weapon even more potent than Orthodox Christianity or Slavic brotherhood to extend its influence abroad and undermine the authority of foreign governments. There is reason to hope that the widespread repudiation of communism in Eastern Europe will have dampened or shattered altogether whatever expectations Russian leaders may have had for further significant extentions of Russian influence abroad through communist revolutions, while in the West this same repudiation may serve to calm Western fears about the threat of communism *as such* to Western security. It may even calm fears about Russia itself, although the problems that will inevitably arise from the revolutionary developments in Eastern Europe may yet make for awkward international complications. In dealing with such complications, however (to return to the point made at the beginning of this essay), our joint possession of nuclear weapons must rule out all consideration of a military response.

There remains only the politics of grouping, of convincing the leaders of Russia and of all other great powers, including our own, that the very survival of the human race depends on their ability and willingness to work together to deal with the world's problems.

The politics of grouping are frustrating, for if successful they are endless, involving as they do the constant need to cope with crisis situations. They are politically unrewarding, for to be successful they require political compromises and the avoidance of all appearance of scoring victories at the expense of one's partners in negotiation. They are distasteful, for they frequently require setting aside the moral values of one's own society, conducting negotiations with and making concessions to statesmen whose own moral values one may despise and governments whose political system one may consider abhorrent. They are politically dangerous, for they expose statesmen engaged in negotiation and compromise to charges on the part of political opponents of appeasement, abandonment of principle, and selling out their country's national interests. And they are difficult to conduct, for they require qualities of patience and tenacity, immense powers of restraint, and a brutally realistic sense of political priorities on the part of the statesmen involved. They require the ability to resist the temptation to exploit situations that offer prospects of unilateral gain (or, perhaps even more difficult to resist, prospects of victories on behalf of cherished ideals such as human rights, the proletarian revolution, or Islam) at the cost of disturbing the international order and arousing the fear and hostility of rival powers. They require a realization of the need for great power cooperation in standing firm against all governments or movements, including those sponsored by one's own government, which seem to pose a threat to the international order. But they also require a willingness to allow for changes in that order and make provisions for reform to deal with injustices and grievances that in themselves constitute a threat to the international system. And they require taking into account the interests of, and if necessary making concessions to, recalcitrant governments and movements in order to persuade them that their own interests are best safeguarded and promoted by cooperating with and working through the existing system.

Above all they require the recognition, already so frequently stressed in this essay, that the preservation of peace is not only the most certain way to safeguard their own interests and security, but that it has now become the fundamental prerequisite to human survival.

If this Cautionary Tale of the Crimean experience contributes at all to awakening or reinforcing that recognition, its purpose will have been well served.

Notes

Chapter 1

1. In human affairs there are inevitably exceptions to such broad generalizations. The statesmen of the concert, like all others, could be tempted to abandon such cooperation when they believed it safe and expedient to do so. The British, for example, condoned or encouraged revolutions against Spanish and Portuguese rule in Latin America that did not appear to threaten the general peace of Europe and that opened up opportunities for the British to extend their political and economic influence in the New World.

2. Contemporary explanations for the war were for the most part variations of the well-worn slogans associated with all modern wartime propaganda, which were confidently set forth at the time and almost certainly sincerely believed by most of the leaders of the belligerent powers and the majority of the people in their respective countries. This was a war of civilization against barbarism, of freedom against tyranny, of self-defense against ruthless aggression, of Christianity (whether Orthodox, Protestant, or Roman) or Mohammedanism against the forces of darkness. Many of these simplistic slogans, though not always so crudely expressed, may still be found in some national histories and even in the works of scholars purporting to seek more profound explanations for the war. In such studies we tend to find Europe divided between the liberal and enlightened nations of the West, Britain and France, and the autocratic "Holy Alliance" powers, Austria, Prussia, and Russia. The war thus becomes one between liberalism and autocracy, a war on behalf of the nationalities of Europe and national self-determination against foreign rule and oppression. All historical judgments, of course, are based on a historian's personal values and prejudices, but ideological explanations for the war must be dismissed for the most part as nonsense. So-called liberal states, Britain and France, were major colonial powers, busily engaged in suppressing freedom and national self-determination in every part of the world and fighting on behalf of the preservation of the Ottoman Empire, a Moslem state whose government was hardly a model of modern enlightenment. The government of Britain itself was as yet a tight aristocratic oligarchy, that of France under Napoleon III a military dictatorship. A far better case can be and has been made that this was a war on be-

half of great power economic and strategic interests in the Near East, and so it was, but all these considerations, it seems to me, may be subsumed under the heading of fear of Russia, which was seen as the primary threat to all the interests of the European powers in this area at that time.

3. On this subject, see the interesting recent work of William E. Echard, *Napoleon III and the Concert of Europe* (Baton Rouge, La., 1983), whose arguments, however, I find unconvincing.

4. In a review article on the foreign policy of Palmerston, the British historian Gavin B. Henderson concludes that the most notable thing about him was his appeal to the popular mind. "If any one theme can be detected running through Palmerston's foreign policy, it was a narrow and bigoted desire to enhance Britain's prestige. In this he was little less than a fanatic" (*History* 20 [1938]: 339, 343).

5. John Howes Gleason, *The Genesis of Russophobia in Great Britain. A Study of the Interaction of Policy and Opinion* (Cambridge, Mass., 1950), especially pp. 272–90.

6. Kingsley Martin, *The Triumph of Lord Palmerston. A Study of Public Opinion in England before the Crimean War* (London, 1924). In his review article on Palmerston's foreign policy, cited in n. 4, Gavin B. Henderson writes that many causes for the Crimean War have been adduced, "the deepest cause, however, lay in that simmering cauldron of evil passions in which public opinion is brewed" (p. 34). It was in his deliberate stimulation of public opinion, Henderson believes, that Palmerston's responsibility for the Crimean War principally rests. On this subject, see the views of another British historian, R. W. Seton-Watson, chap. 6, n. 19.

7. Lynn M. Case, *French Opinion on War and Diplomacy during the Second Empire* (Philadelphia, 1954).

8. Waltraud Heindl, *Graf Buol-Schauenstein in St. Petersburg und London (1848–1852). Zur Genesis des Antagonismus zwischen Österreich und Russland* (Vienna, 1970), pp. 17–18, 114, 120.

9. Metternich to Buol, 9 Feb. 1853, 29 March 1854, 3 June 1854. Prince Metternich, *Aus Metternichs nachgelassenen Papieren,* ed. Prince Richard Metternich-Winneburg, 8 vols. (Vienna, 1880–84), 8: 332–34, 355–56, 360–61. Cited in Winfried Baumgart, *The Peace of Paris, 1856. Studies in War, Diplomacy, and Peacemaking* (Santa Barbara, Calif., 1981), p. 40.

10. Robert J. Kerner, "Russia's New Policy in the Near East after the Peace of Adrianople," *Cambridge Historical Journal* 5 (1931): 286–89.

Chapter 2

1. On the question from the sixteenth to the nineteenth century, see F. von Verdy du Vernois, *Die Frage der Heiligen Stätten* (Berlin, 1901), a somewhat skimpy treatment. On the development of the crisis in the mid-nineteenth century, see Harold Temperley, *England and the Near East: The Crimea* (London, 1936), pp. 280–86; Édouard Antoine Thouvenel, *Nicolas Ier et Napoléon III. Les préliminaires de la guerre de Crimée, 1852–1854. D'après les papiers inédits de M. Thouvenel*, ed. Louis Thouvenel (Paris, 1891), pp. xvii–xxxi; good chronological survey, with documents in German translation, can be found in Julius von Jasmund, ed., *Aktenstücke zur orientalischen Frage. Nebst chronologischer Uebersicht*, 3 vols. in 2 (Berlin, 1855–59), 1: i–v, 1–26.

2. According to the census figures of 1844, which are certainly far from reliable, the total population of the Ottoman Empire was approximately 32 million, 15½ million in European Turkey, slightly more than 16 million in Asiatic Turkey. Of these, 17 million were Moslem (4½ million in European, 12½ million in Asiatic Turkey), 13 million were Orthodox Christian (10 million in European, 3 million in Asiatic Turkey), and well under one million were Roman Catholic (640,000 in European, 260,000 in Asiatic Turkey). The empire also included approximately 70,000 Jews (*The Annual Register, or a View of the History and Politics of the Year 1853* [London, 1854], pp. 263–64). The percentage of Orthodox Christians in the empire in the figures given by Roderic H. Davison, a foremost American authority on Ottoman history, is considerably lower (one-sixth rather than one-third of the total), but the higher estimate was that generally accepted by contemporaries (*Reform in the Ottoman Empire, 1856–1876* [Princeton, N.J., 1963], pp. 61–62; 119, n. 17; 414–15).

3. In the nineteenth century, the tyranny of the Greek clergy over the non-Greek (largely Slavic) membership of the Orthodox church was to lead to demands on the part of the non-Greeks for their own *millets;* hence the later identification of the *millets* as national rather than religious organizations. The Roman Catholic population in the empire had always been so small that it had never been formally recognized as a *millet,* but in 1847, under pressure from the pope and the Catholic powers of Europe, the Roman Catholics too were given their own *millet.*

4. *Within* the Orthodox church, the authority of the patriarch of Constantinople was anything but absolute, and the church was riven by internecine quarrels and doctrinal disputes. These internal divisions were exacerbated by the church's political position within the Ottoman

Empire. The patriarch was obliged to pay heavily for confirmation in office, he in turn exacted payments from his bishops, and so on through the hierarchy to the parish clergy and their congregations. It was thus in the financial interests of the Turks to change patriarchs as frequently as possible. Of the 159 patriarchs who held office between the fifteenth and twentieth centuries, 132 were driven from office or forced to abdicate, several suffered violent deaths, and only 21 died natural deaths while in office. The rapid turnover among patriarchs and the rivalry for the succession contributed to the intrigue and infighting among subordinate leaders in the church hierarchy, which was usually divided into bitterly hostile factions. On the entire question of the Orthodox church under Turkish rule, see the excellent brief discussion by Timothy Ware, *The Orthodox Church* (Baltimore, 1963), pp. 96–111, and his more detailed monograph *Eustratios Argenti. A Study of the Greek Church under Turkish Rule* (Oxford, 1964).

5. Luc Monnier, *Étude sur les origines de la guerre de Crimée* (Geneva, 1977), pp. 22–23. While stressing Napoleon's idealistic goals (the emancipation of the nationalities of Europe), Monnier concedes that his primary objective was the disruption of the international system established after the Napoleonic Wars (pp. 25–26).

6. Anne Pottinger Saab, *The Origins of the Crimean Alliance* (Charlottesville, Va., 1977), pp. 10–13; Monnier, *Étude*, pp. 33–37; Thouvenel, *Nicolas Ier et Napoléon III*, pp. 1–87; Temperley, *England and the Near East*, pp. 287–97; John Shelton Curtiss, *Russia's Crimean War* (Durham, N.C., 1979), pp. 43–47.

7. Thouvenel, French minister to Munich in 1851 and later director of the political affairs department in the ministry of foreign affairs, wrote to an official of the French foreign ministry on 9 December 1851: "What is the significance of this quarrel stirred up in Constantinople over the Holy Places? . . . I know the Orient and I can assure you that Russia will not give in. For her it is a question of life and death and it is to be hoped that one knows this full well in Paris in case one wishes to push the affair to the limit." Thouvenel, *Nicholas Ier et Napoléon III*, pp. 1–2. In an analysis of the dispute over the Holy Places written in January 1853, Buol, the Austrian foreign minister, wrote that if Napoleon refused to recognize the limits of concessions he could secure from the Turks without offending Russia, then Austria would have to conclude that France wanted to promote a dispute between Russia and Turkey. Buol to Leiningen, 22 Jan. 1853. *Akten zur Geschichte des Krimkriegs. Series 1. Österreichische Akten zur Geschichte des Krimkriegs*, ed. Winfried Baumgart, Ana María Schop Soler, and Werner Zürrer. 3 vols. (Vienna, 1979–80), 1:1, #10, pp. 67–70. (Hereafter cited as *Akten*.)

8. As early as January 1850, Napoleon's foreign minister asked the French ambassador to Constantinople whether the Ottoman government would find it desirable to see an increase in French influence in the Near East "to counterbalance the always growing [influence] of Russia." Saab, *Origins*, p. 10.

9. A. M. Zaionchkovskii, *Vostochnaia Voina*, 2 vols. (St. Petersburg, 1903–13), with a two-volume appendix of documents. I have used only the appendix volumes (cited hereafter as Zaionchkovskii), vol. 1, #98, pp. 357–58; Curtiss, *Russia's Crimean War*, p. 62.

10. Memoranda of 25 Dec. 1852 and 1 Jan. 1853. Zaionchkovskii, vol. 1, #96, 97, pp. 351–57.

11. Ibid., vol. 1, #105, pp. 371–74.

12. Ibid., vol. 1, pp. 378–81; Curtiss, *Russia's Crimean War*, p. 90.

13. Austrian documents in *Akten*, 1:1, pp. 59ff.; excellent discussions in Saab, *Origins*, pp. 17–22; Monnier, *Étude*, pp. 53–56; Bernhard Unckel, *Österreich und der Krimkrieg. Studien zur Politik der Donaumonarchie in den Jahren 1852–1856* (Lübeck, 1969), pp. 57–80; and the excellent work of Paul W. Schroeder, *Austria, Great Britain, and the Crimean War. The Destruction of the European Concert* (Ithaca, N.Y., 1972), pp. 24–28.

14. Zaionchkovskii, vol. 1, #103, pp. 368–69; Unckel, *Österreich*, p. 87.

15. Zaionchkovskii, vol. 1, pp. 582–84.

16. Curtiss, *Russia's Crimean War*, pp. 81–82.

17. 28–29 May 1853, communicated to Gorchakov, 9 June 1853. Zaionchkovskii, vol. 1, 603–4.

18. Seymour's reports on his conversations with the tsar are printed in *British Sessional Papers*, House of Commons, 1854, vol. 71, pt. 5. It should be noted that at the time the tsar decided to discuss the Eastern Question with Seymour, the Derby government was still in office, and the tsar did not yet know that Aberdeen would succeed him as prime minister. See Gavin B. Henderson, *Crimean War Diplomacy and Other Historical Essays* (Glasgow, 1947), pp. 5–6.

19. Conversations of 9 and 14 Jan. 1853, reported by Seymour to Russell, 11 and 22 Jan. 1853. *British Sessional Papers*, 1854, vol. 71, pt. 5, pp. 1–6.

20. Seymour to Russell, 12 Jan. 1853. *The Later Correspondence of Lord John Russell, 1840–1878*, ed. G. P. Gooch, 2 vols. (London, 1925), 2:145.

21. Seymour to Russell, 22 Jan. 1853. *British Sessional Papers*, 1854, vol. 71, pt. 5, pp. 3–6.

22. Conversation of 21 Feb. 1853, reported by Seymour to Russell, 22 Jan. 1853. Ibid., pp. 9–12.

23. Memorandum of 5 March 1853. Zaionchkovskii, vol. 1, #100, pp. 362–65.

24. Russell to Clarendon, 20 March 1853. Spencer Walpole, *The Life of Lord John Russell*, 2 vols. (London, 1889), 2:181.

25. Henderson, *Crimean War Diplomacy*, pp. 10–14.

26. Brunnow to Nesselrode, 21 Feb. 1853. Zaionchkovskii, vol. 1, #102, pp. 367–68.

Chapter 3

1. Memoranda of 25 Dec. 1852 and 1 Jan. 1853. Zaionchkovskii, vol. 1, #96, 97, pp. 351–57. Prior to the Menshikov mission, Russia had been represented in Constantinople by a *chargé d'affaires* (Alexander Petrovich Ozerov) who would have lacked the requisite rank and prestige to conduct this kind of diplomatic campaign.

2. Monnier, *Étude*, chap. 4; Saab, *Origins*, chap. 2; Curtiss, *Russia's Crimean War*, chap. 5.

3. All the documents of instruction as well as the draft of a Russo-Turkish convention are printed in Zaionchkovskii, vol. 1, #105–12, pp. 371–87.

4. Theodor Schiemann, *Geschichte Russlands unter Kaiser Nikolaus I*, 4 vols. (Berlin, 1914–19), 4:281–85.

5. Text in Zaionchkovskii, vol. 1, #110, pp. 382–85.

6. French texts in Gabriel Noradounghian, ed. *Recueil d'actes internationaux de l'empire Ottoman*, 4 vols. in 2 (Paris, 1897–1902), 1:319–34; 2:166–73.

7. Article 17, not referred to by the Russians in their draft treaty, dealt with the rights of Christians in the Aegean Islands still under Turkish rule. Article 8, to which the draft treaty did refer, dealt with the rights of Russian pilgrims to the Holy Places.

8. Noradounghian, *Recueil*, 2:86–92.

9. That the Russian government assumed the existence of such rights can be seen from the fact that already in November 1852, in the course of the crisis over the Holy Places, the Russian envoy to Constantinople, Ozerov, had claimed Russia's right to protect the Orthodox religion throughout the Ottoman Empire on the basis of the Treaty of Kutchuk-Kainardji.

10. There is no mention of a lifetime appointment for the patriarchs in any previous treaties, but it is understandable that the Russians should have desired specific provisions to safeguard the patriarchs, whose positions were in constant jeopardy. See chap. 2, n. 4.

11. George Douglas Campbell, Eighth Duke of Argyll, *Autobiography and Memoirs*, ed. Dowager Duchess of Argyll, 2 vols. (London, 1906), 1:447–49.

12. Klezl (Austrian secretary of legation) to Buol, 3 March 1853. *Akten*, vol. 1:1, #34, pp. 109–10; Curtiss, *Russia's Crimean War*, pp. 85, 93; Saab, *Origins*, p. 28; Schiemann, *Geschichte Russlands*, 4: 285–86.

13. Zaionchkovskii, vol. 1, #113, pp. 387–91.

14. The draft treaty presented on March 22 has not been reprinted, but one must assume that it was the draft included with Menshikov's original instructions of 9 Feb. 1853. See chap. 3, n. 5.

15. Zaionchkovskii, vol. 1, #115, 119, pp. 392–93, 397–98.

16. Menshikov to Nesselrode, 10 Apr. 1853. Zaionchkovskii, vol. 1, #121, pp. 399–401; Saab, *Origins*, pp. 36–37; Curtiss, *Russia's Crimean War*, p. 118.

17. Saab, *Origins*, p. 37; Temperley, *England and the Near East*, pp. 317–18.

18. Jean Gilbert Victor Fialin, duc de Persigny, *Mémoires du Duc de Persigny publiés avec des documents inédits* (Paris, 1896), pp. 226–35; Monnier, *Étude*, p. 59.

19. Clarendon to Cowley, 29 March 1853. *British Sessional Papers*, 1854, vol. 71, pt. 1, p. 98.

20. Stanley Lane-Poole, *The Life of the Right Honourable Stratford Canning, Viscount Stratford de Redcliffe. From his Memoirs and Private and Official Papers*, 2 vols. (London, 1888), 2:351–53; E. F. Malcolm-Smith, *The Life of Stratford Canning (Lord Stratford de Redcliffe)* (London, 1933), pp. 241–46; Martin, *Triumph of Lord Palmerston*, pp. 96ff.; Curtiss, *Russia's Crimean War*, pp. 126–27; Saab, *Origins*, pp. 4, 35–36.

21. J. B. Conacher, *The Aberdeen Coalition, 1852–1855. A Study in Mid-Nineteenth-Century Party Politics* (Cambridge, 1968), p. 144; Herbert Maxwell, *The Life and Letters of George William Frederick, Fourth Earl of Clarendon*, 2 vols. (London, 1913), 2:25.

22. 25 Feb. 1853. Harold Temperley and Lillian Penson, eds., *Foundations of British Foreign Policy* (Cambridge, 1938), pp. 138–44; Lane-Poole, *Stratford*, 2:234.

23. Clarendon to Seymour, 5 April 1853. Curtiss, *Russia's Crimean War*, pp. 112–13.

24. 4 April 1853. Lane-Poole, *Stratford*, 2:244–45.

25. Ibid., 2:249, 251–52, 256.

26. Ibid., 2:255–57; Klezl to Buol, 18 April 1853. *Akten*, vol 1:1, #47, pp. 133–35.

27. Menshikov to Nesselrode, 10 April 1853, reporting his conversation with Stratford of 6 April. Zaionchkovskii, vol. 2, #120, pp. 398–99.

28. Menshikov to Nesselrode, 10 April 1853. Zaionchkovskii, vol. 1,

#121, pp. 399–401; Saab, *Origins*, pp. 36–37; Curtiss, *Russia's Crimean War*, p. 118.

29. Nesselrode to Menshikov, 23 April 1853. Zaionchkovskii, vol. 1, #124, pp. 404–5.

30. Ibid., vol. 1, #123, pp. 402–3; Curtiss, *Russia's Crimean War*, p. 119; Lane-Poole, *Stratford*, 2:257.

31. Lane-Poole, *Stratford*, 2:261.

32. Menshikov to Nesselrode, 26 April 1853. Zaionchkovskii, vol. 1, #125, pp. 404–7.

33. Ibid., vol. 1, #128–29, pp. 411–12; Monnier, *Étude*, p. 67; Curtiss, *Russia's Crimean War*, p. 120.

34. Zaionchkovskii, vol. 1, #126–27, pp. 407–10; Menshikov to Nesselrode, 6 May 1853. Zaionchkovskii, vol. 1, #131, pp. 413–15; Curtiss, *Russia's Crimean War*, pp. 120–22.

35. Lane-Poole, *Stratford*, 2:261–65; French translation of Turkish note, Zaionchkovskii, vol. 1, #135, pp. 417–18.

36. Menshikov to Nesselrode. Zaionchkovskii, vol. 1, #139, p. 423.

37. Menshikov to Rifaat, 11 May 1853; Rifaat to Menshikov, 12 May 1853. Ibid., vol. 1, #133, 136, 139, pp. 416, 418–19, 423–25.

38. Menshikov to Reshid, 10 May 1853. Ibid., vol. 1, #134, 138, pp. 416–17, 421–22.

39. Menshikov reports of 16 May 1853. Ibid., vol. 1, #138–39, 141, pp. 420–27; Saab, *Origins*, pp. 39–40; Curtiss, *Russia's Crimean War*, pp. 128–29; Thouvenel, director of the political department of the French foreign ministry, became ambassador to Constantinople in mid-1855. His account of events of May 1853 is thoroughly unreliable. *Nicolas Ier et Napoléon III*, p. 141.

40. Menshikov to Reshid, 15 May 1853; to Nesselrode, 16 May 1853. Zaionchkovskii, vol. 1, #139–40, pp. 423–26.

41. Menshikov report to Nesselrode, 21 May 1853; his note to the Ottoman government, 18 May 1853. Ibid., vol. 1, #142, 145, pp. 428–29, 432–33; Curtiss, *Russia's Crimean War*, p. 133; Saab, *Origins*, pp. 46–47.

42. Lane-Poole, *Stratford*, 2:268–69; Curtiss, *Russia's Crimean War*, p. 135.

43. Zaionchkovskii, vol. 1, #146, pp. 433–34.

44. Ibid., vol. 1, #147, pp. 434–36.

45. This is the opinion of Curtiss, *Russia's Crimean War*, pp. 136–37. Stratford's biographer, Lane-Poole, had a very different view. "What was to be gained by this document, which reiterated the most objectionable parts of the preceding Notes, it is hard to see" (*Stratford*, 2:269). Saab agrees with Lane-Poole that this paragraph reiterated Russia's claim to a protectorate (*Origins*, p. 48).

46. Harold Temperley, "Stratford de Redcliffe and the Origins of the Crimean War," *English Historical Review* 48 (1933):611.

47. Lane-Poole, *Stratford*, 2:270.

48. Zaionchkovskii, vol. 1, #143–44, 146, 148, pp. 429–31, 433–34, 436; Saab, *Origins,* pp. 48–49; Lane-Poole, *Stratford,* 2:271.

49. Buol to Hübner and Colloredo, 14 June 1853. *Akten,* vol. 1:1, #75, p. 189.

50. 2 April 1853. F. de Martens, *Recueil de traités et conventions conclus par la Russie avec les puissances étragères,* 15 vols. (St. Petersburg, 1874–1906), 12:311.

Chapter 4

1. Lane-Poole, *Stratford,* 2:271, 274.

2. 22 May 1853. Curtiss, *Russia's Crimean War,* p. 146.

3. 22 May 1853. Evelyn Ashley, *The Life and Correspondence of Henry John Temple Viscount Palmerston,* 2 vols. (London, 1879), 2:273.

4. Zaionchkovskii, vol. 1, #152, pp. 441–42; Saab, *Origins,* p. 51; Curtiss, *Russia's Crimean War,* p. 173; Monnier, *Étude,* p. 79.

5. The tsar to Paskevich, 28 May 1853. Schiemann, *Geschichte Russlands,* 4:292.

6. Letter of 30 May 1853. Unckel, *Österreich,* p. 89.

7. Brunnow to Nesselrode, 1 June 1853. Martens, *Recueil,* 12:325–26.

8. Conacher, *Aberdeen Coalition,* pp. 151–52; Saab, *Origins,* pp. 53–54; Curtiss, *Russia's Crimean War,* p. 146.

9. Arthur Hamilton Gordon, Lord Stanmore, *Sidney Herbert, Lord Herbert of Lea. A Memoir,* 2 vols. (London, 1906), 1:194; Maxwell, *Clarendon,* 2:25. Clarendon added: "It may do some good to ourselves, which should not be our least consideration." For Aberdeen's sober and thoughtful reply, see Arthur Hamilton Gordon (Lord Stanmore), *The Earl of Aberdeen* (New York, 1893), pp. 223–24.

10. Saab, *Origins,* pp. 53–54.

11. 2 June 1853. Walewski Papers, cited in Monnier, *Étude,* pp. 77–78. Walewski expressed similar satisfaction to the British. *The Greville Memoirs, 1814–1860,* ed. Lytton Strachey and Roger Fulford, 8 vols. (London, 1938) 6:428.

12. Reshid to Nesselrode, 16 June 1853. Zaionchkovskii, vol. 1, #153, pp. 443–44. Monnier, *Étude,* p. 82; Schiemann, *Geschichte Russlands,* 4:294. According to Lane-Poole (*Stratford,* 2:272), Reshid's temperate and reasonable reply to Nesselrode's "arrogant" letter of 31 May 1853 was written under the guidance of Stratford.

13. Nicholas to Francis Joseph, 2 July 1853. Zaionchkovskii, vol. 2, #110, pp. 243–44.

14. Monnier, *Étude,* p. 83; Curtiss, *Russia's Crimean War,* p. 148.

Chapter 5

1. Buol to Prokesch, 1 July 1853. *Akten,* vol. 1:1, #98, p. 233.

2. Stratford's biographer, Lane-Poole, treats these proposals as something of a farce. He has summarized eleven of them on the basis of the evidence available to him (*Stratford,* 2:278, n. 1).

3. Edmond Bapst, *Les origines de la guerre de Crimée. La France et la Russie de 1848 à 1854* (Paris, 1912), pp. 401–2; p. 418, n. 1; Saab, *Origins,* pp. 55ff.; and especially Schroeder, *Austria,* chap. 3.

4. Castelbajac to Napoleon III, 10 June 1853. Monnier, *Étude,* p. 80; Bapst, *Origines,* pp. 386, 390–94, 410.

5. Buol to Hübner and Colloredo, 14 June 1853. *Akten,* vol. 1:1, pp. 186–88.

6. Buol to Bruck, 31 May and 9 June 1853. *Akten,* vol. 1:1, #61, 69, 70, pp. 163–66, 180–82. The official title of the Austrian emissary to Constantinople was *internuntius,* otherwise the title of papal representatives to foreign courts.

7. Buol to Bruck, 31 May, 6 and 9 June, 4 July 1853; Buol to Hübner and Colloredo, 14 June 1853. *Akten,* vol. 1:1, #61, 65, 70, 74, 101, pp. 163–66, 173–74, 181–82, 186–88, 237–39.

8. See chap. 4, n. 12.

9. Bruck to Buol, 23 and 27 June 1853. *Akten,* vol. 1:1, #89, 91, pp. 214–16, 218–19; Curtiss, *Russia's Crimean War,* p. 153; Lane-Poole, *Stratford,* 2:280–81.

10. Stratford to Clarendon, 29 June 1853. Lane-Poole, *Stratford,* 2:280. Bruck, far from being displeased by the activity of Stratford, appears to have been convinced of Stratford's desire to mediate the dispute and approved his plan for a fusion of the latest notes of Menshikov (of 20 May) and Reshid (of 16 June). Bruck to Buol, 27 June 1853. *Akten,* vol. 1:1, #91, pp. 218–19.

11. Stratford to Clarendon, 24, 25, 29 June 1853. Lane-Poole, *Stratford,* 2:280–81.

12. Monnier, Étude, p. 82; Curtiss, *Russia's Crimean War,* p. 148; Schroeder, *Austria,* p. 43; Bapst, *Origines,* p. 425; Vernon John Puryear, *England, Russia and the Straits Question, 1844–1856* (Berkeley, Calif., 1931), p. 281, n. 91.

13. Lane-Poole, *Stratford,* 2:283–84. Stratford informed Clarendon on 23 July that Reshid was also vehemently opposed to the compromise proposals subsequently sent to Constantinople by the French and

British governments, and as Stratford himself did not press them on the Turkish government, these proposals were not acted upon either. Ibid., 2:287; Buol to Bruck, 18 July 1853; Buol to Colloredo, Hübner and Thun, 23 July 1853. *Akten*, vol. 1:1, #115, 122, pp. 256–57, 268.

14. Both letters dated 9 July 1853. Lane-Poole, *Stratford*, 2:282–83.

15. Ibid., 2:283–85; Saab, *Origins*, pp. 57–58.

16. Bruck to Buol, 18 July 1853. *Akten*, vol. 1:1, #118, pp. 260–62; Schroeder, *Austria*, p. 57. On the problem of the conduct of Austrian policy in Constantinople at this time, see Paul W. Schroeder, "Bruck versus Buol. The Dispute over Austrian Eastern Policy, 1853–1855," *Journal of Modern History*, 40 (1968):193–217.

17. 23 July 1853. Lane-Poole, *Stratford*, 2:285–87; Saab, *Origins*, pp. 58–59.

18. On 30 June the Austrian ambassador to Britain reported to Buol that the French government intended to send the Austrian government a draft note to take the place of the Menshikov note rejected by the Porte; the Austrian government should send this French note to St. Petersburg as though it had originated in Vienna and persuade Russia to accept it. This policy had been resolved upon the previous day in agreement with England. The draft note was to be based on a compromise between the Menshikov and Turkish proposals. They (presumably the British and French governments) were certain of the agreement of the Porte. Colloredo to Buol, 30 June 1853. *Akten*, vol. 1:1, #97, pp. 232–33; Bapst, *Origines*, pp. 415–17 and appendix 3, pp. 495–96.

19. Joseph Alexander von Hübner, *Neuf ans de souvenirs d'un ambassadeur d'Autriche à Paris sous le Second Empire, 1851–1859*, ed. Alexander von Hübner, 2 vols. (Paris, 1904), 1:142; Monnier, *Étude*, pp. 81–83; Curtiss, *Russia's Crimean War*, p. 155; Bapst, *Origines*, pp. 415–17; Schiemann, *Geschichte Russlands*, 4:295.

20. Already on 14 July, because negotiations in Constantinople did not seem to be making any progress, Buol had informed the representatives of the great powers in Vienna of his intention to convene a mediation conference in the Austrian capital. The sequence of events is described in Hübner's dispatch to Buol, 25 July 1853. *Akten*, vol. 1:1, #124, pp. 270–71. Hübner suggests clearly that Drouyn, the French foreign minister, did not trust his own emissary to Vienna, Bourqueney, for he asked the Austrian government to send him texts of notes prepared at the conference to verify those sent by Bourqueney.

21. Temperley, "Stratford," *English Historical Review* 49 (1934): 267–68; Bapst, *Origines*, p. 429; Buol to Bruck, 30 July 1853. *Akten*, vol. 1:1, pp. 276–77.

22. Zaionchkovskii, vol. 2, #15, 16, pp. 52–55; *Akten*, vol. 1:1,

#130, 136, pp. 280–81, 289; Saab, *Origins,* pp. 55–61; Unckel, *Österreich,* pp. 96–99; Schroeder, *Austria,* pp. 51–57; Curtiss, *Russia's Crimean War,* pp. 155–56.

23. Buol instructed Bruck to use every conceivable means to put pressure on the Porte, and he informed him that the representatives of Britain, France, and Prussia would also receive the *strictest* orders (Buol's emphasis) to support its acceptance in Constantinople. *Akten,* vol. 1:1, #132, 133, pp. 282–86. For a description of Stratford's behavior, see Lane-Poole, *Stratford,* 2:290–91, and the comments of Schroeder, *Austria,* pp. 57–59.

24. Stratford to Clarendon, 20 Aug. 1853. Lane-Poole, *Stratford,* 2:295.

25. Cowley to Clarendon, 29 Aug. 1853. Maxwell, *Clarendon,* 2: 18–19. Clarendon wrote Lord John Russell on 25 August that Britain's difficulties would now be more Turkish than Russian. "I have all along felt that Stratford would allow of no plan of settlement that did not originate with himself" (ibid., 2:18).

26. Bruck to Buol, 11 Aug. 1853. *Akten,* vol. 1:1, #144, pp. 298–99.

27. Lane-Poole, *Stratford,* 2:292.

28. Temperley, "Stratford," *English Historical Review* 49 (1934): 272. Because Egypt was a vassal state of the Ottoman Empire, an Egyptian fleet could pass through the Dardanelles without violating the Straits Convention of 1841, which prohibited the entry of foreign warships into the Turkish Straits while the Ottoman Empire was at peace.

29. Saab, *Origins,* pp. 70–75.

30. Lane-Poole, *Stratford,* 2:292–93.

31. Zaionchkovskii, vol. 2, #20, pp. 60–63; Curtiss, *Russia's Crimean War,* pp. 160–61; Monnier, *Étude,* p. 88; Saab, *Origins,* 65.

32. Buol to Bruck, 29 Aug. and 13 Sept. 1853. *Akten,* vol. 1:1, #161, pp. 319–20; Unckel, *Österreich,* p. 100.

33. Maxwell, *Clarendon,* vol. 2, pp. 17–18.

34. Aberdeen to Russell, 30 Aug. 1853. Russell, *Later Correspondence,* 2:152.

35. Clarendon to Russell, 27 Aug. 1853. Ibid., 2:151–52.

36. Greville, *Memoirs,* 4:440, 445.

37. Clarendon to Herbert, 11 Sept. 1853. The second part of the quotation was written some time later. Stanmore, *Herbert,* 1:197, n. 1. The British historian Harold Temperley insists that throughout the crisis Stratford acted correctly and carried out the instructions of his government. But to emphasize the perspicacity of Stratford, he cites an article written by Clarendon in 1863 who acknowledged that Russia's subsequent interpretation of the Vienna Note showed that Stratford

had been right. "This is a very remarkable admission," Temperley says, "for Clarendon confesses that Stratford was right in thus disobeying"—whereby Temperley seems to make the even more remarkable admission that Stratford did in fact disobey ("Stratford," *English Historical Review* 49 [1934]:272). Another British historian, R. W. Seton-Watson, has concluded that the evidence about Stratford's desire for war is overwhelming, and he believes it says much about the uncritical character of historical writing on British foreign policy that he should so long have been given the benefit of the doubt. *Britain in Europe, 1789–1914. A Survey of Foreign Policy* (Cambridge, 1937), p. 318.

38. Monnier, *Étude*, p. 90; Bapst, *Origines*, pp. 437–38.

39. Zaionchkovskii, vol. 2, #19, pp. 57–60; Bapst, *Origines*, pp. 438–40; Unckel, *Österreich*, p. 100; Monnier, *Étude*, pp. 93–94; Curtiss, *Russia's Crimean War*, pp. 163–64; Saab, *Origins*, p. 80.

40. Zaionchkovskii, vol. 2, #18, pp. 55–57; Bapst, *Origines*, pp. 497–500; Colloredo to Buol, 20 Sept. 1853. *Akten*, vol. 1:1, #170, pp. 334–36.

41. Monnier, *Étude*, pp. 93–109; Schroeder, *Austria*, p. 68.

42. Buol to Bruck, 13 and 19 Sept. 1853. *Akten*, vol. 1:1, #161, 167, 168, pp. 319–20, 328–30; Zaionchkovskii, vol. 2, #21, 112, pp. 65, 246.

43. Temperley, *Foundations*, pp. 145–52; Bapst, *Origines*, p. 440; Colloredo to Buol, 20 Sept. 1853; Hübner to Buol, 22 Sept. 1853. *Akten*, vol. 1:1, #170, 172, pp. 334–37.

44. Fonton (in Vienna) to Nesselrode, 23 Sept. 1853. Zaionchkovskii, vol. 2, #111, pp. 244–45; Schroeder, *Austria*, p. 68.

45. Clarendon to Cowley, 6 Sept. 1853. Schroeder, *Austria*, pp. 63, 68.

46. Conacher, *Aberdeen Coalition*, p. 180.

47. Schroeder, *Austria*, pp. 63–64.

48. Aberdeen to Russell, 16 Sept. 1853. Walpole, *Russell*, vol. 2, p. 188.

49. *Akten*, vol. 1:1, #161, 167, 168, pp. 319–20, 328–30; Zaionchkovskii, vol. 2, #111, pp. 244–45.

50. Stratford wrote to his wife on 31 August: "The Turks I think are bent on *war, unless their amendments are accepted,* and I fear they cannot help themselves with respect to their army and nation, now thoroughly roused though hitherto well behaved." Lane-Poole, *Stratford*, 2:299–300; Saab, *Origins*, pp. 83–85; Bapst, *Origines*, p. 441 and n. 1, p. 442; Monnier, *Étude*, pp. 92–95; Curtiss, *Russia's Crimean War*, p. 176; Bruck to Buol, 12 Sept. 1853. *Akten*, vol. 1:1, #160, pp. 316–18.

51. Puryear, *England*, pp. 293–95, nn. 146–47; Stratford to Claren-

don, 15 Sept. 1853. Ibid., pp. 445–46. A biographer of Napoleon III, T.A.B. Cowley, believes the emperor urged that the Allied fleets be sent to Constantinople in the interests of peace, convinced that this gesture would awe the Turkish war party and provide a salutary reminder to an overbearing Russia. Concerning Stratford's objection to bringing up the entire British fleet, Cowley cites the opinion of the British historian Harold Temperley that Stratford was also acting in the interests of peace because *he* believed that "to summon the fleet would be to make the Turkish war-party the masters of the situation in Constantinople." Cowley himself makes the interesting case that the reason for Stratford's delay in summoning the fleet was the weather. From July to September the prevailing winds in the Turkish Straits were from the northeast, accompanied by extremely difficult tides and eddies. In October, however, there was a far greater chance of southerly winds that would have facilitated the passage of sailing vessels through the Straits. As the British had a greater proportion of sailing (as opposed to steam) vessels than the French, Stratford wished to postpone their journey to Constantinople until they could expect more favorable winds and thus minimize the risk of their making a poor showing vis-à-vis the French. "Given Stratford's preoccupation with Britain's prestige and the inordinate importance attached by the Turks to outward symbols of power, it was not surprising that he waited until the prevailing wind veered to a southerly direction, which was apparently rather later than usual that year." *Democratic Despot: A Life of Napoleon III* (London, 1961), pp. 385–89. Cowley's information about the winds and tides in the Straits came from *The Black Sea Pilot.* Although it is possible that Stratford, with his long experience in Constantinople, took such calculations into account, I have found no evidence that he did so.

52. Monnier, *Étude,* p. 95; Bapst, *Origines,* p. 441.

53. Puryear, *England,* p. 295; Schroeder, *Austria,* p. 73; Bapst, *Origines,* p. 442; Temperley, *Foundations,* pp. 145–52.

54. Conacher, *Aberdeen Coalition,* p. 188.

55. Temperley, "Stratford," *English Historical Review* 49 (1934): 276.

56. Conacher, *Aberdeen Coalition,* p. 192, n. 1; Schroeder, *Austria,* pp. 77–82; Curtiss, *Russia's Crimean War,* pp. 174, 182–83.

57. *Akten,* vol. 1:1, #175, 176, pp. 342–45.

58. Schroeder, *Austria,* pp. 77–82; Curtiss, *Russia's Crimean War,* pp. 190–96; Bapst, *Origines,* pp. 446, 451.

59. Conacher, *Aberdeen Coalition,* p. 192; Schroeder, *Austria,* p. 81.

60. Conacher, *Aberdeen Coalition,* p. 197.

61. Edward Hertslet, ed., *Map of Europe by Treaty,* 4 vols. (London, 1875–91), vol. 2, pp. 1171–76.

62. Puryear, *England,* p. 298; Saab, *Origins,* p. 88; Monnier, *Étude,* p. 95; Curtiss, *Russia's Crimean War,* p. 183.

63. Saab, *Origins,* p. 91.

64. Puryear, *England,* p. 300; Saab, *Origins,* pp. 88–92; Lane-Poole, *Stratford,* 2:300.

65. 4 Oct. 1853. J. L. Herkless, "Stratford, the Cabinet, and the Outbreak of the Crimean War," *Historical Journal* 28 (1975):520.

66. Jasper Ridley, *Lord Palmerston* (London, 1970), p. 417.

67. Hertslet, *Map of Europe,* 2:1177; Lane-Poole, *Stratford,* 2:301; Monnier, *Étude,* p. 111; Curtiss, *Russia's Crimean War,* pp. 185, 203.

Chapter 6

1. Conacher, *Aberdeen Coalition,* pp. 195–96. Aberdeen prepared a shorter account of this meeting for the queen. *The Letters of Queen Victoria. A Selection from Her Majesty's Correspondence between the Years 1837 and 1861,* ed. A. C. Benson and Viscount Esher, 3 vols. (London, 1907), 2:551–52, where part of the letter to Graham is printed in a footnote.

2. Memorandum of 10 Oct. 1853. Victoria, *Letters,* 2:552–54.

3. Ibid., 2:554–55.

4. Memorandum of 16 Oct 1853. Ibid., 2:555–58.

5. Gordon, *Aberdeen,* pp. 232–33.

6. Victoria, *Letters,* 2:560–61.

7. Maxwell, *Clarendon,* 2:29.

8. Ashley, *Palmerston,* 2:285–87.

9. Martens, *Recueil,* 12:330–31.

10. Ibid., 12:343–45; Zaionchkovskii, vol. 2, #139, pp. 321–22.

11. Martens, *Recueil,* 12:345–47; Zaionchkovskii, vol. 2, #140, pp. 322–26.

12. Buol to Nesselrode, 6 Oct. 1853. Zaionchkovskii, vol. 2, #113, pp. 248–49; *Akten,* vol. 1:1, #184, pp. 357–58; Schroeder, *Austria,* p. 86.

13. Zaionchkovskii, vol. 2, #114, pp. 249–50; *Akten,* vol. 1:1, #200, 201, pp. 381–83.

14. 16 Nov. 1853. Conacher, *Aberdeen Coalition,* pp. 210–11.

15. Buol to Colloredo and Hübner, 21 Nov. 1853; Buol to Colloredo, 29 Nov. 1853; Buol to Bruck, 5 Dec. 1853. *Akten,* vol. 1:1, #239, 248, 249, pp. 435, 450–53; Zaionchkovskii, vol. 2, #116, pp. 252–53; Conacher, *Aberdeen Coalition,* p. 213; Schroeder, *Austria,* pp. 104–14; Monnier, *Étude,* pp. 124–25.

16. Zaionchkovskii, vol. 2, p. 219.

17. According to Russian sources, the Turkish squadron consisted of seven frigates, one sloop, one steamer, and five transports (Menshikov

to Gorchakov, 8 Dec. 1853). Figures on Turkish losses from Allied sources, which use slightly different terms to describe the Turkish vessels, are almost identical. Allied as well as Russian sources agree that it was the Turks who fired first, just as the Russian ships had taken up their battle positions. The Turks reported losses of about four thousand men. One Turkish vessel, the steamer, escaped and brought the news of the Sinope disaster to Constantinople (*Annual Register . . . 1854,* pp. 488–90). Although these figures on the size of the Turkish fleet and Turkish losses were given out shortly after the Sinope incident, the popular press grossly exaggerated the extent of the disaster, and a number of historians have accepted these inflated figures.

18. Victoria, *Letters,* 2:564–65. This was also the opinion of Prince Albert. Theodore Martin, *The Life of His Royal Highness the Prince Consort,* 5 vols. (London, 1875–80), 2:532–33; Stanmore, *Herbert,* 1:198. Gordon, *Aberdeen,* pp. 242–43. The British historian, R. W. Seton-Watson, writing in 1937, says about the Battle of Sinope: "The two countries had been at war for over a month, and if the Turks were justified in attacking and defeating the Russians by land on the Danube, the Russians were equally justified in retaliating by sea. Nor can there be much doubt that the Turks, though of course not prepared for such condign punishment, had deliberately aimed at provoking a conflict between Russia and the Allies" (*Britain in Europe,* p. 320). Also Saab, *Origins,* pp. 113ff., 127; Curtiss, *Russia's Crimean War,* pp. 206–7; Schroeder, *Austria,* pp. 116–20.

19. Martin, *Triumph of Lord Palmerston,* pp. 148ff.; Gordon, *Aberdeen,* p. 255. On this subject Seton-Watson writes: "If ever a war was made by an ill-informed but ardent public opinion against the better judgment of a divided Government, it was the Crimean War. It is the classic disproof of the view that peoples are always pacific and only the statesmen or financiers warlike. . . . [The Crimean War] will remain beyond all question as the classical proof that in foreign policy the voice of the people is not necessarily the voice of God, and that an ill-informed and excitable public opinion can plunge a country into a war no less effectually than a dictator or a crowned autocrat" (*Britain in Europe,* pp. 325, 359).

20. Case, *French Opinion,* pp. 17–18; Monnier, *Étude,* pp. 128–29.

21. Conacher, *Aberdeen Coalition,* pp. 215–32; Herbert C. F. Bell, *Lord Palmerston,* 2 vols. (London, 1936), 2:94–102; Ridley, *Palmerston,* p. 421.

22. Charles Stuart Parker, *Life and Letters of Sir James Graham, Second Baronet of Netherby, P.C., G.C.B., 1792–1861,* 2 vols. (London, 1907), 2:226.

23. Conacher, *Aberdeen Coalition,* p. 240.

24. Ibid., pp. 241–42; Schroeder, *Austria,* pp. 121, 126–27.

25. Parker, *Graham*, 2:226, 242; Schroeder, *Austria*, p. 126.

26. Maxwell, *Clarendon*, 2:41. The text is slightly different in Parker, *Graham*, 2:242.

27. Nesselrode to Buol, 17 Oct. 1853. Zaionchkovskii, vol. 2, #114, pp. 249–50.

28. Victoria, *Letters*, 2:559–60.

29. 26 Nov. 1853. Zaionchkovskii, vol. 2, #115, pp. 250–51.

30. 14 and 24 Dec. 1853. Victoria, *Letters*, 2:565–66; Zaionchkovskii, vol. 2, #99, 100, 117, pp. 203–5, 253–54.

31. Zaionchkovskii, vol. 2, #86, pp. 181–82; Monnier, *Étude*, pp. 119, 125.

32. Monnier, *Étude*, pp. 119–22, 125.

33. Nicholas to Francis Joseph, 24 Dec. 1853. Zaionchkovskii, vol. 2, #117, pp. 253–54; Lebzeltern to Buol, 26 Dec. 1853. *Akten*, vol. 1:1, #261, pp. 477–79; Henderson, *Crimean War Diplomacy*, p. 155.

34. Lane-Poole, *Stratford*, 2:330; Bruck to Buol, 19 Dec. 1853, 9, 16, and 30 Jan. 1854. *Akten*, vol. 1:1, #258, 273, 282, 306, pp. 472–73, 497–98, 513–14, 549–50; Bapst, *Origines*, appendix 6, pp. 501–4.

35. Buol to Bruck, 2 and 16 Jan. 1854. *Akten*, vol. 1:1, #266, 278, pp. 486–87, 503–5.

36. Buol to Lebzeltern, 13 Jan. 1854; Buol to Esterházy, 24 Jan. 1854. *Akten*, vol. 1:1, #275, 292–95, pp. 499–501, 528–38; Stanmore, *Herbert*, 1:189; Monnier, *Étude*, pp. 131–32; Conacher, *Aberdeen Coalition*, pp. 244–45. Clarendon was indignant with France for supporting the Constantinople Note and for bringing heavy pressure to bear on Austria to accept it, evidently fearing that France as well as Austria might now be prepared to make dangerous concessions to Russia to avoid war. "It is terrible," he wrote to Cowley, the British ambassador to Paris, "to think of the dangerous ground on which we are standing" with the French "preparing to back out of the war they have done even more than us to provoke" (Schroeder, *Austria*, p. 132).

37. Lebzeltern to Buol, 19 Jan. 1854. *Akten*, vol. 1:1, #285, p. 519; Zaionchkovskii, vol. 2, #119, 122–24, pp. 257, 262–70; Schroeder, *Austria*, pp. 139–41; Monnier, *Étude*, pp. 131, 134.

38. Buol to Hübner, Colloredo, and Thun, 3 Feb. 1854. *Akten*, vol. 1:1, #314, pp. 561–62. Evidently in the hope of keeping negotiations open, Nesselrode was later to deny that they were a response to the note of 13 Jan. 1854 (Esterházy to Buol, 5 Feb. 1854. *Akten*, vol. 1:1, #320, pp. 572–74), but this denial had no effect on the immediate (negative) reaction in Vienna.

39. Orlov to Nesselrode, 3 Feb. 1854; to the tsar, 4 Feb. 1854. Zaionchkovskii, vol. 2, #122–24, pp. 262–70; Austrian ministerial con-

ference, 31 Jan. 1854; Francis Joseph to the tsar, [5] Feb. 1854. *Akten*, vol. 1:1, #308, 319, pp. 551–54, 570–72.

40. Buol to Hübner, Colloredo, and Thun, 3 Feb. 1854; Buol to Esterházy, 5 Feb. 1854. *Akten*, vol. 1:1, #314–18, pp. 561–70; Bapst, *Origines*, pp. 478–79, 485; Curtiss, *Russia's Crimean War*, pp. 215–17.

41. Zaionchkovskii, vol. 2, #89, pp. 184–86.

42. Case, *French Opinion*, pp. 25–27; Monnier, *Étude*, pp. 136–37; Curtiss, *Russia's Crimean War*, p. 232; Saab, *Origins*, p. 133.

43. Zaionchkovskii, vol. 2, #89–90, pp. 186–91; Curtiss, *Russia's Crimean War*, pp. 233–34; Schroeder, *Austria*, p. 133.

44. Zaionchkovskii, vol. 2, #102–3, pp. 219–21; Martens, *Recueil*, vol. 12, pp. 337–40; Conacher, *Aberdeen Coalition*, pp. 246–49; Schroeder, *Austria*, p. 131; Curtiss, *Russia's Crimean War*, p. 230.

45. Zaionchkovskii, vol. 2, #93, 104, pp. 192–93, 221–22; Conacher, *Aberdeen Coalition*, p. 249; Schroeder, *Austria*, p. 145; Curtiss, *Russia's Crimean War*, p. 235.

46. Buol to Hübner, Colloredo, and Thun, 10 Feb. 1854; Buol to Esterházy, 11 Feb. 1854. *Akten*, vol. 1:1, #326, 328, pp. 579–82.

47. Buol to Esterházy, 5 March 1854. *Akten*, vol. 1:1, #361, pp. 637–39.

48. Stanmore, *Herbert*, 1:189–92.

49. Hertslet, *Map of Europe*, 2:1191, note; Zaionchkovskii, vol. 2, #141, pp. 327–28; Curtiss, *Russia's Crimean War*, p. 235.

50. Hertslet, *Map of Europe*, 2:1181–84, 1193–95.

51. 31 March 1854. G. D. Clayton, *Britain and the Eastern Question: Missolonghi to Gallipoli* (London, 1971), p. 109.

Chapter 7

1. There was much less general enthusiasm for war in France, owing in part to a profound dislike for the alliance with Britain. Case, *French Opinion*, pp. 18–25.

2. *Annual Register . . . 1854*, pp. 57–58; Schroeder, *Austria*, p. 146.

3. Russell, *Later Correspondence*, 2:160–61; Walpole, *Russell*, 2:213–14; Frances Balfour, *The Life of George, Fourth Earl of Aberdeen*, 2 vols. (London, 1922), 2:205–6; Henderson, *Crimean War Diplomacy*, p. 199. Lansdowne, a member of the cabinet without office, commented in a memorandum of 20 March: "I say nothing of Lord Palmerston's suggestions as they open so wide a field, and all imply previous successes the extent of which either by war or negotiation we cannot now anticipate." Russell, *Later Correspondence*, 2:161.

4. A.J.P. Taylor, *The Struggle for Mastery in Europe, 1848–1918* (Oxford, 1954), p. 67, n. 1.

5. Bell, *Palmerston*, 2:104–5.

6. Lane-Poole, *Stratford*, 2:354–58.

7. 3 April 1854. Zaionchkovskii, vol. 2, #161, pp. 362–65.

8. *Akten*, vol. 1:2, #64–66, pp. 192–97; Schroeder, *Austria*, p. 178; Unckel, *Österreich*, p. 135; Curtiss, *Russia's Crimean War*, pp. 258–60.

9. Buol to Francis Joseph, 21 March 1854; ministerial conferences of 22 and 25 March 1854. *Akten*, vol. 1:1, #393, 395, 399, pp. 688–93, 697–702, 708–713.

10. Ministerial conferences of March 22 and 25, cited above; Hess to Francis Joseph, 25 March 1854; instructions for Hess, 25 March 1854. Ibid., vol. 1:1, #400, 402, pp. 713–18, 723–24.

11. Ernst Rudolf Huber, ed., *Dokumente zur deutschen Verfassungsgeschichte*, vol. 2, *1851–1918* (Stuttgart, 1964), pp. 11–13. The German Confederation joined the Austro-Prussian alliance on 24 July 1854. Ibid., 2:13–14.

12. *Akten*, vol. 1:2, #56, pp. 178–81.

13. See chap. 7, n. 8.

14. Letter of 3 Nov. 1983.

15. Henderson, *Crimean War Diplomacy*, pp. 155–56. For the tsar's summary of Russian grievances against Austria, see Zaionchkovskii, vol. 2, #163, pp. 368–69. According to the Soviet historian, E. V. Tarle, the tsar turned Francis Joseph's picture to the wall and wrote across the back in his own hand *"Du Undankbarer!"* ("You Ingrate!"). See Albert Seaton, *The Crimean War. A Russian Chronicle* (London, 1977), p. 48.

16. Esterházy to Buol, 6 July 1854. *Akten*, 1:2, #97, pp. 247–49.

17. Nesselrode to Gorchakov, 29 June 1854. Zaionchkovskii, vol. 2, #158, pp. 357–59; Buol to Hübner and Colloredo, 9 Aug. 1854. *Akten*, vol. 1:2, #143, p. 336; Curtiss, *Russia's Crimean War*, pp. 260–68, 276–79; Schroeder, *Austria*, p. 207; Unckel, *Österreich*, p. 138.

18. Hertslet, *Map of Europe*, 2:1213–15; Zaionchkovskii, vol. 2, #159, pp. 359–61. Moldavia was to be occupied exclusively by Austria, Wallachia was to be occupied jointly, the city of Bucharest was to be occupied exclusively by Turkey.

19. Letter of 3 Nov. 1983.

Chapter 8

1. For much of the information in this chapter, I am indebted to the help of Mr. Peter Harrington and Mr. Richard Harrington, curators

of the Anne S. K. Brown collection of military history at Brown University.

2. See p. 98. Sir Edmund Lyons, British commander in the Black Sea, to Graham, first lord of the admiralty, 6 April 1854; Graham to Raglan, British commander in the Crimea, 8 May 1854. Parker, *Graham,* 2:243; Palmerston memorandum for the cabinet, 15 June 1854. Ashley, *Palmerston,* 2:295–98.

3. Argyll, *Autobiography,* 1:474.

4. Christopher Hibbert, *The Destruction of Lord Raglan. A Tragedy of the Crimean War* (Baltimore, 1963), pp. 244–58, 287.

5. W. H. Russell, *The British Expedition to the Crimea* (London, 1858), pp. 207, 212. For statistics on muskets, rifles, their size and range, see Michael Barthorp, *Crimean Uniforms. British Infantry* (London, 1977), pp. 74–75; Robert Wilkinson-Latham, *Uniforms and Weapons of the Crimean War* (London, 1977), pp. 92–94.

6. Robert Wilkinson-Latham, *Crimean Uniforms 2. British Artillery* (London, 1973), pp. 51–64; Seaton, *Crimean War,* pp. 60, 95; Curtiss, *Russia's Crimean War,* p. 334.

7. Hibbert, *Destruction,* p. 342 and entire volume; Brison D. Gooch, *The New Bonapartist Generals in the Crimean War. Distrust and Decision-Making in the Anglo-French Alliance* (The Hague, 1959), pp. 59–60; W. Baring Pemberton, *Battles of the Crimean War* (New York, 1962), pp. 163, 170–73, 207–8; Philip Warner, *The Crimean War. A Reappraisal* (New York, 1972), pp. 13–17.

8. Pemberton, *Battles,* p. 208.

9. Gooch, *New Bonapartist Generals:* on Saint-Arnaud, pp. 18–23, 42–45, 116, 121; on Canrobert, pp. 133–34, 196–201, 265–66; on Pélissier, pp. 176ff. Pemberton, *Battles:* on Canrobert, pp. 34, 37, 42–43; on Pélissier, pp. 184–85, 192.

10. In general, Seaton, *Crimean War,* pp. 15–16, 98, 186–87; Curtiss, *Russia's Crimean War:* on Menshikov, pp. 305–7, 312, 329, 332–34; on Gorchakov, pp. 427, 440.

11. Seaton, *Crimean War,* pp. 15–16, 99; Curtiss, *Russia's Crimean War,* pp. 302, 314–18.

12. According to some observers, "a vast deal of the sickness was brought on by the men themselves by excessive drinking" (Hibbert, *Destruction,* pp. 43, 54, 260, 285). In fact, alcohol was probably the only safe drink available, though it was clearly not consumed for this reason. On the Russian situation, Curtiss, *Russia's Crimean War,* pp. 459–71.

13. Among many studies, the very readable Cecil Woodham-Smith, *Florence Nightingale, 1820–1910* (New York, 1951).

14. Warner, *Crimean War,* pp. 191–93, 212–14. See p. 183.

15. Wilhelm Treue, *Der Krimkrieg und die Entstehung der modernen Flotten* (Göttingen, 1954).

16. Actually this railway was nothing more than a pair of iron tracks and trucks with grooved wheels to run on them. Constructed by the firm of Peto, Betts, and Brassey early in 1855, it was an enormous improvement over transportation via the mud and ruts of the regular road. There is a pencil sketch of a railway engine on the Balaclava railway dated 18 Nov. 1855 (thus after the fall of Sebastopol) by the British war artist William Simpson in an unpublished sketchbook that he called "Crimea. Constantinople. Voyage Home, 1855" (Anne S. K. Brown Military Collection, Brown University.) Throughout most of its operation during the siege, however, the power of the railway was supplied by horses, mules, seamen yoked in gun harness, and by a steam engine driving a windlass, because the gradients to the heights above Balaclava were too steep for an ordinary railway engine. There is a drawing of the horse-drawn Balaclava railway by the French artist Constantin Guys in Pemberton, *Battles*, p. 102. See also Hibbert, *Destruction*, p. 304, and George Brackenbury, *The Campaign in the Crimea. An Historical Sketch* 2 vols. (London, 1855–56), illustrated by 40 color plates from the drawings of William Simpson, pp. 96–97.

17. 4 Jan. 1855. From the Raglan Papers, quoted in Hibbert, *Destruction*, p. 194; Gooch, *New Bonapartist Generals*, p. 116.

18. Gooch, *New Bonapartist Generals*, pp. 107, 114; Hibbert, *Destruction*, pp. 48–49, 56; on the Allied landings and the entire course of the war, see the excellent contemporary British account in the *Annual Register*, which includes official dispatches about the major engagements and some important diplomatic documents.

19. Gooch, *New Bonapartist Generals*, p. 117; Warner, *Crimean War*, p. 25; Hibbert, *Destruction*, pp. 61–76.

20. The Russians also appear to have thought it was too late in the season for the Allies to initiate a military campaign, although they had been receiving information that such a campaign was imminent for weeks. The failure of the government in St. Petersburg to send a greater proportion of its mighty armies to the Crimea from the Baltic and Poland was a major reason for the Russian defeat. Curtiss, *Russia's Crimean War*, p. 303; Gooch, *New Bonapartist Generals*, p. 118.

21. Seaton, *Crimean War*, pp. 59–61.

22. Ibid., pp. 50–103, esp. pp. 89–91, 99; Gooch, *New Bonapartist Generals*, pp. 121–28; Warner, *Crimean War*, pp. 24–47.

23. Gooch, *New Bonapartist Generals*, pp. 130, 135; Hibbert, *Destruction*, pp. 119–35; Seaton, *Crimean War*, pp. 96, 108–25; Curtiss, *Russia's Crimean War*, pp. 316–18.

24. Curtiss, *Russia's Crimean War*, pp. 313–14; Hibbert, *Destruction*, pp. 136–37; Gooch, *New Bonapartist Generals*, p. 129.

25. Hibbert, *Destruction*, pp. 136–63, 164–87; Pemberton, *Battles*, pp. 71–116; Seaton, *Crimean War*, pp. 138–56. In notable contrast to writers who see Balaclava from the Western point of view, Curtiss describes it as a demonstration rather than a battle and severely criticizes Menshikov for not waiting for the reinforcements that might have given him the decisive victory he sought. Curtiss regards Inkerman as the truly decisive battle of the campaign. *Russia's Crimean War*, pp. 321–28.

26. Seaton, *Crimean War*, pp. 157–78; Hibbert, *Destruction*, pp. 198–232; Pemberton, *Battles*, pp. 117–64.

27. Gooch, *New Bonapartist Generals*, pp. 150–52; Hibbert, *Destruction*, pp. 233–43.

28. Gooch, *New Bonapartist Generals*, pp. 153–65; Pemberton, *Battles*, pp. 165–84.

29. Gooch, *New Bonapartist Generals*, pp. 196–201, 205–8. Raglan had favored and in fact initiated the expedition.

30. Curtiss, *Russia's Crimean War*, pp. 440–59; Gooch, *New Bonapartist Generals*, pp. 231–51.

31. Curtiss, *Russia's Crimean War*, pp. 341, 469–71; Seaton, *Crimean War*, pp. 15–16.

32. Treue, *Krimkrieg*, pp. 117–21.

33. Warner, *Crimean War*, pp. 195–96; Seaton, *Crimean War*, p. 49; Curtiss, *Russia's Crimean War*, pp. 287, 419–21.

34. Warner, *Crimean War*, pp. 197–210; Curtiss, *Russia's Crimean War*, pp. 408–19, 424; *Annual Register . . . 1854*, pp. 370–78; . . . *1855*, pp. 270–78.

Chapter 9

1. *Akten*, vol. 1:2, pp. 67ff.

2. Hübner to Buol, 15 July 1854. Taylor, *Struggle*, p. 65; *Akten*, vol. 1:2, p. 290, n. 1. D'Harcourt quotes an identical remark made by Drouyn to Emperor Francis Joseph in April 1855. Bernard Hippolyte d'Harcourt, *Diplomatie et diplomates: les quatre ministères de M. Drouyn de Lhuys* (Paris, 1882), pp. 130–35. Drouyn evidently convinced Palmerston that he agreed with the British minister's more extreme views, for Palmerston recorded that Drouyn had told him that the war must bring about great territorial changes; if the war achieved nothing more than the destruction of Sebastopol and the Russian fleet, "the French nation would say they had been made the Cats Paw of England, who always wanted the destruction of the Fleet of other

Countries." Palmerston commented: "What of course these remarks pointed out to were Georgia and Circassia, the mouths of the Danube, Poland and Finland, matters on which he said his opinion had for two years been the same as those which I told him were mine personally." Conacher, *Aberdeen Coalition*, pp. 441–42.

3. Schroeder, *Austria*, pp. 182–83, 192–94; Henderson, *Crimean War Diplomacy*, pp. 99, 166–67; Curtiss, *Russia's Crimean War*, pp. 277–89; Buol to Hübner and Colloredo, 21 and 31 July 1854; Colloredo to Buol, 28 July 1854. *Akten*, vol. 1:2, #120, 121, 128, 132, pp. 290–93, 308–11, 317–18.

4. Text in Hertslet, *Map of Europe*, 2:1216–18.

5. Buol to Esterházy, 10 Aug. 1854; Nesselrode to Gorchakov, 26 Aug. 1854; Esterházy to Buol, 30 Aug. 1854. *Akten*, vol. 1:2, #147, 174, pp. 341–43, 387–89.

6. Conacher, *Aberdeen Coalition*, p. 435.

7. 24 October 1854. Taylor, *Struggle*, p. 69.

8. Esterházy to Buol, 17 Nov. and 2 Dec. 1854; Buol to Hübner and Colloredo, 3 Dec. 1854. *Akten*, vol. 1:2, #277, 279, pp. 580, n. 4, 593–94, 597–98; Curtiss, *Russia's Crimean War*, pp. 350–53; Taylor, *Struggle*, pp. 69–70.

9. Hertslet, *Map of Europe*, 2:1221–24; Schroeder, *Austria*, pp. 224–26; Conacher, *Aberdeen Coalition*, p. 440.

10. 22 Nov. 1854. Schroeder, *Austria*, p. 237. Buol to Hübner and Colloredo, 23 Dec. 1854. *Akten*, vol. 1:2, #304, p. 646 and n. 3.

11. 10 Dec. 1854. Henderson, *Crimean War Diplomacy*, pp. 185–86.

12. Ibid., pp. 154, 186–89.

13. The entire episode is described by Henderson in ibid., pp. 105–14, 122.

14. Hertslet, *Map of Europe*, 2:1225–26; Buol to Hübner and Colloredo, 23 Dec. 1854. *Akten*, vol. 1:2, #304, p. 646.

15. Buol to Esterházy, 3 Jan. 1855. *Akten*, vol. 1:2, #315, pp. 666–68.

16. This reaction of Gorchakov was reported by Bourqueney, the French ambassador to Vienna, to his foreign minister, Drouyn de Lhuys, 28 Dec. 1854. D'Harcourt, *Drouyn*, pp. 89–92. In describing the same conference to Esterházy, the Austrian ambassador to St. Petersburg, Buol reported that Gorchakov had merely said that he would neither accept nor reject the proposals but was disposed to refer them to his government. Buol described Gorchakov's reservation about the third point in greater detail in a dispatch to Hübner and Colloredo of 4 Jan. 1855. *Akten*, vol. 1:2, #320, pp. 675–77.

17. Henderson, *Crimean War Diplomacy*, pp. 115–16.

18. Buol to Hübner, Colloredo, and Esterházy, 8 Jan. 1855. *Akten,* vol. 1:2, #322, pp. 678–80; Bourqueney to Drouyn, 7 Jan. 1855. D'Harcourt, *Drouyn,* pp. 95–97; Henderson, *Crimean War Diplomacy,* pp. 120–21; Schroeder, *Austria,* pp. 243–44.

19. On British opposition to negotiations, see Colloredo to Buol, 12 Feb. 1855. *Akten,* vol. 1:2, #369, pp. 760–62. Cowley, the British ambasador to Paris, reported to Clarendon on 21 Jan. 1855, that he had had a two-hour conversation with Napoleon that morning. The emperor's "principal preoccupation at present appears to be to escape from all further negotiations with Russia." Napoleon had a scheme that he thought would put an immediate end to the negotiations. "The truth begins at last to ooze out," Cowley continued. "Drouyn has been amusing Austria with visions of peace in order to get her alliance . . . Austria has fallen into the snare." Victor Wellesley and Robert Sencourt, eds., *Conversations with Napoleon III. A Collection of Documents, mostly unpublished and almost entirely Diplomatic* (London, 1934), p. 69. This policy toward Austria appears to have been Napoleon's own. Later in that same year he informed Prince Albert of his scheme for catching Austria as an ally in the war—and then declining to make peace when the Allies' *avowed* objectives had been attained. Argyll, *Autobiography,* 1:555.

20. Hertslet, *Map of Europe,* 2:1228–29.

21. Franco Valsecchi, *L'alleanza di Crimea. Il Risorgimento e l'Europa* (Milan, 1948); Luigi Chiala, *L'alleanza di Crimea* (Rome, 1879); Conacher, *Aberdeen Coalition,* pp. 444–46; Taylor, *Struggle,* pp. 71–72.

22. Conacher, *Aberdeen Coalition,* chap. 18; Bell, *Palmerston,* 2:106–17; Henderson, *Crimean War Diplomacy,* p. 142; Argyll, *Autobiography,* 1:561–62.

23. Schiemann, *Geschichte Russlands,* vol. 4, chap. 14.

24. Buol to Hübner, Colloredo, and Esterházy, 8 Jan. and 19 March, 1855. *Akten,* vol. 1:2, #322, 397, pp. 678–80, 810–11.

25. Drouyn, who did not come to Vienna until 6 April after previous consultations with the British government, took a hard line in the early stages of the conference, perhaps in response to orders from Napoleon to keep French policy in line with that of Britain. Hübner to Buol, 16 Jan. and 14 March 1855. *Akten,* vol. 1:2, #331, 394, pp. 695–97, 804–6. Also Drouyn to Bourqueney, 17 March 1855; Drouyn to Napoleon, 1 April 1855. D'Harcourt, *Drouyn,* pp. 110–25; Cowley to Clarendon, 18 March 1856. Wellesley, *Conversations,* pp. 76–77. In a letter to Clarendon of 27 March, Cowley said he thought Drouyn would try to get the best conditions possible but that in the end he was for "peace at any price." Henderson, *Crimean War Diplomacy,* pp. 47–48.

26. Russell, *Later Correspondence*, pp. 184–207; Henderson, *Crimean War Diplomacy*, pp. 37–38, 41; Schroeder, *Austria*, pp. 249–50.

27. Napoleon appears to have been tempted by the favorable terms worked out in Vienna but in the end adhered to his policy of cooperation with Britain, which accorded with the advice of his military leaders. See p. 152.

28. Buol to Hübner and Colloredo, 21 and 28 March 1855. *Akten*, vol. 1:2, #399, 410, pp. 813–15, 830–31; Drouyn to Napoleon, 1 and 6 April 1855. D'Harcourt, *Drouyn*, pp. 113–29; Schroeder, *Austria*, pp. 265–66; Henderson, *Crimean War Diplomacy*, pp. 47–50.

29. Buol to Francis Joseph, 15 April 1855; Buol to Hübner and Colloredo, 15, 16, and 23 April 1855. *Akten*, vol. 1:2, #431–35, 440, pp. 864–70, 877–79; D'Harcourt, *Drouyn*, pp. 140–41; Henderson, *Crimean War Diplomacy*, pp. 52–54; Schroeder, *Austria*, pp. 270–73.

30. Drouyn's policy throughout seems to have been to secure the cooperation of Austria to impose satisfactory peace terms on Russia, or Austria's entry into the war if Russia rejected them. D'Harcourt, *Drouyn*, pp. 140–41, 143–47; Hübner to Buol, 30 April 1855. *Akten*, vol. 1:2, #443–44, pp. 884–87.

31. Schroeder, *Austria*, p. 273.

32. Argyll, *Autobiography*, 1:552–53.

33. Henderson, *Crimean War Diplomacy*, p. 57. Both Henderson and Schroeder (*Austria*, p. 276) think the resolution of the British cabinet weakened over the next two days and that the British government might have accepted the Austrian Ultimatum if Napoleon had done so. This is possible, but in view of the prevailing attitude of Palmerston and Clarendon it is more probable that the British would simply have posed new—and unacceptable—conditions of their own.

34. Cowley to Clarendon, 4 May 1855. Schroeder, *Austria*, p. 277.

35. Cowley to Stratford, 5 May 1855. Wellesley, *Conversations*, p. 82. "Playing old Gooseberry" means making mischief, or wreaking havoc. Henderson, *Crimean War Diplomacy*, pp. 60–63; Schroeder, *Austria*, pp. 277–78, 282–84; Argyll, *Autobiography*, 1:554.

36. Argyll, *Autobiography* 1:555.

37. Maxwell, *Clarendon*, 2:82.

38. Ashley, *Palmerston*, 2:315–16.

39. Maxwell, *Clarendon*, 2:82.

40. 27 May 1855. Ibid., 2:82.

41. 20 May 1855. Ridley, *Palmerston*, p. 446.

42. Buol to Hübner and Colloredo, 6 June 1855. *Akten*, vol. 1:2, #478, pp. 946–47; Curtiss, *Russia's Crimean War*, pp. 399–400; Schroeder, *Austria*, pp. 299, 303.

43. Palmerston to Clarendon, 20 May 1855. Ridley, *Palmerston*, pp. 445–46.

44. Bell, *Palmerston*, 2:130–31.
45. D'Harcourt, *Drouyn*, pp. 143–47.
46. Maxwell, *Clarendon*, 2:80; Henderson, *Crimean War Diplomacy*, p. 142; Schroeder, *Austria*, p. 299; Ridley, *Palmerston*, p. 447.
47. *Akten*, vol. 1:2, #448, p. 905.

Chapter 10

1. To Michael Gorchakov, 15 Sept. 1855. Baumgart, *Peace of Paris*, p. 58; Unckel, *Österreich*, pp. 227–28.
2. Napoleon to Walewski, 14 Sept. 1855. "Les papiers inédits du Comte Walewski. Souvenirs et correspondance (1855–1868)" ed. G. Raindre, *Revue de France* 5 (1925):489–90.
3. Hübner to Buol, 21 Sept. 1855. *Akten*, vol. 1:3, #9, pp. 59–65; Baumgart, *Peace of Paris*, p. 25.
4. Palmerston to Cowley, 22 Sept. 1855. Schroeder, *Austria*, p. 315, note.
5. Palmerston to his brother William, 25 Aug. 1855. Ashley, *Palmerston* 2:320.
6. C. C. Bayley, *Mercenaries for the Crimea. The German, Swiss, and Italian Legions in British Service, 1854–1856* (Montreal, 1977).
7. See p. 147.
8. Hertslet, *Map of Europe*, 2:1241–42; Curtiss, *Russia's Crimean War*, p. 479; Schroeder, *Austria*, p. 330; Carl Hallendorff, ed., *Konung Oscar I: s politik under Krimkriget* (Stockholm, 1930).
9. Palmerston to Clarendon, 25 Sept. 1855. Bell, *Palmerston*, 2:138.
10. Marquess of Lorne, *Viscount Palmerston, K.G.* (New York, 1892), pp. 174–77.
11. 13 Sept. 1855. Lane-Poole, *Stratford*, 2:413–14.
12. A. Pingaud, "La politique extérieure du Second Empire," *Revue Historique* 156 (1927):41–68; Baumgart, *Peace of Paris*, p. 25; Prince Albert to Stockmar, 29 Oct. 1855, summarizing Napoleon's views as presented most recently to the British government. Martin, *Prince Consort*, 3:385.
13. Bayley, *Mercenaries*, pp. 26, 35.
14. 20 Jan. 1856. Victoria, *Letters*, 3:211–13.
15. Walewski, "Papiers inédits," p. 488.
16. 14 Sept. 1855. Ibid., pp. 489–90. See above p. 157.
17. Hübner to Buol, 13 and 21 Sept., 2 Oct. 1855; Buol to Hübner, 1 Oct. 1855. *Akten*, vol. 1:3, #3, 9, 13, 18, pp. 51–52, 59–65, 71–72, 78–80.
18. Baumgart, *Peace of Paris*, p. 46.
19. Karnicki to Buol, 22 Sept. 1855. *Akten*, vol. 1:3, #10, pp. 66–

67; W. E. Mosse, *The Rise and Fall of the Crimean System, 1855–1871. The Story of a Peace Settlement* (London, 1963), p. 16.

20. Friedrich Ferdinand Count von Beust, *Memoirs of Friedrich Ferdinand Count von Beust*, 2 vols. (London, 1887), 1:142–43, 384–89; Charles Morny, *Extrait des mémoires du duc de Morny. Une ambassade en Russia, 1856* (Paris, 1892), pp. 7ff.; Curtiss, *Russia's Crimean War*, pp. 480–91; Baumgart, *Peace of Paris*, pp. 54–68.

21. Hübner, *Neuf ans*, 1:343; Schroeder, *Austria*, pp. 312–13. In the publication of Austrian diplomatic documents for this period, there is an inexplicable gap between 2 October, when Hübner reported a confidential statement of Walewski relative to peace negotiations, and 29 October, when Hübner reported on Bourqueney's return to Vienna. *Akten*, vol. 1:3, #18, 21, pp. 78–80, 83.

22. Mosse, *Crimean System*, p. 18; Hübner, *Neuf ans*, 1:349–50.

23. Clarendon to his wife, 23 Oct. 1855. Maxwell, *Clarendon*, 2:102.

24. 17, 20, and 23 Oct. 1855. Schroeder, *Austria*, pp. 321–22.

25. 22, 24, and 29 Oct. 1855. Hübner, *Neuf ans*, 1:353–55.

26. Wellesley, *Conversations*, p. 97; Schroeder, *Austria*, p. 313; Baumgart, *Peace of Paris*, p. 48.

27. Baumgart, *Peace of Paris*, pp. 48–50.

28. See p. 174.

29. Puryear, *England*, pp. 131–38.

30. *Akten*, 1:3, #32, pp. 103–4; Unckel, *Österreich*, pp. 230–33; Schroeder, *Austria*, pp. 314–15.

31. *Akten*, vol. 1:3, #34, pp. 106–7; Baumgart, *Peace of Paris*, pp. 50–51.

32. Austro-French memorandum, 14 Nov. 1855; Buol to Hübner and Colloredo, 17 Nov. 1855. *Akten*, vol. 1:3, #33, 39, 40, pp. 104–5, 116–19.

33. Hübner, *Neuf ans*, 1:358–60.

34. Palmerston to Clarendon, 20 Nov. 1855. Schroeder, *Austria*, p. 325.

35. Palmerston to Persigny, 21 Nov. 1855. Ashley, *Palmerston*, 2:322–23.

36. Clarendon to Palmerston, 18 Nov. 1855. Schroeder, *Austria*, p. 324.

37. 19 Nov. 1855. Victoria, *Letters*, 3:193.

38. Argyll, *Autobiography*, 1:596–97; Baumgart, *Peace of Paris*, p. 36; Schroeder, *Austria*, pp. 329–30 and note.

39. Victoria to Clarendon, 23 Nov. 1855. *Letters*, 3:194–96.

40. Colloredo to Buol, 24 Nov. 1855; Hübner to Buol, 26 Nov. and

3 Dec. 1855. *Akten*, vol. 1:3, #43, 46, 58, pp. 122–23, 126–29, 152–55; Hübner, *Neuf ans*, 1:359–60, 362–63.

41. Palmerston to Clarendon, 20 Nov. 1855; Clarendon to Stratford, 28 Dec. 1855. Schroeder, pp. 323, 325; Granville to Stratford, 20 Dec. 1855. Edmond Fitzmaurice, *The Life of Granville George Leveson Gower, Second Earl of Granville K. G. 1815–1891*, 2 vols. (London, 1905), 1:133; Greville, *Memoirs*, 7:169–76; Baumgart, *Peace of Paris*, pp. 14, 86, n. 133.

42. The queen had warned that such a provision would be so humiliating to Russia that Austria would probably decline to propose it. (Victoria to Clarendon, 23 Nov. 1855. *Letters*, 3:194–96). The British were to raise this demand again at the peace conference. See p. 191.

43. The course of Walewski's negotiations with the British, insofar as Hübner was informed of them, is described in Hübner's dispatch to Buol of 3 Dec. 1855. *Akten*, vol. 1:3, #58, pp. 152–55; Hübner, *Neuf ans*, 1:367–68; Argyll, *Autobiography*, 1:599.

44. Clarendon sheds some interesting light on the state of the international money market of that time. On 19 November he wrote to his wife that the feeling in England about the fall of Kars was very strong and that he believed there would be "the devil to pay when parliament meets." He then went on to add: "Only think of the Russian loan being levied here! in the ordinary way of business, too, so that I don't see how it can be interfered with! £200,000 left London yesterday, and the pressure on the money market will be great." Maxwell, *Clarendon*, 2:107.

45. Hübner to Buol, 3 Dec. 1855. *Akten*, vol. 1:3, #58, pp. 152–55; Hübner, *Neuf ans*, 1:367–68.

46. Buol to Colloredo, 9 Jan. 1856. *Akten*, vol. 1:3, #107, pp. 222–23; Schroeder, *Austria*, p. 321; Baumgart, *Peace of Paris*, pp. 92, n. 226, 101.

47. 13 Dec. 1855. Maxwell, *Clarendon*, 2:107.

48. Hübner, *Neuf ans*, 1:370.

49. Buol to Hübner and Colloredo, 17 Dec. 1855. *Akten*, vol. 1:3, #73, pp. 175–76; Hübner, *Neuf ans*, 1:370–71.

50. Victoria, *Letters*, 3:194–97.

51. Buol to Hübner and Colloredo, 17 Dec. 1855. *Akten*, vol. 1:3, #73, pp. 175–76; Hübner, *Neuf ans*, 1:370–71.

52. Colloredo to Buol, 1 Jan. 1856. *Akten*, vol. 1:3, #99, pp. 213–14.

53. Schroeder, *Austria*, pp. 327–36.

54. Text in *Akten*, vol. 1:3, #65, pp. 162–63.

55. Ibid., vol. 1:3, #88, p. 196.

56. Buol to Esterházy, 16 Dec. 1855. Ibid., vol. 1:3, #66, 67, pp. 164–67; Baumgart, *Peace of Paris*, pp. 51–52; Unckel, *Österreich*, pp, 237–38.

57. Baumgart, *Peace of Paris*, pp. 68–69; Curtiss, *Russia's Crimean War*, pp. 495–98.

58. Buol to Esterházy, 12 Jan. 1856. *Akten*, vol. 1:3, #115, pp. 232–33.

59. Esterházy to Buol, 29 Jan. 1856. *Akten*, vol. 1:3, #178, pp. 314–15; Curtiss, *Russia's Crimean War*, pp. 499–500; Baumgart, *Peace of Paris*, pp. 68–80; Mosse, *Crimean System*, pp. 28–31.

60. Palmerston to Clarendon, 7 Jan. 1856. Bell, *Palmerston*, 2:140.

61. Colloredo to Buol, 1 and 4 Jan. 1856. *Akten*, vol. 1:3, #99, 102, pp. 213–14, 216–17.

62. Schroeder, *Austria*, pp. 334–36; Colloredo to Buol, 6 Jan. 1856; Hübner to Buol, 17 Jan. 1856. *Akten*, vol. 1:3, #131, 135, pp. 249, 253–55.

63. Buol to Hübner and Colloredo, 9, 18, 21, and 22 Jan. 1856. *Akten*, vol. 1:3, #107–8, 140–41, 147–50, pp. 223–24, 261–63, 271–73; Hübner, *Neuf ans*, 1:380; Baumgart, *Peace of Paris*, p. 102.

64. By now British statesmen generally had the lowest possible opinion of Walewski. Lord Greville described him in his diary (entry for 17 Jan. 1856) as "an adventurer, a needy speculator, without honour, conscience, or truth, and utterly unfit both as to his character and his capacity for such an office as he holds." *The Greville Diary. Including Passages Hitherto Withheld from Publication*, ed. P. W. Wilson, 2 vols. (New York, 1927), 2:522.

65. Napoleon to Victoria, 14 Jan. 1856. Victoria, *Letters*, 3:205–7. Persigny addressed his appeals to Clarendon. Palmerston commented on them in the letter cited in n. 66.

66. Palmerston to Victoria, 17 Jan. 1856. Victoria, *Letters*, 3:209–11.

67. 24 Jan. 1856. Ridley, *Palmerston*, p. 448.

68. 19 Jan. 1856. Baumgart, *Peace of Paris*, p. 101.

69. Colloredo to Buol, 24 Jan. 1856. *Akten*, vol. 1:3, #159, 161, pp. 285–86, 288–90; Hübner, *Neuf ans*, 1:383–85; Baumgart, *Peace of Paris*, p. 102.

70. Hübner to Buol, 15, 25, 27, and 28 Jan. 1856; Colloredo to Buol, 16 Jan. 1856. *Akten*, vol. 1:3, #129, 131, 172–75, pp. 246–47, 249, 304–9; Hübner, *Neuf ans*, 1:387; Schroeder, *Austria*, p. 350.

71. Buol to Hübner and Colloredo, 1 Feb. 1856. *Akten*, vol. 1:3, #188, pp. 328–29.

Chapter 11

1. According to Hübner, the Austrian ambassador to Paris, Cowley had been "absolutely bowled over [*bouleversé*] by Russia's acceptance of our proposals." Hübner, *Neuf ans*, 1:382–83. On 12 March 1856, Clarendon wrote to Granville: "The negotiations are a year too soon, and I have no doubt that another campaign would have enabled us to impose very different conditions on Russia." Maxwell, *Clarendon*, 2: 118–19.

2. 18 Jan. 1856. Lane-Poole, *Stratford*, 2:434.

3. 21 Jan. 1856. Ibid., 2:435–36.

4. 25 April 1856. Ibid., 2:436. On the catastrophic health situation of the French army, Baumgart cites even more alarming figures: in the French army of 150,000 in the Crimea, 42,000 were on sick leave, and 250 were dying every day (*Peace of Paris*, p. 106).

5. Bell, *Palmerston*, 2:146; Ridley, *Palmerston*, pp. 449–51; Argyll, *Autobiography*, 2:22.

6. Clarendon to Palmerston, 29 Feb. and 3 March 1856. Maxwell, *Clarendon*, 2:116–18.

7. To Granville, 12 March 1856. Ibid., 2:118–19. Relations between Britain and the United States at this time, already strained by conflicting claims in Latin America and disputes over trading and fishing rights, were exacerbated further by British efforts to recruit soldiers in the United States for the war in the Crimea. Bayley, *Mercenaries*, pp. 87–94; Alan Dowty, *The Limits of American Isolation: The United States and the Crimean War* (New York, 1971), pp. 189–202.

8. Buol and Hübner to Francis Joseph, 19 March 1856. *Akten*, vol. 1:3, #306, pp. 535–36.

9. Baumgart provides an insightful analysis in *Peace of Paris*, pp. 130–34.

10. Buol and Hübner to Francis Joseph, 24 Feb. 1856. *Akten*, vol. 1:3, #234, pp. 409–13.

11. See n. 7.

12. Articles 3, 4, and 30. An English text of the final treaty can be found in Hertslet, *Map of Europe*, 2:1250–65; French text in Martens, *Recueil*, 15:307–25.

13. 22 March 1856. Lane-Poole, *Stratford*, 2:435.

14. See above, p. 167.

15. *Akten*, 1:3, pp. 413ff.

16. 9 March 1856. *Akten*, vol. 1:3, #279, pp. 484–88. This report was a summary of the negotiations over Bessarabia.

17. Articles 20 and 21. Hertslet, *Map of Europe*, 2:1259–60; Baumgart, *Peace of Paris*, pp. 108–11.

18. *Akten*, vol. 1:3, #279, 281, 286, 293, pp. 484–88, 489–91, 498–99, 508–10.

19. Articles 22–29. Hertslet, *Map of Europe*, 2:1260–62; Baumgart, *Peace of Paris*, pp. 116–25.

20. Baumgart, *Peace of Paris*, p. 125.

21. *Akten*, 1:3, #275, 295–97, pp. 479–81, 511–19; Baumgart, *Peace of Paris*, pp. 125–28.

22. Articles 15–19. Hertslet, *Map of Europe*, 2:1257–59.

23. *Akten*, vol. 1:3, #272–73, 275, pp. 473–76, 479–81; Baumgart, *Peace of Paris*, pp. 113–16.

24. Articles 11–14. Hertslet, *Map of Europe*, 2:1256–57.

25. Article 12, which provided for freedom of commerce on the waters of the Black Sea.

26. Article 14 of the final Treaty of Paris and the Russo-Turkish Convention, signed 30 March 1856. Hertslet, *Map of Europe*, 2: 1270–71,

27. Article 10 of the final Treaty of Paris and the Straits Convention of 30 March 1856. Ibid., 2:1266–69.

28. Article 33 of the Final Treaty of Paris and the Aaland Islands Convention, signed 30 March 1856. Ibid., 2:1272–73; Baumgart, *Peace of Paris*, pp. 112–13.

29. Preamble and Articles 7 and 8. Hertslet, *Map of Europe*, 2: 1251–53, 1254–55.

30. English text in ibid., 2:1243–49.

31. Davison, *Reform*, pp. 53, 60–61. A detailed account of Stratford's activity on behalf of reform is provided by Harold Temperley, "The Last Phase of Stratford de Redcliffe, 1855–1858," *English Historical Review*, 47 (1932):216–59, who stresses the rivalry between British and French influences in Constantinople.

32. Article 9. Hertslet, *Map of Europe*, 2:1255.

33. Baumgart, *Peace of Paris*, p. 130.

34. Beust, *Memoirs*, 1:144.

35. Text in Hertslet, *Map of Europe*, 2:1280–81; Schroeder, *Austria*, 381; Curtiss, *Russia's Crimean War*, pp. 524–25; Unckel, *Österreich*, pp. 278–81; Mosse, *Crimean System*, chap. 2.

36. 16 April 1856. *Akten*, vol. 1:3, #358, pp. 606–7.

37. Seton-Watson, *Britain in Europe*, p. 349; Schroeder, *Austria*, p. 365.

Chapter 12

1. Harold Temperley, "The Treaty of Paris of 1856 and Its Execution," *Journal of Modern History*, 4 (1932):529.

2. After Napoleon's escape from Elba and his defeat at Waterloo, somewhat harsher peace terms were imposed on France, including reparations.

3. The statesmen of the concert, of course, could differ amongst themselves as much as statesmen of any era and their policies frequently seem inconsistent and contradictory—but the methods described here were those employed by the most influential among them, in particular by Metternich and Castlereagh.

4. In the brilliant conclusion to his own book on Crimean War diplomacy, Paul Schroeder draws attention to the crucial importance of this problem of change and observes that "the problem of reconciling order and change has been the bane of every great plan for world peace ever devised" (*Austria*, p. 426).

5. Michael Hurst, in a review of Conacher's *Aberdeen Coalition*, *Historical Journal*, 12 (1969):722–23.

Bibliography

Akten zur Geschichte des Krimkriegs. Series 1. *Österreichische Akten zur Geschichte des Krimkriegs.* Edited by Winfield Baumgart, Ana María Schop Soler, and Werner Zürrer, 3 vols. Munich and Vienna, 1979–80. An invaluable source collection.

Anderson, M. S. *The Eastern Question, 1774–1923.* New York, 1966. Excellent overall survey.

————, ed. *The Great Powers and the Near East, 1774–1923.* New York, 1971. Valuable brief collection of documents.

Anderson, Olive. *A Liberal State at War: English Politics and Economics during the Crimean War.* London, 1967. Stimulating interpretation.

Annual Register. Published annually in London in the year after the events covered. Valuable contemporary appraisals, with numerous documents, dispatches, statistics.

Argyll, George Douglas Campbell, Eighth Duke of. *Autobiography and Memoirs.* Edited by the Dowager Duchess of Argyll. 2 vols. London, 1906.

Ashley, Evelyn. *The Life and Correspondence of Henry John Temple, Viscount Palmerston.* 2 vols. London, 1879.

Bailey, F. E. *British Policy and the Turkish Reform Movement, 1826–1853.* Cambridge, Mass., 1942.

Balfour, Frances. *The Life of George, Fourth Earl of Aberdeen.* 2 vols. London, 1922.

Bapst, Edmond. *Les origines de la guerre de Crimée. La France et la Russie de 1848 à 1854.* Paris, 1912. Contains valuable documentary material on French policy.

Barthorp, Michael. *Crimean Uniforms. British Infantry.* London, 1977. Includes information on weaponry.

Baumgart, Winfried. *The Peace of Paris, 1856. Studies in War, Diplomacy, and Peacemaking.* Santa Barbara, Calif., 1981. Full of valuable information and interesting interpretations, but so crowded with detail and so poorly organized that the main themes and lines of argument are often difficult to follow.

————. "Probleme der Krimkriegsforschung. Eine Studie über die Literatur des letzten Jahrzehnts (1961–1970)." *Jahrbücher für Geschichte Osteuropas* 19 (1971):49–109, 243–64, 371–400. A massively detailed bibliography, with valuable commentaries.

Bayley, C. C. *Mercenaries for the Crimea. The German, Swiss, and Italian Legions in British Service, 1854–1856.* Montreal, 1977. Fascinating work on a little-known subject.

Bell, Herbert C. F. *Lord Palmerston.* 2 vols. London, 1936. Fine biography with valuable extracts from documents.

Beust, Friedrich Ferdinand Count von. *Memoirs of Friedrich Ferdinand Count von Beust. Written by Himself.* 2 vols. London, 1887.

Bolsover, G. H. "Nicholas I and the Partition of Turkey." *Slavonic and East European Review* 27 (1948):115–45. Ascribes tsar's policy not to Machiavellian expansionism but to natural desire to safeguard Russian interests and avoid risk that Turkey's collapse might take the powers unaware and provoke a general war.

Borries, Kurt. *Preussen im Krimkrieg, 1853–1856.* Stuttgart, 1930.

Brackenbury, George. *The Campaign in the Crimea. An Historical Sketch.* 2 vols. London, 1855–56. Illustrated by forty color plates from the drawings of the war artist William Simpson.

Bruck, Karl Ludwig von. *Memoiren des Baron Bruck aus der Zeit des Krimkriegs.* Edited by Isidor Heller. Vienna, 1877.

Byrne, Leo Gerald. *The Great Ambassador. A Study of the Diplomatic Career of the Right Honourable Stratford Canning, K.G., G.C.B., Viscount Stratford de Redcliffe, and the Epoch during which he served as the British Ambassador to the Sublime Porte of the Ottoman Empire.* Columbus, Ohio, 1964. Simplistic popularization and uncritical eulogy, based largely on Lane-Poole.

Case, Lynn M. *Edouard Thouvenel et la diplomatie du second Empire.* Paris, 1976. Thin on the Crimean War but contains interesting details on question of Turkish reform.

————. *French Opinion on War and Diplomacy during the Second Empire.* Philadelphia, 1954. Valuable and original analysis.

Chiala, Luigi. *L'alleanza di Crimea.* Rome, 1879.

Clayton, G. D. *Britain and the Eastern Question. Missolonghi to Gallipoli.* London, 1971.

Conacher, J. B. *The Aberdeen Coalition, 1852–1855. A Study in Mid-Nineteenth-Century Party Politics.* Cambridge, 1968. First-class monograph.

Cowley. *The Paris Embassy During the Second Empire. Selections from the Papers of Henry Richard Charles Wellesley, 1st Earl Cowley. Ambassador at Paris, 1852–1867.* Edited by F. A. Wellesley. London, 1928. So severely edited as to be of little value.

Cowley, T.A.B. *Democratic Despot. A Life of Napoleon III.* London, 1961.

Curtiss, John Shelton. *Russia's Crimean War.* Durham, N.C., 1979. Excellent and important monograph, on which I have relied heavily.

Davison, Roderic H. *Reform in the Ottoman Empire, 1856–1876.* Princeton, N.J., 1963. First-class monograph, with valuable insights into the operations of the Ottoman government.

Dowty, Alan. *The Limits of American Isolation: The United States and the Crimean War.* New York, 1971.

Echard, William E. *Napoleon III and the Concert of Europe.* Baton Rouge, La., 1983. Deals with the emperor's efforts to redraw the map of Europe on the basis of the principle of nationality through agreements arranged at international conferences.

Eckart, Ferenc. *Die deutsche Frage und der Krimkrieg.* Berlin, 1931.

Engel-Janosi, Friedrich. *Der Freiherr von Hübner, 1811–1892. Eine Gestalt aus dem Österreich Kaiser Franz Josephs.* Innsbruck, 1933.

Ernst II, Herzog von Saxe-Coburg-Gotha. *Aus meinem Leben und aus meiner Zeit.* 3 vols. Berlin, 1888–89.

Euler, Heinrich. *Napoleon III in seiner Zeit.* Vol. 1. *Der Aufstieg.* Würzburg, 1961.

Fitzmaurice, Edmond. *The Life of Granville George Leveson Gower, Second Earl of Granville K.G. 1815–1891.* 2 vols. London, 1905.

Gleason, John Howes. *The Genesis of Russophobia in Great Britain. A Study of the Interaction of Policy and Opinion.* Cambridge, Mass., 1950. Concentrates on the period between the Napoleonic Wars and 1841, when he thinks the foundations of Russophobia in Britain were laid.

Golder, Frank A. "Russian-American Relations during the Crimean War." *American Historical Review,* 31 (1925–26):462–76. Deals with Russian quest for American involvement, American mediation efforts, international shipping rights.

Gooch, Brison D. "A Century of Historiography on the Origins of the Crimean War." *American Historical Review.* 63 (October 1956): 33–58. Somewhat disjointed and not always accurate.

———. "The Crimean War in Selected Documents and Secondary Works since 1940." *Victorian Studies.* 1 (1958):271–79. Deals almost entirely with military problems and contains a long critique of Cecil Woodham-Smith's book *The Reason Why.*

———. *The New Bonapartist Generals in the Crimean War. Distrust and Decision-Making in the Anglo-French Alliance.* The Hague, 1959. Gives appropriate emphasis to the importance of the French army and leadership in the war, so often neglected in British works on the subject.

Goriainov, S. M. *Le Bosphore et les Dardanelles.* Paris, 1910. A compendium of documentary evidence put together by the director of the Russian state archives.

Gordon, Arthur (Lord Stanmore). *The Earl of Aberdeen.* New York,

1893. Brief, but with numerous quotations from Aberdeen's private papers, most of them undated.

Greville. *The Greville Diary, Including Passages Hitherto Withheld from Publication.* Ed. P. W. Wilson. 2 vols. New York, 1927.

Greville. *The Greville Memoirs, 1814–1860.* Edited by Lytton Strachey and Roger Fulford. 8 vols. London, 1938.

Guichen, Eugène. *La guerre de Crimée (1854–1856) et l'attitude des puissances européennes.* Paris, 1936.

Halicz, Emanuel. *Danish Neutrality during the Crimean War, 1853–1856. Denmark between the Hammer and the Anvil.* Odense, 1977.

Hallberg, Charles W. *Franz Joseph and Napoleon III, 1852–1864. A Study of Austro-French Relations.* New York, 1955.

Hallendorff, Carl, ed. *Konung Oscar I: s politik under Krimkriget.* Stockholm, 1930. Valuable collection of Swedish government documents.

Harcourt, Bernard Hippolyte d'. *Diplomatie et diplomates: les quatre ministères de M. Drouyn de Lhuys.* Paris, 1882. With extensive quotations from documents, including dispatches from Bourqueney.

Heindl, Waltraud. *Graf Buol-Schauenstein in St. Petersburg und London (1848–1852). Zur Genesis des Antagonismus zwischen Österreich und Russland.* Vienna, 1970. A valuable monograph on a much neglected figure.

Henderson, Gavin B. *Crimean War Diplomacy and Other Historical Essays.* Glasgow, 1947. Penetrating analyses of key problems.

———. "The Foreign Policy of Lord Palmerston." *History* 20 (1938): 335–44. Brief review article.

Herkless, J. L. "Stratford, the Cabinet, and the Outbreak of the Crimean War." *Historical Journal.* 28 (1975):497–523. Agrees fully with Temperley's interpretation of Stratford's behavior, and in this article discusses Stratford's differences with the British cabinet.

Hertslet, Edward, ed. *Map of Europe by Treaty.* 4 vols. London, 1875–91. Contains English translation of texts of all major European treaties as well as maps.

Hibbert, Christopher. *The Destruction of Lord Raglan. A Tragedy of the Crimean War.* Baltimore, 1963. Well-written narrative, sympathetic to Raglan.

Hösch, Edgar. "Neuere Literatur (1940–1960) über den Krimkrieg." *Jahrbücher für Geschichte Osteuropas* 9, n.s. (1961):399–434.

Hoffmann, Joachim. "Die Politik der Mächte in der Endphase der Kaukasuskriege." *Jahrbücher für Geschichte Osteuropas* 17, n.s. (1969): 215–58. Deals with period after 1856 Peace of Paris.

Huber, Ernst Rudolf, ed. *Dokumente zur deutschen Verfassungsgeschichte.* Vol. 2, 1851–1918. Stuttgart, 1964.

Hübner, Joseph Alexander von. *Neuf ans de souvenirs d'un ambassa-*

deur d'Autriche à Paris sous le Second Empire, 1851–1859. Edited by Alexander von Hübner. 2 vols. Paris, 1904. Important source, with many documents.

Hurewitz, J. C. "Ottoman Diplomacy and the European State System." *Middle East Journal.* 15 (1961):141–52. Important introduction to the subject, which remains to be investigated on the basis of Ottoman records.

————. "Russia and the Turkish Straits. A Reevaluation of the Origins of the Problem." *World Politics.* 14 (1961–62):605–32. Deals entirely with early nineteenth-century treaties and their interpretation. Calls the Goriainov volume, cited above, "a political tract disguised as scholarship" (p. 610).

Hurst, Michael. Review of *Aberdeen Coalition,* by J. B. Conacher. *Historical Journal* 12 (1969):722–23.

Jasmund, Julius von, ed. *Aktenstücke zur orientalischen Frage. Nebst chronologischer Uebersicht.* 3 vols. in 2. Berlin, 1855–59. Useful collection, with particularly valuable chronological survey. Unfortunately most of the documents are in German translation with no indication of their provenance.

Jomini, A. G. *Diplomatic Study on the Crimean War (1852 to 1856). Russian Official Publication.* 2 vols. London, 1882. A production of the Russian foreign ministry, virtually without documentation and inadequately dated.

Kerner, Robert J. "Russia's New Policy in the Near East after the Peace of Adrianople." *Cambridge Historical Journal* 5 (1937): 280–90.

Krautheim, Hans-Jobst. *Öffentliche Meinung und imperiale Politik. Das britische Russlandbild, 1815–1854.* Berlin, 1977. Builds on works of Gleason and Martin. Adds little of significance.

Lane-Poole, Stanley. *The Life of the Right Honourable Stratford Canning, Viscount Stratford de Redcliffe. From his Memoirs and Private and Official Papers.* 2 vols. London, 1888. Admiring and uncritical, but full of important material drawn from Stratford's private papers, most of them now apparently destroyed.

Lincoln, Bruce. *Nicholas I. Emperor and Autocrat of all the Russias.* Bloomington, Ind., 1978.

Lorne, Marquess of. *Viscount Palmerston, K.G.* New York, 1892.

Luxenburg, Norman. "England and the Caucasus during the Crimean War." *Jahrbücher für Geschichte Osteuropas.* 16, n.s. (1968):499–504. Contains interesting details but fails to deal with central issues.

Malcolm-Smith, E. F. *The Life of Stratford Canning (Lord Stratford de Redcliffe).* London, 1933. Uncritical eulogy, but contains information that supplements Lane-Poole.

Mange, Alyce Edythe. *The Near Eastern Policy of the Emperor Napo-*

leon III. Urbana, Ill., 1940. Pedestrian, based on previously published works without providing fresh interpretations.

Mardin, Şerif. *The Genesis of Young Ottoman Thought. A Study in the Modernization of Turkish Political Ideas.* Princeton, N.J., 1962. Important monograph.

Martens, F. de. *Recueil des traités et conventions conclus par la Russie avec les puissances étrangères.* 15 vols. St. Petersburg, 1874–1906. Official publication of the Russian foreign ministry, with a running commentary based on Russian archival sources.

Martin, Kingsley. *The Triumph of Lord Palmerston. A Study of Public Opinion in England before the Crimean War.* London, 1924. An analysis of the power of public opinion to influence government and Palmerston's ability to influence public opinion. Of great value for understanding Britain's entry into the war.

Martin, Theodore. *The Life of His Royal Highness the Prince Consort.* 5 vols. London, 1875–80. Full of important information.

Marx, Karl. *The Eastern Question. A Reprint of Letters Written 1853–1856 Dealing with the Events of the Crimean War.* Edited by Eleanor Marx Aveling and Edward Aveling. London, 1897.

————. *The Story of Lord Palmerston.* London, 1969. Originally published in 1853 in the *New York Tribune* and, in England, in the *People's Paper.* A denunciation of Palmerston as a sham liberal. Instead of being a champion of constitutionalism, he was in reality "the unflinching and persevering advocate of Russian interests." Only goes to 1838.

Maxwell, Herbert. *The Life and Letters of George William Frederick, Fourth Earl of Clarendon.* 2 vols. London, 1913. Based on his private correspondence. Important source.

Metternich-Winneburg, Prince Clemens Lothar Wenzel von. *Aus Metternichs nachgelassenen Papieren.* Edited by Prince Richard Metternich-Winneburg. 8 vols. Vienna, 1880–84.

Meyendorff. *Peter von Meyendorff. Ein russischer Diplomat an den Höfen von Berlin und Wien. Politischer und privater Briefwechsel, 1826–1863.* Edited by Otto Hoetzsch. 3 vols. Berlin, 1923. Important source.

Monnier, Luc. *Étude sur les origines de la guerre de Crimée.* Geneva, 1977. Valuable short monograph.

Morny, Charles duc de. *Extrait des mémoires du duc de Morny. Une ambassade en Russie. 1856.* Paris, 1892.

Mosse, W. E. *The European Powers and the German Question, 1848–1871.* Cambridge, 1958.

————. *The Rise and Fall of the Crimean System, 1855–71. The Story of a Peace Settlement.* London, 1963. Draws moral that a peace settlement that cannot be enforced is useless.

Nesselrode, Charles Robert, Count. *Lettres et papiers du chancelier comte de Nesselrode, 1760–1856.* Edited by A. Nesselrode. 11 vols. Paris, 1904–12. Important source.

Noradounghian, Gabriel, ed. *Recueil d'actes internationaux de l'empire Ottoman.* 4 vols. Paris, 1897–1900.

Parker, Charles Stuart. *Life and Letters of Sir James Graham, Second Baronet of Netherby, P.C., G.C.B., 1792–1861.* 2 vols. London, 1907.

Pemberton, W. Baring. *Battles of the Crimean War.* New York, 1962. Intelligent analysis that corrects many misconceptions.

Persigny, Jean Gilbert Victor Fialin, duc de. *Mémoires du Duc de Persigny publiés avec des documents inédits.* Paris, 1896.

Pingaud, A. "La politique extérieure du Second Empire." *Revue Historique* 156 (1927):41–68.

Pradier-Fodéré, Paul Louis. *M. Drouyn de Lhuys.* Laval, 1871.

Puryear, Vernon John. *England, Russia, and the Straits Question, 1844–1856.* Berkeley, Calif., 1931. Valuable monograph. Emphasis on economic factors, with a wealth of information and statistics. Very critical of Stratford.

————. *France and the Levant, 1820–1854.* Berkeley, Calif., 1941.

————. *International Economics and Diplomacy in the Near East. A Study of British Commerical Policy in the Levant, 1834–1853.* Stanford, Calif., 1935.

Ramm, Agatha. "The Crimean War." *The New Cambridge Modern History.* 10. *The Zenith of European Power, 1830–1870.* Edited by J. P. T. Bury. Cambridge, 1960, pp. 468–92. Brief and somewhat superficial.

Ridley, Jasper. *Lord Palmerston.* London, 1970.

Riker, Thad Weed. *The Making of Roumania. A Study of an International Problem, 1856–1866.* London, 1931.

Russell. *The Later Correspondence of Lord John Russell, 1840–1878.* Edited by G. P. Gooch. 2 vols. London, 1925.

Russell, W. H. *The British Expedition to the Crimea.* London, 1858. By the correspondent of *The Times.* Lively and readable.

Saab, Ann Pottinger. *The Origins of the Crimean Alliance.* Charlottesville, Va., 1977. Excellent monograph on which I have relied heavily. Especially valuable for its attention to the Turkish role.

Schiemann, Theodor. *Geschichte Russlands unter Kaiser Nikolaus I.* 4 vols. Berlin, 1904–19. Detailed and authoritative.

Schlitter, Hans. *Aus der Regierungszeit Kaiser Franz Joseph I.* Vienna, 1919. Contains text or summary of important documents from Austrian archives.

Schmitt, B. E. "Diplomatic Preliminaries of the Crimean War." *American Historical Review* 25 (1919–20):36–67. Now badly out of date.

Schroeder, Paul W. "Austria and the Danubian Principalities, 1853–1856." *Central European History* 2 (1969):216–36.

———. *Austria, Great Britain, and the Crimean War. The Destruction of the European Concert.* Ithaca, N.Y., 1972. Original and important work on which I have relied heavily. Theme that Buol followed a consistent policy in trying to mobilize the concert to prevent the war and then end it. Very critical of Britain. Brilliant final chapter examines principles of nineteenth-century European diplomatic relations.

———. "Bruck versus Buol: the Dispute over Austrian Eastern Policy, 1853–1855." *Journal of Modern History* 40 (1968):193–217.

———."A Turning Point in Austrian Policy in the Crimean War. The Conferences of March, 1854." *Austrian History Yearbook.* 4–5 (1968–69):159–202.

Seaton, Albert. *The Crimean War. A Russian Chronicle.* London, 1977. Valuable account from Russian point of view; emphasis on military history.

Seton-Watson, R. W. *Britain in Europe, 1789–1914. A Survey of Foreign Policy.* Cambridge, 1937. Balanced and intelligent analysis.

Shaw, Stanford J., and Ezel Kural. *History of the Ottoman Empire and Modern Turkey.* Vol. 2. *Reform, Revolution, and Republic: The Rise of Modern Turkey, 1818–1875.* Cambridge, 1977. Poorly organized and uncritically pro-Turkish. Valuable though often confusing descriptions of Ottoman institutions. Weak and often inaccurate on foreign policy.

Simpson, F. A. *Louis Napoleon and the Recovery of France.* London, 1923. Superbly written; somewhat weak on foreign policy.

Southgate, Donald. *"The Most English Minister . . ." The Policies and Politics of Palmerston.* London, 1966.

Stanmore, Arthur Hamilton Gordon, Lord. *Sidney Herbert. Lord Herbert of Lea. A Memoir by Lord Stanmore.* 2 vols. London, 1906. Important source.

Stephen, John J. "The Crimean War in the Far East." *Modern Asian Studies* 3 (1969):257–77. Almost entirely devoted to military and naval questions.

Sturdza, D., ed. *Recueil de documents relatifs à la liberté de navigation du Danube.* Berlin, 1904. Covers period 1814–1902.

Taylor, A. J. P. *The Struggle for Mastery in Europe, 1848–1918.* Oxford, 1954. Brilliant, provocative, and full of original insights but also many errors and some curiously distorted interpretations.

Temperley, Harold. "The Alleged Violations of the Straits Convention by Stratford de Redcliffe between June and September, 1853." *English Historical Review* 49 (1934):657–72. Defense of Stratford against Puryear's charges.

————. "Austria, England, and the Ultimatum to Russia, 16. December, 1855." In *Wirtschaft und Kultur. Festschrift zum 70. Geburtstag von Alfons Dopsch*, pp. 626–37. Berlin, 1938.

————. *England and the Near East: The Crimea*. London, 1936. Staunch defense of British policy. Seemingly authoritative but contains numerous errors and misconceptions.

————. "The Last Phase of Stratford de Redcliffe, 1853–1858." *English Historical Review* 47 (1932):216–59.

————. "Stratford de Redcliffe and the Origins of the Crimean War." *English Historical Review*. 48 (1933):601–21; 49 (1934):265–98. Detailed defense of Stratford.

————. "The Treaty of Paris of 1856 and Its Execution." *Journal of Modern History* 4 (1932):387–414, 523–43. Pro-British and not altogether accurate.

————, and Penson, Lillian, eds. *Foundations of British Foreign Policy from Pitt (1792) to Salisbury (1902)*. Cambridge, 1938. Useful collection of documents and commentaries.

Testa, I. de, ed. *Recueil des traités de la Porte Ottomane avec les puissances étrangères*. 11 vols. Paris, 1864–1911. From the year 1535. Includes correspondence and memoranda.

Thouvenel, Édouard Antoine. *Nicolas Ier et Napoléon III. Les préliminaires de la guerre de Crimée, 1852–1854, d'après les papiers inédits de M. Thouvenel*. Edited by Louis Thouvenel. Paris, 1891.

Treue, Wilhelm. *Der Krimkrieg und die Entstehung der modernen Flotten*. Göttingen, 1954. Important monograph.

Unckel, Bernhard. *Österreich und der Krimkrieg. Studien zur Politik der Donaumonarchie in den Jahren 1852–1856*. Lübeck, 1969. Valuable monograph.

Valsecchi, Franco. *L'Alleanza di Crimea. Il Risorgimento e l'Europa*. Milan, 1948.

Verdy du Vernois, F. von. *Die Frage der Heiligen Stätten*. Berlin, 1901. A slim survey.

Victoria. *The Letters of Queen Victoria. A Selection from Her Majesty's Correspondence between the Years 1837 and 1861*. Edited by A. C. Benson and Viscount Esher. 1st ser., 3 vols. London, 1907.

Walewski. "Les papiers inédits du Comte Walewski. Souvenirs et correspondance (1855–1868)." Edited by Gaston Raindre. *Revue de France* 5 (1925):485–510. Immense gaps; contains only a few documents of interest.

Walpole, Spencer. *The Life of Lord John Russell*. 2 vols. London, 1889.

Ware, Timothy. *Eustratios Argenti. A Study of the Greek Church under Turkish Rule*. Oxford, 1964. Important monograph.

————. *The Orthodox Church*. Baltimore, 1963. Lucid brief survey.

Warner, Philip. *The Crimean War. A Reappraisal.* New York, 1972. Contains extensive quotations from contemporary sources.

Wellesley, Victor, and Sencourt, Robert, eds. *Conversations with Napoleon III. A Collection of Documents, mostly unpublished and almost entirely Diplomatic.* London, 1934.

Wieczynski, Joseph L. "The Myth of Kuchuk-Kainardja in American Histories of Russia." *Middle Eastern Studies* 4 (1968):376–79. Analysis based on English translation of the document with no attention to its ambiguities and the interpretations deriving from them.

Wilkinson-Latham, Robert. *Crimean Uniforms 2. British Artillery.* London, 1973.

————. *Uniforms and Weapons of the Crimean War.* London, 1977.

Woodham-Smith, Cecil. *Florence Nightingale, 1820–1910.* New York, 1951.

Zaionchkovskii, A. M. *Vostochnaia Voina.* 2 vols. St. Petersburg, 1908–13. With a two-volume appendix of documents. Invaluable source for Russian policy.

Index

Aaland Islands, 108, 124, 137, 143, 170, 173, 179, 192–93
Aali Pasha, 184
Abdul Medjid I (sultan of Turkey), 19, 77, 86–87; role during Menshikov Mission, 51–53, 56–57
Abereen, George Hamilton Gordon, Earl of, 25, 29, 32, 36, 63, 97, 98, 109, 148; confusion in diplomacy, 89, 90, 91–92, 93; interpreting Vienna Note, 77, 81, 82, 83; reaction to Salamis, 43, 44
Albert (prince-consort of England), 90, 153
Alexander I (tsar of Russia), 14, 16
Alexander II (tsar of Russia), 149, 157
Alma River, Battle of the, 133, 143
Anglo-French alliance, 50, 66, 104–6, 125, 143; Allied troop landings in Crimean campaign, 132–36; Austria in, 142–43, 144–47; equipment and leadership of, 126–32, 133; fleets dispatched to Near East, 63–64, 65, 82–84, 86, 90, 93, 103, 104; interpretation of Four Points, 145–47; Napoleon III's hope for, 42–43; response to Austrian Ultimatum, 118, 120, 122, 123; shortage of troops, 148, 158; Stratford on, 44, 45
Argyll, George Douglas Campbell, Duke of, 40, 125, 153
Austria, 3, 11–12, 22, 55, 67, 190; changing stance, 111–16; at Congress of Vienna, 185–86; consequences of war for, 117–18, 197–98, 200–1; desire for peace, 11–12, 13; early efforts to preserve peace, 99–100, 101–3, 104–6; early wartime position, 140–43; final peace efforts, 67–68, 69, 70–73; joins Anglo-French alliance, 144–45, 166; post-Sebastopol ne-

gotiations, 166–69; relations with Russia, 10, 14, 18, 30, 31, 33, 36
Austrian Ultimatums: final ultimatum to Russia, 168, 174, 179; to Russia in June 1854, 111, 116–17, 118–23; from Vienna Conference, 151, 152–54, 162
Azov, Sea of, 135, 171, 173, 191

Balaclava, Battle of, 131, 133, 134, 135
Balkans, 2, 28, 30, 62, 88, 124, 151, 206; importance in war, 125, 132, 137
Baltic Sea, 2, 124, 136–38, 143, 173
Bavaria, 189
Belgium, 36
Benedetti, Vincent, Count, 144–45
Besika Bay, 64, 66, 70, 81
Bessarabia, 109, 154, 157, 166, 168, 169, 177; as issue in Treaty of Paris, 187–89, 196
Beust, Friedrich Ferdinand, Count von, 164
Black Sea, 22, 62, 84, 146–47; importance in war, 124–25, 126, 134, 135, 138, 139; as issue in Treaty of Paris, 188, 191–92, 197; neutralization of, 149, 150, 168, 169–70
Bomarsund, 124, 137, 143
Bosnia, 94
Bosporus. See Straits
Bourquency, François Adolphe, Count de, 162, 184, 196. See also Buol-Bourquency Negotiations
Britain, 7–8, 22, 36, 59; after Crimean War, 200, 201, 206; desire to extend war, 157–60, 174, 175, 179–81, 238n44; final peace efforts, 66, 67, 68; making peace, 182–86, 193, 240n1; partisan neutrality, 89–93, 94; public opinion,